"It's Jacqui's engagingly frank voice and fierce self-enquiry that drive this fast-paced gripping tale through all its spirited twists and turns."
Nina Geraghty

———◆———

"On one level, this is a tale of looking for love in all the wrong places, but on a deeper level, it's a story of how adversity, viewed through the lens of insight and wisdom, leads to hope and redemption. It's a tumultuous, terrifying, frustrating journey, as Jacqui struggles to uncover the heroine within. The miracle is that she comes out the other side alive—and willing to use her life story to inspire others to survive and flourish."
Giles Griffin

To my Grandmother, my Guardian Angel.
To my mother for your courage to Be Love, no matter the turmoil.
To Amanda and Jill, for loving me unconditionally.

CONTENTS

AUTHOR'S NOTE

WRITING A MEMOIR WHILE TRYING to disguise the nature and character of the people who have inspired and shaped me proved impossible. So, to preserve anonymity, I have changed the names of most people and some places. To further protect their identity, I have also modified details that might identify these individuals, when it did not impact the narrative.

I have made six exceptions. I have used the real names of Amanda and Jill, my two closest friends, as I wish to honour and celebrate them sincerely and publicly for their consistent and unconditional loving presence in my life. Without them, this book would not be in your hands. I have their consent and blessing for this decision. I have also used Mrs Hope and Blues' real names, as I believe some angels should have the light shone on them.

I have also chosen not to change the real name of Don Johnson (not the actor) and I thank the Me Too movement for giving me the courage to speak out in this instance.

Finally, I have used Deloitte's name as the story of our struggle with them is a matter of public record in South Africa and I am not bound by a non-disclosure agreement. I have not disclosed the names of the Deloitte employees involved in the matter.

At times I have omitted people and events, but only when that omission had no impact on the substance of the story or its authenticity. To write this book, I have relied on my memory, my personal notes, correspondence and journals. The views, feelings, opinions, philosophies, emotions and recollections expressed in this book are my own and do not necessarily reflect the views or recollections of my family, friends, clients, associates or any other individuals in this book. I have researched facts where I could and I have consulted with several of the people who appear in the book.

The characteristics of my four brothers are composite, as are the events in chapter 1 to 4, and chapter 41. Where necessary, some letters have been edited and/or shortened. While my brothers and I grew up listening to a fear-based racist narrative under Apartheid in the 1960s, '70s and '80s, I personally believe none of my brothers to be racist by nature.

To my ex-husband 'Michael', thank you for generously giving me your blessing so that I could be fully myself with this project, despite any discomfort that might cause you.

To my mother, my ultimate teacher in this life, thank you for being my mother. I love you, and I know as angels we will fly together again someday. Mom, you have your wings. I still have to earn mine.

PROLOGUE

THERE ARE A THOUSAND WAYS you can stare up at a snow-capped peak, but there's only one way you can lie up there dead in the ice. The mountains aren't here simply for our enjoyment. They are sublime and I am a dead woman walking through the snow, trying and failing to touch that other-worldly power. I am standing 11,000 feet above the world and staring down at the wreckage of my life. I came into this life as a stranger and now, after eight near-death experiences and 15 years of marriage, I am leaving as a stranger. My husband does not know me and I do not want to know myself. I avert my eyes from what lies inside, the way one looks away from a mangled body at the scene of a car accident. I want to keep speeding down the highway and put it all out of my mind, but I can't do that anymore. It's screaming to be let in. It's hammering on the windows and smashing through the doors to be let in, to be let out. I am frozen and the wind tugs at my clothing. If I stayed here and did not move, at last I would die. Now I know why I travelled over 15 000 kilometres to get to these mountains in Colorado. I am running away from the person I have become. I have been trapped inside someone else's idea of myself, which bears no relation to the truth of who I am, and I ache for someone to tell me what to do. I ache for someone to explain to me how I became like this. The snow keeps falling and I am alone.

PART ONE

BURNING SHAME

For My Father

my imperfections
are my beauty spots
along life's mirrored wall

i wear their scars
externally
so you can see them all

my shame, my guilt, my blame
my doubt
my inner critic's plea

the freedom from
their sight and sound
projections gift to be

i know now that
your mirrors' truth
reflects the perfect me

uncomplicated
for its grace
my heart gives thanks to thee

CHAPTER ONE

*We're not on our journey to save the world but to save
ourselves. But in doing that you save the world. The
influence of a vital person vitalizes. – Joseph Campbell*

A LTHOUGH NO ONE LIKES TO admit it, growing up white in
small-town apartheid South Africa was nice. As a six-year-old
tomboy in the early '70s, I thought my life was perfect. My family
loved Jesus, the National Party and Sunday roasts followed by vanilla
ice cream. We believed without a doubt in white supremacy.

My Dad was the perfect father of five robust children, from
helping my four brothers and I win the soapbox car derby to taking
us all camping and fishing. My mother was also perfect. All born
within six years of each other, my parents had no choice other than
to bring us up as a pack. My parents' marriage was perfect too. They
held hands in public when no one else's parents did and my mother
told me that she had married well. Even after everything that
happened, it was clear Mom loved Dad beyond reason, beyond sense.
As a child I thought theirs was the most wonderful union in the
world.

We never wanted for anything, at least not in the material sense,
and our house was always open for the neighbours to pop by for a

visit. We had the-more-the-merrier *braais* (barbecues) in the sunshine beside the pool with friends and family, complete with peppermint crisp tart or steamed pudding. The men stood around the fire drinking beers and the women stood inside on the vinyl kitchen floor making salad drowned in mayonnaise.

On Sundays, we went to church. While my brothers stood patiently for Dad to help them with their safari suits, Mom fought to get me into a much-hated dress. She was desperate to play doll with her only daughter, but I refused to cooperate. One Sunday Mom even coaxed me into a dress with chocolate, but the moment I'd finished it I wanted to whip the dress off again.

'God won't listen to your prayers if you don't wear a dress,' she said to me, while my grandmother watched the battle with amusement.

I started to cry. The injustice and the betrayal were too much. I hadn't realised I was meant to keep wearing the dress. But I loved Sunday school and I loved God. Him not hearing my prayers was my biggest fear.

'My dear,' Granny said to my mother, 'Jacqueline is a spirited child. Think before you say "no" to her, otherwise the two of you will be at each other's throats for the rest of your life.'

———◆———

Sundays seemed to last a hundred years when I was young. By the time evening came, I was numb from trying to be good. In the week, my four brothers and I, along with the other neighbourhood kids, would walk home from school, change and then play games in the field until sunset, where I would try my hardest to prove that, despite being a girl, I was the toughest and could keep up with their games.

'Jacqueline! What have you done?' Mom sighed when I arrived home after playing outside one day, my clothes muddied and shins scraped.

She was never a *shouter*, unlike Dad, but her sweet calmness made it hard to tell if she was upset. Since my brothers and I were always getting up to no good, Mom must have had a heck of a lot of unspoken anger in her. I hung my head and examined the new living room carpet. It was cream and shaggy like a dog. Dad had just bought it and, like so many things in the seventies, it was the height of cool and absolutely hideous.

'I'm at my wits' end,' she said. 'What I wouldn't give for you to behave like a normal girl. You come home with grazed knees. Your shorts are ripped – and you've bruised your fingers. For a girl like you to be fighting, I don't know *what* the neighbours will –'

'I haven't been fighting! It was Mrs le Roux!' I blurted out.

My father had entered the living room. He flopped down onto the couch and loosened his tie. Dad was handsome, powerfully built and charming, but my favourite things about him were that he spoke his mind and was spontaneous. That was what made him such fun.

He winked at me. I hid a smile. The only thing that gave me a bigger kick than my father calling me his tomboy was when someone outside of the family mistook me for a boy. I wanted to grow up to be just like my father.

'Jacqueline's been telling me that she got into a fight with her class teacher, Mrs le Roux.'

'No, Mrs le Roux hit me over the hands with her ruler.'

'What happened?' asked my father.

My teacher had instructed us to draw a picture of our family and had hit me because I'd included our maid, Sara.

'Mrs le Roux said Sara's a coloured, and she's not part of the family, and I said, no, Sara's not a coloured, and then she smacked me on the hand.'

Mom glanced at Dad before speaking, something she did often.

'Well, you shouldn't speak back to your teacher like that,' she said, and left Dad to deal with me.

'Sara is not a part of this family,' Dad said, picking me up and putting me on his lap. 'She's a maid.'

'But I love Sara and she lives with us.'

'Sara is a coloured. She's not black, but they're all the same. They're not like us, they're like animals.'

'But why?'

'Because that's the way God made it. Do you hear me?'

I shrunk back from him. There was something in his voice that I had never heard there before – fear.

'I don't get it.'

He grabbed me by the arm so that I knew who was in control— as if I could forget. He was like God in our house. We respected him and lived by his rules.

'I don't want to hear another word about it, okay? We're white, they're not. God only knows that if we pushed them all into the sea and let them drown, the world would be a better place.'

I imagined Sara drowning.

'Do you understand?'

'Yes Dad,' I whispered.

I couldn't understand what my father had said. I thought if anyone could explain, it would be my eldest brother Mark. By nature he was gentle and kind. I found Mark outside throwing a tennis ball against the garage wall. He tossed the ball to me. I caught it left-handed and threw it back.

'Mark,' I said, as we flung the ball between us, 'why are the coloureds and black people different from us?'

'Oh, that's easy. We're smarter. We look different and that's the proof. You've heard the joke, haven't you? Why did God give black people short curly hair? Because he knew they would ride in the back of *bakkies* (trucks).'

'I don't understand.'

'Because they are labourers and you know that they don't sit in the front of the *bakkie* with the driver, they sit in the back,' he laughed. 'They've got curly hair so that it won't blow in their faces when they are on the back of the *bakkie*.'

I clearly didn't understand.

'Oh, forget about it. You'll understand when you're older.'

'Why can't they sit with the driver in the front?'

'Jeez, Jacqueline, stop asking questions all the time. Go find the others, then we can play a game of rugby before dinner,' he said.

But I wasn't in the mood for a game.

———◆———

As time went on, I pressed down my questions so that I wouldn't provoke Dad, whom I adored. But my silence was also for Mom's sake. She loved me, but I was a disappointment as a girl and I didn't want to it make worse. Although the word was not in her vocabulary, I'm sure that she had night terrors of her only daughter being lesbian. These fears were unfounded. I soon had my first crush on a boy and on the last day of my first year of school, he asked if we could swop photos. When a boy asked you to swop school portrait photos with you, everyone knew you were boyfriend and girlfriend.

That evening, before she tucked me in bed, my mother asked to see the photographs and noticed that one was missing.

'Jacqueline, one of your small portraits is missing. There should be six.'

I burrowed deeper under my blankets.

'Jacqueline?'

'I gave it to my boyfriend.'

'You've got a boyfriend? What's his name?'

'James.'

She knew him well as we all played together after school. She giggled and I couldn't help but smile.

'One of the older boys, hey?' she teased.

'Promise you won't tell anyone.'

'I promise.'

'Not a soul. You *can't* tell anyone, Mommy, okay? *Please?*'

'I won't tell, I promise!'

We clasped our little fingers together. It was sealed. Then she kissed me on both cheeks and turned out the lights.

The next morning, I sat still while my mother blow-dried my hair with a bright red hairdryer that made an awful noise. Mom was dedicated to the red beast and every morning she would blow and tease her own hair into a giant pile on top of her head. Dad was lying on his back on the bed, reading the weekend paper, cursing under his breath.

'Bloody *kaffirs* (an insulting term for a black African),' he said, and threw the newspaper onto the floor.

'What's wrong, Daddy?' I shouted over the noise of the hairdryer.

'Nothing.' He sighed, then smiled. 'So, Mom tells me you have some exciting news?'

'No?'

'Something to do with a certain older boy?'

I stiffened.

'Word on the street is that you have a bo-o-yfriend.'

I smashed my fist into the hairdryer, shoving it away from my head and screamed.

'*YOU LIAR! YOU PROMISED YOU WOULDN'T TELL!*

'*JACQUELINE, DON'T YOU SPEAK TO YOUR MOTHER LIKE THAT!*

'Jacqueline,' Mom said, 'Daddy's teasing you.'

'It was a secret and you *promised!*

I ran out of the room. She ran after me and caught me by my arm.

'I'm sorry, Jacqueline,' she said, crouching down in front of me. 'But you've got to understand that there are no secrets between Daddy and me. One day when you're married you'll understand.'

'But you promised,' I whispered.

'I'm sorry, Jacqueline. But Daddy and I made a promise to one another in front of God on our wedding day not to have secrets. Our promise to each other came first, before my promise to you last night.'

Her eyebrows were pushed together, making little worry creases between her eyebrows, and she was biting her bottom lip. A smear of pink lipstick marked one tooth.

'I'll make you peppermint crisp tart for Sunday lunch tomorrow.'

I brightened.

'Really?'

'Yes. Off you go now.'

The whole gang was in the fort we'd built in the field. We were lying on our stomachs waiting, but we had no enemies against which to defend our camp. No one wanted to admit that it was boring.

'Maybe we could get some snacks,' said Mark.

Mark was always eating.

'I'll go,' I offered.

At the house, Sara was mopping the floor in the hall. She knew I'd come to steal food and held a finger up to her lips. I could hear Mom and the neighbour, Mrs West, in the lounge, laughing over their tea. Sara motioned for me to wait there while she went to go and get us food.

'Oh, dear me, that is too funny,' Mrs West was saying.

'So, young Jacqueline has a boyfriend.'

'You should have seen her when her father was teasing her about it. Bright red in the face. Spitting mad! She has a temper like her father.'

'Oh, precious! Children are too funny!'

'I know. She is so serious about it, I had to stop myself from giggling the entire time she was telling me!'

I went cold and then hot again. I didn't wait for Sara to come back with the food, but ran down the driveway and out into the road to hide.

I'd often heard Dad say, one should never trust a woman. No wonder he checked on where Mom went and with whom. I made a promise to myself: I would never trust my mother again in my life or anyone else who lied to me.

CHAPTER TWO

---

*Love one another. As I have loved you, so you must
love one another. – Jesus*

IT SEEMED LIKE IT WAS always summertime when I was growing up. The summer of my tenth year was a particularly happy one as we kids were packed off to my grandparents' fruit farm while my parents went to visit their friends Pat and Harry in Johannesburg. Everything about Granny and Oupa, my Dad's parents, was wonderful – they were refined but warm and did not subscribe to the idea that children should be seen and not heard.

They weren't religious in the way we were, even though I knew they believed in God. Who didn't? Without Jesus Christ our Lord and Saviour, we would all be lost. Yet my relationship with God was becoming more complicated. We were all bright children, but I felt stupid for not being able to understand our church's case for segregation. It didn't make sense to me that the few people of colour I came across weren't even allowed to cross the threshold of our church. They weren't allowed anywhere that we were.

Once, when Ouma, my other grandmother, and I were at the post office on a rainy day, the coloured and black families were forced to stand outside in the downpour to queue for their stamps, even though Ouma and I were practically the only customers in the huge post office. There was ample space for them inside.

'Why can't they come in?' I'd asked.

'Because they're black,' she muttered and then silenced me.

While wandering around the orchards with my three elder brothers, I asked them what they thought about blacks and whites being separate.

'I mean, doesn't God say we should all share and love one another?' I asked.

'It's simple, Jacqueline,' said Alan, who always knew everything. 'The Bible teaches us that God created different races. The story of Babel clearly states that it was God's will that the people in His Kingdom be divided into different races with different languages.'

'But I can speak English and Afrikaans – and I could probably learn other languages.'

'The Bible says, "From our one ancestor God made all nations to inhabit the whole earth, and He allotted" – I can't remember the next part – but then it goes on to say that He made the boundaries of the places where they would live. That clearly shows that it's God's will that the blacks live in the *Bantustans* (a partially self-governing area set aside during apartheid for a particular indigenous African people: a so-called homeland) or, like, townships outside of the city, and that they go to different churches and all that.'

'But what about in John where it says, "The one who hates his brother is in the darkness and walks in the darkness"?'

I had been doing my Bible study, too. I'd been searching for anything that would explain the way things were. Alan swelled with indignation as if to say, don't you come and out-Bible *me*.

'They're not our brothers, Jacqueline!'

'They are. They have to be, because Jesus loves everyone and says everyone is our brother and Jesus says we must love one another as He has loved us, and hate is a sin and –'

'No one is suggesting hatred here, just segregation.'

'But that's not love! My Sunday school teacher says that God is love and this proves that God is in all of us, even in the plants and the animals. So that means God is inside the blacks, too, and that they're our brothers.'

'It's simple. Separate churches and missions are supported by the Bible and mixing of the races is not. Either you learn to embrace God's word or you oppose Him. And if you oppose Him, you'll go to hell.'

But it didn't seem simple to me, although the thought of hell shut me up for the rest of the walk back to Granny and Oupa's farmhouse.

Granny was a spiritual woman who seemed to see eternity in even the littlest things, but she was a straight talker. Maybe I could ask her, I thought. Oupa on the other hand was gentle and serious. He loved to read and didn't talk much. When he did, we all listened.

The days flew by with us racing one another through the vineyards to where the peach trees grew. We filled our T-shirts with fruit from low-hanging branches. The peaches were soft and sunny and the juices ran down my chin.

I couldn't seem to find a moment to speak to Granny alone. By Sunday I was running out of time, so I went to her bedroom in the hopes that she'd turn up there and I could ask her. I waited and waited and soon found myself looking through her things and slipping my hands into her fur-lined leather gloves. She always dressed beautifully, but, unlike my mother, she hardly wore any lipstick.

'No matter if you're wearing wellington boots or stilettos, it's all about confidence,' she'd once told me.

Even I, who thought that girls' clothing was made to get in the way of normal activity, wished I could look like her, but my father might hate it if I wore girls' clothes. He didn't like girls who dressed sexily, but he also didn't seem to like the fact that I wanted to look like a boy. I sometimes wondered how he had fallen in love with my mother, the picture of femininity, if he hated women so much.

I picked up a pair of clip-on earrings and held them to my ears.

I would never risk wearing earrings, not even clip-ons. My father believed that if God wanted holes in your ears, He would have given them to you at birth. Only whores pierced their ears. Whores also painted their nails.

As I ran my hands over a string of pearls, I slid the top drawer of her dresser open, but saw only folded scarves – light, airy ones; thick, sumptuous ones; striped and spotted and floral ones. Granny knew I loved her scarves and told me that when I was older, she would give me one of hers. The second drawer contained mountains of pantyhose, over which I ran my hands. I kneeled on the carpet and opened the last drawer.

'*Jacqueline!*'

I hadn't heard her come into the bedroom. She was towering above me, her hands on her hips. I leaped to my feet, my heart racing.

'How would you feel if you caught me snooping through your drawers?'

'Upset,' I whispered.

'Very upset. I don't appreciate you looking through my things. It's disrespectful. Is that understood?'

'Yes, Granny. I know.'

I felt so ashamed, but Granny looked me in the eyes and said.

'If you would like to know what I keep in my drawers, you can ask me. You know you can ask me anything.'

'Yes, Granny. I'm sorry, Granny.'

'That's all right. Now, off you go. The boys are outside at the dam. I'm making *melkkos* (a traditional meal: a porridge of flour, butter, milk, sugar and cinnamon) for lunch before your parents arrive.'

I hugged her and then ran out the room to find my brothers. *Melkkos* was my favourite. All thoughts of asking about God's love for black people were driven from my mind.

Later that day, when my parents came to fetch us, my father was grinning and swaggering as he always did after a visit with his cool friends and my mother – I could scarcely believe it – had painted her finger nails.

'Mom – your nails,' I said.

'Mm-hmm, I painted them.'

I looked towards Dad. He was chatting to Oupa about television broadcasting finally coming to South Africa and bragging about how he was going to buy us a TV to be sure we were the first in our neighbourhood to own one. He had unbuttoned one more button on his shirt than usual and was laughing too loudly.

'*You* painted them?' I asked, suspicious.

'Auntie Pat painted them for fun,' she said.

I clung to Granny's hand as Dad packed our bags into the boot. I stared at my mother. I knew she wasn't a whore – I was ten, I wasn't stupid – but something terrible had gone wrong within her soul for sure. As we drove back home, I wracked my brain for reasons how this could have happened. The only plausible explanation was that Auntie Pat was a bad influence and so I thanked God that night that she lived far away and I prayed for her and my mother.

The next day, Mom's fingernails were shell pink and natural again and Dad's shirt was buttoned to the top. God had heard me and locked away the scandalous, free versions of my parents. They had snapped back to reality and I was grateful that my mother would never dare put nail polish on all by herself. She was a good wife and mother and would never not honour and obey my perfect father.

CHAPTER THREE

There is no coming to consciousness without pain. – Carl Jung

THE OLDER I GOT, THE more growing up seemed like being pulled up against my will. I fought hard, but I lost more ground each year.

I was twelve and was sitting on the steps near the pool of 1 Van der Merwe Street in my bikini bottoms, feeling confused about the previous day's events. My father had screamed at his foreman, '*YOU STUPID KAFFIR, YOU'VE BUILT THE FUCKING WALL HALF A METRE TOO LONG!*' I kept seeing his fist colliding with the coloured man's face in my mind.

If adults were required to act the way he did towards his foreman, I had no interest in becoming one. He muttered something that sounded like a curse word under his breath and hit the steering wheel hard.

'Dad, why did you hit that man?' I'd asked, once we were on our way home.

'Jacqueline, that man had no right to talk back to me, so don't ask me about things you don't understand. You think I like being the bad guy, huh? But it's the only way to get these lazy *kaffirs* to listen. I didn't make the world like this, but that's how it is, so you'd better get on board and show your father the respect he deserves.'

I pushed the memory to the back of my mind and tried to focus on the sun on my stomach and thighs as I watched Alan and his friend Gary try to drown one another in the pool. Gary came over and sat down beside me on the front steps.

'Hey bro,' he said. 'How's your preparation for athletics day going?'

I had been training hard at sprinting the 100 metres and knew I would be selected for the Western Province team. I wanted to win my race at the South African Junior Schools Sports Association meeting and break the record. After that, it would be a short and tough journey to the Olympics. That was the plan, in any case. I outlined my training plan to Gary (it wasn't very sophisticated, but I thought it would work: run, run more, run faster, win) and soon I'd forgotten all about my father.

'Jackie (as my friends called me), shouldn't you start wearing a bikini top now?' he faltered.

I hadn't expected him to say that. I looked down at my chest. My nipples, which had looked like everyone else's – 'everyone else' being the boys – seemed bigger. A few weeks previously one had been lumpy. Now there were two of them and they looked a little bit pointy, even. I poked one with my finger.

'Do you think so?' I asked, sceptically.

'Yes, I do.'

'What a bummer.'

He laughed and then sprinted off to dive back into the pool with Alan. Life looked easy from their perspective.

To hide my changing body, I developed a stoop and wore oversized T-shirts and each evening I would check on my body in the mirror. Over time I saw that, despite my prayers, Gary was right: I was getting boobs and they seemed to have a mind of their own. If my mother had noticed the abhorrence I had for anything girly, including my body, she said nothing. Occasionally she would smile and correct the bank tellers, who said to her what a fine job she was doing of teaching her son about banking, or the sales assistants who would inform us where the men's changing rooms were. She would nod ruefully at friends who said I was a real tomboy. But for my mother, life was a watercolour. Unpleasantness could be blotted away or lifted off and then painted afresh in her mind. Facts ruled her life, but the facts needed to match one another to form a pretty picture. She would not investigate anything that did not align with this picture, but instead rearranged things to suit her picture: Jacqueline was going through a phase as a result of having four brothers and a talent for athletics. Yes, the phase had lasted her entire life so far, but Jacqueline was only twelve and did not know herself. And there was no connection between Jacqueline's desperation to be one of the boys and her father's treatment of women. Her father treated women respectfully – had he not been the perfectly loving, loyal and hardworking husband since the very beginning? He was a gentleman, through and through. Mom was proud that she had married well. It's all a phase, an exaggeration, a natural acting-out. After all, she's nearly a teenager.

And even if I had confessed to her how much I hated my body, and later myself, she would never have believed a word I'd said.

———◆———

Despite my battle against time and my body, I couldn't help being enthusiastic about life. It was my final year of primary school and I couldn't wait to start high school. I was a top student and I had made it into both the Boland Athletics Squad and the Western Province Platteland team and it was a matter of time before the big win that would really put me on the map, or so said my athletics coach. My father hadn't shown up to the prize-giving, but the thought of my Olympic Gold made it hurt less. A win at the Olympics would make him prouder than he had ever been.

I had gone for a run early one Saturday morning and came home to find my favourite brother Steve, with whom I shared everything, flopped on the couch in the lounge with his feet up, which meant that our parents were still asleep. I made us each a cup of tea and then, pushing Steve's feet off the couch, sat down next to him.

'So, listen,' said Steve. 'I've been wanting to ask you. Do you have any pubic hairs?'

'*What?* Ew! No, man, gross!'

'Well, I've got three or four.'

'Oh. Me too.'

'Cool.'

Dad walked in and we both jumped. He was wearing his dressing gown and was smiling. It made me happy to see him like that. When he was happy, it made the whole world a better place.

'It's a beautiful day,' he said.

We followed him into the kitchen and Steve put bread into the toaster. My father had been tense because of work and I hoped this meant things were looking up. I dreaded problems at work because it always meant that a big change was coming – a move of house, Dad's raised voice behind closed doors, or someone getting fired. Number 1 Van der Merwe Street was the eighth house I'd lived in by the time I was twelve and it was my favourite. Although I didn't remember it, we'd left Krugersdorp, just as my parents had left Cape Town, Pietermaritzburg and Pretoria before that. In Somerset West alone I'd lived in six houses, but 1 Van der Merwe Street was more than a house. It was a home. Aunt Lilly, my favourite, lived down the street and I had other uncles, aunts and cousins close by. Ouma and Oupa Bunny, my Mom's parents, were ten minutes away in the Strand at their house on the beachfront, called Pop Inn, where my cousins and all our friends hung out all the time. Granny and Oupa had recently retired and moved to the Strand as well. My best friend Leigh and all my school friends were dotted around us and we lived ten minutes away from the Helderberg Nature Reserve. I loved hiking in the Hottentots Holland mountains and was known as a tour guide of sorts – one who would go off the steep mountain paths and into uncharted territory. It was all perfect.

'For you,' said Steve, handing me a plate with a slice of hot buttered toast on it.

'I got good news from Uncle Harry yesterday,' Dad said.

Dad worked in the accounts department for a timber company, but had started his own business with Uncle Harry from Johannesburg.

'Business is going well,' said my father.

'But Dad, how come Mom said business wasn't good?'

'I never said that,' said my mother from behind me.

She'd stepped into the kitchen unheard, dressed as if she were about to go out.

'Where do you think you're going, dressed like that?'

'I'm going out for tea with the girls.'

'You should have asked first, but fine. Be back by eleven.'

'Thank you,' she said, and then she was gone.

'As I was saying, business is going very well. And I wouldn't be able to do any of it without my little champion supporting me,' he said, ruffling Steve's hair.

'I support you too, Dad,' unable to stop fawning over my hero.

'Of course you do. And because you're such great kids, I'm going to give you a surprise.'

'But you just bought us the new TV,' said Steve.

'But the best kids in the world deserve another treat, don't they? Hey?'

We grinned.

'What's the surprise?'

'You'll see,' he winked and left the kitchen with his half-eaten toast in hand.

———◆———

Weeks later Steve and I were still waiting for the surprise to materialise. The whole lot of us were sitting in the lounge chatting while the radio played. The South-Easter was howling outside and

Night Fever by the Bee Gees was playing loudly, but we could still hear Dad's raised voice from his bedroom. Steve turned the volume louder to block out his words. The front door banged open and my father stormed out, got into his car and drove away. I got up and went to their room. Mom was slumped forwards, her head in her hands. She never slouched; she was never anything but the straight-backed picture of composure and I was worried.

'Mom, are you okay? What happened?'

'It's nothing.'

If my father had tried to set her on fire, she would have smiled and said, 'It's nothing'. I despised that side of her.

'What's wrong with Dad?'

'He has a bit of a headache, that's all.'

I wanted to shout, don't you think I know when you're lying? But I remained silent.

A week later, I found out the typical way: through the long chain of family members. Ouma had somehow found out and, being the gossip that she was, had told a cousin who told Alan who told me. I then confronted Granny about it and Granny, who never lied, told me that Dad had been fired for doing something bad at work. Since there was only a tiny chance that Mom didn't already know, I asked her about it one day when she was reading in the lounge.

'Fired? Why would you ask me that? You mustn't tell lies. Your father has not been fired.'

'Mom, he has. Granny told me. He was fired,' I whispered, not wanting my brothers to hear us, although I suspected all of them already knew. 'Why was he fired?'

'Jacqueline, don't talk nonsense: I'm not going to discuss this with you anymore! Why can't you ever stop asking questions?'

She put her book down and left. She'd spoken somewhat hysterically, which was unlike her. It reminded me of what I already knew so well: don't trust her; her word is no good. But I still hoped that someone would tell me the rest of the story. I wondered what my brothers knew. Had Dad confided something in one of them? If he had, not one of them would break and tell.

I didn't think I asked too many questions, but compared to my brothers, who never asked *any* questions, I guessed that it must frustrate my mother. I doubted she had any answers, because I knew what my father was like. If I were a wife with five children and my husband had been fired, I'd have been mad as hell, even if it wasn't his fault, which of course it wasn't. I didn't want to consider what it would be like if we had to move again. We had never been so happy, and the happiness, I was sure, was caused by the house itself. But we'd all be okay. God would watch over us, I knew it. And if Mom was secretly mad at Dad, she would forgive him – she probably already had. For better, for worse, she was always there for him and no one could say a word against him, no matter what he did or said. Apart from me, she was his biggest champion. Their love was true love. I convinced myself that I was being suspicious and decided that maybe this time I did not need an answer.

No one said anything. It was a time of awkward silences that would stretch into adulthood. I wished I had told Steve what I was feeling – then we would have been in it together, like we always used to be.

CHAPTER FOUR

*For what shall it profit a man, if he gain the whole
world, and lose his own soul?* – Jesus

I WAS SITTING ON THE floor of Marsha's room reading *Heidi.* Marsha
had been our maid at 1 Van der Merwe Street since we'd moved in
and even though I was now old enough to know that she wasn't family,
I loved her. She didn't mind me coming to lie on her floor and read. I was
reading the part where Heidi returns to her grumpy grandfather in the
Alps and teaches him that it's never too late to turn to God and ask for
his forgiveness. I knew this to be true from personal experience, as God
had forgiven me for talking back to my parents, playing catch with the
china, exploding a Coca-Cola bomb in the lounge, trying to make my
guinea pig race my Scalextric cars, making my yo-yo hit my little brother
David in the back of the legs repeatedly until he cried, prank-calling the
police on the telephone and making them call back, putting dishwashing
liquid on Leigh's trampoline and then jumping on it until someone
sprained an ankle – well, the list was long, but I turned to God with an
open heart and He forgave me.

'Do you know, Marsha,' I said, 'that if you pray to God, even the
worst things will go away. No matter what you've done, God will save
you.'

Marsha raised her eyebrows and looked down at me from where she sat on her bed.

'Don't you believe me?' I asked.

'I do believe in prayer. And in God. But I think that for some people, it's too late. Some people have gone too far,' she said darkly.

'What do you mean? Who's gone too far?'

'Never mind, now. I've got to get back to work. You make sure you put that book back in the bookcase, okay?'

I nodded and followed Marsha out into the house through the back door. She stayed in the kitchen and I went to the front of the house where the bookshelf stood outside my father's office. I'd read *Heidi* many times before and knew, as I put it back on the bookshelf, that it wouldn't be long before I read it again. I put it next to another book called *Mein Kampf.* It was a huge book so I bet it was boring. My father said it was a book written by a great man. I wanted to be an author one day – once I retired from my athletics career, that is.

I could hear my father talking on the telephone while I browsed for a new book to read in bed that night. There was nothing that caught my eye. I would have to ask Mom to take me to the library. My father raised his voice. My thoughts interrupted, I couldn't help but hear what he was saying.

'Don't fuck with me, Martin!'

I tried to ignore him, but his words forced themselves on me.

Dad was telling Martin to make sure the fire destroyed the paperwork in his study, if he wanted the rest of the money.

The door banged open before I'd had a chance to think of running away.

'Were you eavesdropping on me?' he whispered, while towering over me.

'No – no – I swear –' I stammered.

'*Were you eavesdropping on me?*'

I cowered to the ground, as shame cast its shadow over me.

'You heard nothing? Swear to me that you heard nothing, Jacqueline?'

'Nothing. I heard nothing, I swear.'

'Good.'

He straightened his tie and walked away, his leather shoes clacking on the floorboards.

That night I couldn't sleep. I knew it was wrong to eavesdrop and snoop and I felt ashamed that I had, even though it was by accident. My father was a good Christian: it wasn't his fault that he'd gotten so angry, so whatever fire or paperwork he was talking about couldn't be bad. I kept telling myself this as I tried to drift off, but it didn't help. Sleep wouldn't come. My mouth felt dry. I got out of bed and tiptoed down the passage to the bathroom. A strip of light shone under the door. I was not about to be caught lurking outside another door. I turned to go back to bed.

'What are you doing up so late?'

Mom was wearing her nightdress and her face was covered with white cream.

'I couldn't sleep.'

'Did you have a nightmare?'

'No. I couldn't fall asleep.'

'Was it your back that was hurting you?'

I had back pain that had been getting worse over the months and my training schedule didn't seem to be helping.

'My back is always hurting me, but it's not that.'

'It's probably the start of your period.'

I frowned. I didn't understand what a period was, but I didn't want one. I had been begging God not to let that happen to me and so far He'd answered my prayers.

'Well, do you want to tell me why you think you couldn't sleep?'

'No,' I said, too quickly.

She looked hurt, but I couldn't tell her. Not this, not anything.

'Why don't you think of nice things then, Jacqueline? It's almost

Easter and we will be camping in Hermanus and your birthday is around the corner.'

'I'll try,' I said, but I couldn't.

———◆———

'I want to sleep in the tent,' said David.

'There's no space. You and I have to sleep in the caravan with Mom and Dad,' I snapped.

David looked like he was going to start crying and I felt guilty for being short-tempered with him, even though he irritated me in a way only a little brother could. I'd been struggling to sleep every night since I'd overheard my father's conversation. David stormed off.

It was Easter Friday and my father had taken us to Hermanus for a weekend of camping. Alan and Mark were busy organising the fire for that evening's *braai* while Steve and I were setting up the tent, and David was getting in the way. My mother sat on a plastic chair at the campsite next door to us, chatting to her friends. Her hair was still wet from our afternoon swim and it struck me that she looked like a much younger woman, almost girlish. I'd only ever thought about her as our mother. I wondered what was on her mind – did she know things that kept her up at night?

'Jacqueline, you're not paying attention there,' called Steve.

A gust of wind had blown our half-erected tent over. Steve was struggling under a sheet of tarpaulin. Mark, now seventeen and well over six foot tall, lumbered over and helped Steve.

'Where's Dad?' he asked. 'The meat and the fire are ready, so we can start *braaing*.'

'I dunno. Mom, where's Dad?' I called.

'He's gone perlemoen diving with his friends,' she said. 'He's late but he should be back soon.'

Dad arrived at dusk. He had no perlemoen. He and his friends had been pulled over by the police and their perlemoen had been confiscated because they were over the legal fishing limit. I sensed they were a little over the beer limit as well. We spent the evening laughing and joking about Dad getting bust. Later, when my parents went to sleep in the caravan, Steve and I sat outside chatting by the fire.

'Listen,' I whispered. 'Do you know why Dad was fired?'

Steve was silent and seemed nervous.

'Come on, tell me.'

'You know I can't. He made me promise. It's between us, no one else can know. I'm going to bed,' he said, and walked off.

When I woke the next morning, I felt dull and headache-y. I'd had nightmares of crows picking at my skin and my brothers being melted like plastic dolls in a fire. I blinked blearily at the sink where a large pile of dirty camp plates sat ready to be washed. I got up, got dressed and started washing up with David under my mother's instructions.

A knock sounded on the side of the caravan. The door was open, but I couldn't see who it was.

'Good morning, officer,' my mother said politely.

I froze, let the plate I was holding slide back into the sink and listened carefully.

'Good morning, ma'am. I'm looking for your husband?'

'He is currently at the ablution block. Would you mind waiting for him?'

'Ma'am, I need to speak to your husband urgently. I have some bad news.'

No one spoke on the drive home. A cold, heavy liquid seemed to have filled my stomach and throat. I didn't think I could speak, even if I'd wanted to. I gazed out of the window as we drove down Sir Lowry's pass towards our home. Dad parked the car in the driveway and got out, followed by my mother and brothers. I kept my eyes on my knees, not wanting to get out, afraid of what I would see.

'Come on, Jacqueline,' Steve whispered.

As I walked slowly up the driveway, I was aware of other

people, strangers and neighbours and policemen and fireman, crowding around the house, but I didn't look at them. All I could see was the blackened ruin that was our home. The front door had been burned away, leaving a gaping black mouth through which the charred interior was visible. Many of the brick walls were still standing. Blistered beams and remnants of household appliances littered the open spaces. I walked around the garden, examining the shattered walls from every angle. I was looking for a sign that this had nothing to do with my father; a signal that he was innocent, that it was a simple accident. But there was no sign. I looked at the remains of his office and saw that the window was wide open. I looked at each window in turn and wondered why they were all open. I knew that we'd shut and locked all the windows as usual when we left the house. I finally got to the back of the house. My bedroom had simply ceased to exist. It was an empty block of air; it was a piece of grey sky on a misty morning. A gust of wind kicked up some ash and the smell of smoke pricked my nose.

———◈———

We stayed at Ouma's house in the Strand because we had nowhere else to go. My Ouma was nothing like Granny. While Granny could wax lyrical on the benefits of owning the perfect scarf or single piece of fine jewellery, she was not a natterer like Ouma. Ouma never stopped gossiping, loved junk jewellery, or junk anything for that matter, and her every second word was Jesus. She was even more religious than my parents, which was no mean feat, and had covered every inch of the back window of her little orange Datsun with 'God is Love', 'Jesus is My Co-Pilot' and 'Honk if You Love Jesus' stickers. The stickers painted a forgiving image of her Christianity, which in fact was far more aligned with hellfire and brimstone – and, of course, the 'you' in 'Jesus Loves You' referred only to white people. On top of all of that, my Ouma was a girly girl. She had a purple bedroom and her house was a riot of clashing colours. In short, I didn't understand her the way I understood Granny and even though we both loved Jesus, having to move in with her made the fact that we had just lost our house and all our possessions even more unbearable. My brothers and I were slouched around the cluttered living room, waiting for a word from our parents, who had gone again to inspect the ruined house. All attempts at conversation had fizzled out within seconds and we sat staring at one another blankly. Then we heard the scraping of keys. My father walked in backwards, carrying a big box.

'Got some good news,' he said, when he'd put the box down on the coffee table.

We looked at him eagerly.

'We've got the TV back!'

We all shouted our excitement.

'But how come it didn't burn down like everything else?' I asked.

My father narrowed his eyes.

'Jeez, Jacqueline,' Alan muttered.

'For your information, Jacqueline, I lent the television to Harry for the weekend.'

'But, why? Doesn't he have his own TV —'

Steve slammed his elbow into my ribs. I was aching to shout that I knew, *I knew* what he had done, but shame bit my tongue as fear pushed down my words. Ouma bustled in with a tea tray.

'What you children need to cheer you up is a nice cup of tea and a whole lotta Jesus. We should all thank Him that none of you were in the house,' she said cheerfully.

The sticky moment evaporated. We, masters of the art of pretending that everything was okay, sat down for tea. I looked at my father properly for the first time over the rim of my teacup. He had tried to fluff his thinning hair over his forehead. His lips were slack over his teacup, showing small, gapped teeth. That smile could be so warm and winning, if you had pleased him. We locked eyes for a second. His blue eyes had that open frankness, that happily clear conscience of the righteous damned. I wanted to shatter my teacup on the floor and run to him, put my arms around him, close his eyes gently with my fingertips and tell him that everything would be fine. But mine were human hands. He needed hands other than mine to make him see that he had done wrong, to make him step into his fear and surrender. He needed God's hands. But my faith did not help me when I finally confronted him.

CHAPTER FIVE

---

*Darkness cannot drive out darkness; only light can do
that. Hate cannot drive out hate; only love can do that.*
— *Martin Luther King Jr*

ON THE DAY I DECIDED to speak my mind, my father was lying
slumped in bed wearing nothing but sleep shorts. He closed his
eyes when he saw me. I guess he should've been looking for another
job but I heard him shout at my mother one evening that 'no one is
fucking hiring at the moment'. Weeks had passed since the fire. He
kept his eyes shut and pulled the duvet over his feet.

'Dad, I need to talk to you.'

'Not now. I'm exhausted. The police are trying to find the person
who burnt the house down and then we can lock him up for good.'

I played along. It was a strange game; he knew I had overheard
his conversation on the telephone.

'Are they sure the fire wasn't an accident?'

'They're dead sure. All the windows were open and your
mother's jerseys were doused with petrol.'

I hesitated. Perhaps the phone call had had nothing to do with
the fire and maybe it was true what my father kept on saying:
someone had it in for him. He seized his advantage.

'Now we all need to stick together. We're not going to let this tear our family apart. I know you loved that house, but you're going to have to be a big girl for me now, because −'

'Dad, I know it was you.'

'Excuse me?'

'I know you paid someone to burn the house down.'

His eyes narrowed and his face grew red. I immediately wanted to go back in time and unsay it.

'*How dare you?* How dare you speak to me like that and accuse me of a crime when all I've ever done is worked day and night for you kids? You stand there and tell me I burned our house down! Have you no shame?'

He stood up in front of me, pointing his finger in my face. If I leant forward a centimetre he would have touched my cheeks. I began to cry.

'You don't understand, you don't get to stand there and pass judgment as if you were some kind of a fucking saint and now look at you − crying like a little girl −'

'I know you did it,' I sobbed, 'I don't mind Daddy, I forgive you. God will forgive you too, but you need to tell the truth.'

He walked away from me and his turned back was a punch to the gut.

'Don't you even think about telling your mother about this.'

Then he turned to face me and for a second I thought that we were going to forget all about it, but the moment I saw his twisted smile I knew there was no chance.

'Not that it matters if you did. She doesn't believe a word you say.'

I reeled, knowing he was right, knowing I was completely alone in this. It was on me to save him from himself.

'Please Dad,' I said taking a deep breath, 'I love you, but admit −'

'Admit it? You want me to incriminate myself and go to jail for no reason? Who will then work and earn money to feed you and your brothers? Your mother?'

'I'll work, I'll get a job, I promise, I'm so sorry!'

'That's ridiculous!'

He started to laugh.

'You started the fire, I know you did it!'

'So what? They can't prove a thing.'

We looked at each other, breathing heavily. It was as good as an admission.

'What are you going to do about it? Tell the police, huh?'

His mouth had formed a contemptuous little smile and he was shaking his head.

'Well guess what, Jacqueline? They probably already know. They know it was me. So, don't think you're so clever.'

'But what if they do find proof, Dad? Maybe they'll be less angry if you come forward before they find out. We'll stick together, we always do.'

'Come forward and it will be okay? Jesus Christ Jacqueline, how naïve are you?'

'Jesus will forgive you.'

'You know I'll go to jail if I admit it,' he whispered.

He looked scared and vulnerable. I wanted to reach out to him and hug him, but I feared he'd push me away.

'If you do, I'll visit you every single day, twice a day. Sometimes people who go to jail get out really soon if they're actually good people who made a mistake. I'll pray for you, I'll stand by you.'

But the moment of vulnerability had been strangled by shame.

'Don't be fucking naïve, Jacqueline. Get out of my room.'

'But –'

'*Get out!*'

The next day he came to find me while I was reading on the couch in the lounge. He sat down beside me and put his arm around my shoulder. He rubbed my shoulder with his hand and then my arm.

'Jacqueline, I didn't mean any of those things I said yesterday.'

'I know.'

'You know that sometimes it's hard to love you, right?'

It was true: I was hard to love. I imagined my father drawing up a pros and cons list of having me as his daughter. On the good side, I was tough. Pain was nothing to me. I was smart. Dad said that women weren't cut out for working with numbers, but I was excellent at maths and science. I wasn't a loose girl like some of the high school girls that Alan and Mark hung around. They were all flirtatious and wore sexy bikinis and Alan's friend Amy was a bra model, which my father said was disgusting. I would never shame my father that way. I prayed and I read my Bible and enjoyed it. I wasn't vain – in fact, I never bothered to look in the mirror.

I wracked my brain trying to think of more reasons for him to love me, but came up blank. The negatives crowded in.

The first negative was the biggest and the rest all stemmed from it: I was an outspoken girl and there was nothing my father hated more than females with opinions. Women were made by God to only be involved with children, kitchen and church – and nothing else. God, as he had told me many times, made Man superior to Woman like White is superior to Black. Girls should be married, barefoot and pregnant by nineteen – and that was that. I wasn't sure why we had to be barefoot.

He thought I was too sensitive, even though I could count the number of times I had cried in front of him on one hand. I was too inquisitive and I didn't respect my parents enough – I was always asking questions and interfering with adult things. I was disobedient. He'd told me that countless times. I caused him constant worry because I was a girl.

I guess he worried that I would become immoral and stray from the path that God had laid out for me; that I would become superficial from all the TV I watched; that I would become arrogant if I won too many races; that I would damage my brothers if I did better than they had done at school or in sports; that I would prove to be a selfish woman if I didn't put him and my brothers first or help my mother in the kitchen; that I would never marry because I was a tomboy. The endless worry must have exhausted him and I didn't know how to stop, to be better, to reassure.

'I know it's hard to love me.'

'Now we're in this together, Jacqueline. You're the only one that knows the truth. You're the only one who really understands. This means we've got a special bond now. You're my only daughter after all, so I know I can trust you with this secret.'

I looked up into his clear blue eyes and knew I would do anything for him.

'So, you'll go to the police then?'

'I'll have to choose the right time. But you can't tell anyone about the phone conversation, okay?'

'I promise I won't.'

'Not a single soul. We're partners now.'

'But you're going to admit it, hey?'

'Of course, Jacqueline, of course. The Lord our God is merciful and forgiving.'

I beamed.

Months later, I was no longer beaming. It was almost the end of the school year and the guilt of keeping our secret gnawed at me all day, but still he hadn't gone to the police. He avoided being alone with me. One morning, when everyone was asleep, I snuck into the kitchen to talk to him.

'What do you want, Jacqueline?' he sighed. 'Can't you see I'm tired?'

'Dad, you need to own up to what you did,' I said quietly.

'I told you I would, didn't I? But it has to be at the right time. Don't you trust your father?'

'Of course I do.'

'Then stop checking up on me! Remember, Jacqueline, the fire was as much your fault as mine. When you are a parent one day, you'll understand that sometimes you have to do whatever it takes to protect your family.'

'I know, Dad, but —'

To silence me he promised that he would confess once the insurance company had paid him. I believed him after he reminded me that I should be ashamed for doubting my father.

'We won't have to leave Somerset West, will we Dad?'

He didn't answer.

———

Oupa, my Dad's father, died a few months later. For a while thereafter, things seemed to go back to normal. I started high school and we rebuilt our house with the insurance money. I was finally feeling happy again when my father called us all inside one evening and announced to the family that we would be moving to Ladysmith, some godforsaken town over 1400 kilometres away. He tried to sell the idea to us, but I saw right through him.

I couldn't believe that he was my father, the same father who protected me in the waves at the Strand beach, taught me to ride a bike, tucked me in bed at night. The house was sold and we moved in with Granny, into her house in the Strand. I tried not to think about the secret, but it was only when I was running that I could get it out of my mind.

'Jacqueline, honestly, haven't you had enough of running?' Granny asked as I flopped down next to her on the *stoep* (verandah). 'You need to take up a community sport, like tennis, something that you can play for the rest of your life. All of this solitary exercise won't serve you.'

I grinned at her and she smiled back. She knew I'd never stop running, but that wouldn't stop her from speaking her mind. I wished more adults were like her — always ready to listen and given advice when asked. Two of my favourite pearls of wisdom were 'A woman needs only two things in life, her dignity and a pair of fur-lined gloves' and 'Never blame others for your own failings.' I didn't feel like I had much dignity left and I'd failed at getting my father to admit what he'd done, but Granny wouldn't judge me if I told her about it. In the past I would have talked to Steve, but things were different now. I was too ashamed to tell him that I'd overheard that phone call and I could've done something to save our house. In a time when I should have acted, I hadn't had the courage.

'Granny, can I ask you something?'

'You can ask me as many questions as you like, my dear, but I can't guarantee that you'll like the answer. Shoot – isn't that what you young people say?' she laughed.

'Actually, I want to tell you something.'

But as I opened my mouth to speak, the telephone rang and she went inside to answer it. Long after she'd gone inside, I stayed sitting on the *stoep* in the cold wind. I knew that I'd never be able to break my word to my father and tell her. Dad had told me not to judge him, as only God could judge him. I prayed every night for a miracle that would make life go back to how it was before the fire. I prayed for God to somehow let us go back to 1 Van der Merwe Street, where we had been happy. But God didn't hear me.

CHAPTER SIX

The important thing is not to stop questioning. Curiosity has
its own reason for existing. – Albert Einstein

THE CAR JOURNEY FROM SOMERSET WEST to Ladysmith, Natal
(now KwaZulu-Natal) lasted sixteen hours and I refused to say
a word for the entire trip. There was no reason for me to be dragged
away from my friends, from my athletics team and from everything I
loved. Mark had been allowed to stay with my Ouma because he only
had one year of school left. I'd begged my parents to let me stay too.

'You'll love it,' said my father from behind the wheel as we
neared Ladysmith. 'Did I tell you that Ladysmith is on the banks of
the Klip river? And the Drakensberg mountains are in the distance.
Did I tell you that? I know how much you love the mountains,
Jacqueline.'

He caught my eye in the rear-view mirror and I looked away.

The closer we got to Ladysmith, the thicker the air became. It
was hot and heavy when we arrived at our rental house and my
clothes stuck to my back. Thirty degrees in Somerset West felt
nothing like this. This was hell. We unpacked sullenly, each wrapped
in a world of our own, and spent the next few days moping. On the
third day, Dad called us outside to introduce us to two boys he'd

persuaded to come and meet us. The kids attended the only high school in town, like we would, and the next day they invited us to the public pool to meet the rest of their friends.

At the pool the guys introduced me to a gang of girls. Claire, Lisa, Nicole and the others weren't like girls I knew from home. They spoke about sex and they actually had sex, too. They drank, smoked and they swore, chewed with their mouths open and burped, had painted nails, wore short skirts and flashed their panties. Bewildered, I watched and listened, too scared to participate. They found my naivety hilarious. Before Lisa told the story of how she and Claire had figured out how to use tampons, I didn't even know what a tampon was. Lisa explained in fits of laughter how she had made Claire lift her one foot up onto the toilet seat while she crouched on the bathroom floor and tried to stuff the tampon into Claire. I was shocked that one girl had seen another girl's you-know-what. I'd never even dared to look at my own. Still, by the time the first term had started, I was one of the gang.

One night, months later, I got drunk with them. The next morning, a Sunday, my mother kept glancing at me over the cereal box at the breakfast table. My tongue felt as if it were made of leather. I kept my eyes cast down, hoping she wouldn't figure it out. I was fourteen. There was no reason for her to suspect me of having been drunk and vomiting on Nicole's shoes at a complete stranger's wedding the night before.

'Jacqueline, what happened last night. I practically dragged you from the bathroom to your bedroom so that your father didn't see.'

I hazily remembered that I had fallen flat on my face on the bathroom floor in front of Mom.

'Your father thinks you and Alan were drinking. Is that true?'

'No way,' I lied. 'Mom, you know I would never do that. It was something I ate.'

If she caught me in a lie, I'd face the consequences, but my mother evoked none the gut-twisting guilt that my father could with one glance.

'Your father and I have been thinking that perhaps it would be better if you spent time with a different group of children for a while.'

'Why?'

'They come from a different background to us and they're – Jacqueline, they're –'

'But Mom, they are my friends.'

'We hope that you'll consider finding new friends, friends who, let's say, match your own status in life. That's why we're moving to a better area in Ladysmith next month, just until Dad can buy a house on the hill. Everyone who is anyone lives on the hill, you know.'

I ignored this, as we had moved too many times for me to care.

'What do you mean, 'My own status in life?''

'We may be facing difficult times, but that does not mean your father's family name need fall into disrepute. We can't have you playing with children who literally live on the wrong side of the railway tracks.'

'Granny doesn't give a hoot about our stupid family name, especially since the very reason all of us including her are facing difficult times is because of Dad! I know that he got fired and I know what he did to the house! I'd rather hang out with real friends who actually like me than –'

'*JACQUELINE!*

I was surprised. She was angry.

'*Don't you ever speak like that again!*

I watched her compose herself, wiping away her anger.

'Don't you ever say a word against your father in my presence! I don't know who has been telling you these lies, but I refuse to listen to a single word. Go to your room. Now!'

Mom never got angry and I felt a stab of savage pleasure knowing I had finally gotten a reaction out of her. Mom didn't even react when Dad was picking on her. Bitter thoughts coursed through my mind as I lay on my bed, watching the fan carve its way through the muggy air. My father had been behind the whole conversation. My mother would never have confronted me about my friends unless commanded to by her husband, but I had no intention of giving up the gang, no matter what either of them said about it. As the months sped by in Ladysmith, I grew closer to my friends and drifted further from my brothers – and my father didn't like it one bit. While me being a tomboy wasn't ideal, me having a close group of wild girlfriends must've been his nightmare.

——◆——

A few weeks after moving houses yet again, my father found me completing the last of my chores on the roster for that day. It was my duty day in the kitchen and I was unpacking the dishwasher. He gave me such a fright when he said my name that I screamed.

'Afraid of your dad?' he laughed.

The week before I'd come home with a pair of pink jeans that I'd bought and he'd told me I looked like a fucking whore and should be ashamed to walk around in public in them. It wasn't the first time he'd lost it with me since we'd moved to Ladysmith. I was now used to being called a little bitch, but a fucking whore? I should have sensed his warning signs when he came out onto the *stoep* that day and found my mother painting. He told her it was a waste of time and money. I had started defending her of late, which made him turn on me. I shouldn't have bothered. It didn't change anything, it only made him mad, but I wasn't thinking straight. I was too excited about the jeans. When he saw the jeans, he screamed at me as if I'd come home pregnant, screamed until his veins started pulsing and his spit flew, screamed until I was shaking and begging him to stop. I was terrified of this new, angry Dad.

'I didn't know they were slut's jeans,' I'd sobbed. 'It's not for the boys, I promise it's not for the boys!'

'Well it sure as hell fucking *looks* like it's for the boys! Don't you know what kind of message you're sending? But I suppose women never do, do they?'

And then he'd said it. '*You fucking whore!*'

I would never wear pink again, I'd thought.

I unpacked the plates one by one, still not looking at him.

'Jacqueline, I might've overreacted last weekend by making you take those jeans back to the store. It's not easy being a dad, you know. I've got to try and make the best decisions for you all the time and I want to protect you. I don't want you hanging out with that gang of girls as they are only interested in boys.'

'I know, Dad.'

'If I did overreact, it's because I love you. You know that, right? You're my little girl and I've got to look out for you.'

He smiled his most winning smile at me and I softened. I had recently become anxious and scared of him. I was grateful he wasn't screaming or doing any of the other things I had on my imagined-worst-things list, as it was better than being taken by surprise by a new insult. But today, he was the best of Dads, the warmest and the most caring.

He wrapped his arm around my waist and pulled me close to him. He'd always been affectionate. I was wearing a pair of loose shorts and he slid his hand under the waistband and patted me on my bum, underneath my panties. This was also new behaviour and I hated it when he did this, but I didn't move because it felt like he loved me and the past week had been hell with him refusing to look at me or talk to me.

'You and I, we've got to look out for one another, hey? Jacqueline, you know I will protect you from anything.'

'I get that you were trying to protect me, Dad.'

He squeezed my bum, took his hand away and gave me a one-armed hug.

'If you want, you can buy the jeans. I won't say a word. You're a big girl now and I've got to trust you to look after yourself.'

'Really? Like, really really?'

'Really. Besides, you're strong enough to break any boy who tries to touch you, right?'

He laughed and turned to leave.

'Wait, Dad.'

'Yes,' he said.

Dad was being nice to me, so I thought it was a good time to ask.

'Dad you haven't confessed about the fire yet. I want to know when you will.'

'Jacqueline, don't *fucking* push me.'

I shut my mouth instantly. I couldn't face him screaming again.

'If you trust me, you know I'll do it in my own good time like I promised. Now finish your chores. When you're done, I'll drive you to town and we can buy the jeans together. Whaddaya say?'

That evening I stared at the pink jeans he'd bought me, but didn't bother to take the price tag off them. I knew I'd never be able to wear them. I no longer believed I could trust him.

A few weeks later my father and I were driving to get milk.

'Listen, Jacqueline,' he said, 'Your mother and I have been thinking.'

'You know the way we feel about your friend group. We want you to give some other kids a chance, okay? That's all we ask.'

'What other kids?'

'Well, I met a great guy, a lawyer, actually. He's also involved in politics with the National Party and he's going to help me find a bigger house to buy in a better area. We won't have to rent this small one anymore. He has a daughter a year younger than you and he has asked her to invite you to tea.'

Oh, here we go again. My parents were obsessed with trying to find me 'Nice Kids from Good Families' to hang out with.

'Who's the girl?'

'Hannah Meyer,' he said. 'Do you know her?'

I tried not to roll my eyes. Hannah Meyer was the tennis champ with the high ponytail that she was always swishing in other people's faces. I could imagine what the gang would say.

But as it turned out, I liked being with Hannah.

Her house was at least four times the size of ours. When I arrived, she had just finished a tennis match against her brother and was wearing a white tennis dress. She looked like she had stepped off the court at Wimbledon, except that she wasn't sweaty. She took me up to her bedroom, where we chatted about our favourite teachers. It was a relief not to talk about boys, which was the only topic with the gang. Hannah's bedroom walls were plastered with magazine pictures of Lady Diana, her heroine.

'I'm probably going to marry a prince or something one day,' she said, watching me stare at the photographs, 'So I've got to be, like, ready. I'm having my hair cut like Lady Di next week.'

'Cool,' I said. I made a mental note never to tell Claire or Nicole or anyone about this, because they would never stop teasing her.

We went down to the lounge. The maid brought a tea tray, complete with a teapot and a selection of freshly baked biscuits. It felt posh and reminded me of how we did things at my Granny's house.

'You know,' Hannah said, 'These are supposed to be the best days of our lives.'

We looked at one another and then snorted with laughter.

Being with Hannah made me think of my friends back in Somerset West. Maybe I could be happy again.

CHAPTER SEVEN

*The way to gain a good reputation is to endeavour to
be what you desire to appear. – Socrates*

ON THE FACE OF IT, I was settling in well, despite the fact that
we had moved again and the fights that kept flaring up between
my father and me. I was getting good marks, I'd found friends my
father was not ashamed of, while secretly staying close with the gang,
and I had joined the netball team even though my parents muttered
that netball was only for trashy girls. Proper young ladies from good
families played hockey. Nevertheless, life felt toneless. All I wanted
was to be like other kids, but my father policed everything. I was
pushing myself to be the best at every sport I was involved in, and
most of all in my running, because I wanted him to look up from the
newspaper he was cursing and tell me I'd done a good job. But he'd
changed, I told myself, and it wasn't fair to expect him to notice things
I did. He had more important things to do: I just couldn't figure out
what they were. He'd lost interest in being the coolest guy around
and, aside from Hannah's father and one or two other men, he hadn't
bothered to make new friends. I prayed for him every night and for
my brothers, too. They were bearing the physical brunt of his changed
mood. While I got screamed at, they got hidings. It was particularly

hard on David, because he got a bit of both.

Whenever friends from out of town came to visit, you'd swear he was Dad-of-the-year – he was chilled out, happy to toss a ball with us, or let us go off with our friends without checking on where we were going or when we were coming back. It was confusing as hell, but it felt like old times and I loved it. One evening when Uncle Harry had come to Ladysmith for a visit, my father invited his handful of friends over for dinner. I knew they would have drinks in the lounge afterwards, so I lay down behind the couch, hoping he might tell them why he'd changed.

'What can I say?' he said, cracking open a beer. 'I've bought this beautiful home, one of the finest old homes in Ladysmith. I'm blessed.'

'Ja, you're really living the life out here,' Uncle Harry said.

'Ja no, it's lekker in Ladysmith. We're having a ball. The kids are loving it, man.'

'They're great kids,' said another man.

'Don't I know it! You should see Jacqueline on the athletics field. She's a sportswoman and a half. And academic as anything!'

'She must get it from her mother,' joked Uncle Harry, and they all burst out laughing.

I lay behind the couch until well past my bedtime, my parents thinking I was asleep in bed. He had admitted to others that he was proud of me. Why couldn't he tell me that? But it was better than nothing and I held onto that moment whenever I feared he would explode, because it showed that he really did love me.

But it wasn't enough to keep me safe. I walked on eggshells and soon I was in a state of perpetual exhaustion. At night I lay awake thinking of ways to get him to confess and of ways I could improve myself – then maybe we'd all be happy again. The chant 'sticks and stones may break my bones but words will never hurt me' had slowly stopped making sense to me. I used to be able to brush off the insults and take pride in being able to ignore them and move on. But over time

– fucking bitch, slut, whore – built into a weight on my chest that I felt too weak and worthless to lift. I envied my elder brothers their beatings, and perhaps David did too, but more than anything I missed the happy person I used to be. There was nothing I wouldn't give to change myself and make it all go away, but even the littlest things made him angry. If Steve or David watched *The Brady Bunch* too loudly, he would snap and turn it off – and then complain about the humidity or something equally irrelevant. And the blacks – most of all, he complained about all the black people. I think we'd all been shocked when we first arrived in Ladysmith, as there seemed to be millions of them and only a few of us. In contrast to Somerset West, we were a very small group of whites – tiny and out of place – and these black people weren't scared of us.

'Aren't we supposed to be the majority? Why else are we the only ones in government?' I'd asked when we first arrived.

'We're in charge,' snapped my father. 'We might be a minority but we've got brains, unlike these stupid kaffirs. If it weren't for us, they'd still be living in mud huts and trading chickens.'

'And what about the Indians?' I asked. 'Where do all of the Indians come from?'

'India, obviously.'

'But why?'

'To build railways and things. What else are they good for? Now stop asking questions, for God's sake, Jacqueline.'

In Somerset West, I'd lived under the happy illusion that I was an insider and meant to be there, while in Ladysmith I was an interloper. The villages surrounding Ladysmith had names I could not pronounce, like Ekuvukeni, Nxamalala, Emachunwini and Phuthaditjhaba. Not three hours away was the independent Kingdom of Lesotho. I had heard from one of the girls at school that Lesotho was where you went if you were an enemy of the state or planning an uprising. I thanked God my father didn't have to live in a country where black people were in control, because he would have choked to death on his rage.

'We should push these kaffirs and coolies into the sea and let them drown. It's not like they can swim,' he'd say again and again.

It had been his mantra since I was little. When I was younger, I'd had suspicions that apartheid was not in line with God's plan, but due to the overwhelming whiteness of my life in Somerset West, it had been easy to forget. Now it was clear to me that what was happening was plain wrong. It all felt like a lie and I was sick of lies, but I had no idea how to change any of it.

I tried to outrun the way I was feeling by training harder than before. I would practise sprinting up the hill that overlooked Ladysmith and then I'd sit at the lookout point, with the whole town below me, and think of how to help my father. I knew with a conviction as strong as if God Himself had commanded me that if I could only become a sniper and shoot down every single black person in Ladysmith, my father would be okay again. But God would never command me to do that because God was Love and no matter what my family said, this applied to everyone, no matter their colour. But why couldn't He help my father stop being so angry all the time? Why weren't my prayers being answered? I couldn't bring any of this up with my father without driving him over the edge and I couldn't ask my mother because, as Dad said, she was a woman and couldn't understand important matters. The questions rolled around my head, making it pound.

———◆———

I got home from a run one afternoon and found Dad asleep on the couch, snoring. My insomnia was driving me mad and his snoring even madder. I was pretty sure the whole town could hear it, but Dad had always insisted that he didn't snore. This was the perfect opportunity to catch him at it. I went to fetch the video recorder, clicked the cassette into place and started recording. He gave a massive, guttural snore and I had to fight back a laugh. Since we'd arrived in Ladysmith he had gotten fat and his last shirt button had popped open to show his hairy, white belly. He continued snoring and muttering in his sleep and, after a few minutes, I turned off the video, pushed the tape into the video player and waited for him to wake up. He must have sensed my presence. In a few minutes, he was awake and complaining that my mother was ten minutes late.

'Dad. Do you snore?' I interrupted him, excited to show him the video and have a good laugh together.

'Nope,' he said, smiling.

'Are you sure?' I said, fighting to keep my face serious.

He seemed to know there was a joke afoot and grinned up at me from the couch. It was my favourite smile of his – the cheeky one – as he gave his standard answer to this question.

'I've never heard myself snore in my life!'

'Watch this,' I said, and pressed play.

The image of him lying on the couch flickered for a moment and then settled. He looked even worse on the television screen than in real life. His face was red and swollen and his fat body heaved with guttural snores. His mouth hung open and his lips were sucked back to show his front teeth. Before the tape ended, he stood up and started shouting. *'HOW DARE YOU! YOU FUCKING LITTLE BITCH!'*

My brain, working in slow motion, couldn't piece together why this was happening. It was supposed to be funny. I backed away, bumping the TV to get further from him. He kept the words raining down on me like lashes, until I wanted to lie at his feet and beg him to hit me instead. He suddenly became quiet and then started walking away from me across the living room. When he got to the door, he turned back to look at me.

'You can't say those things to me,' I whispered, but he didn't hear.

I let myself slide down to the floor and crouched on my knees, sobbing. I could hardly think straight as I stumbled to my bedroom. I wished I could control the blood in my cheeks, but they had started pulsing with shame as I lay on my bed. I wished he'd hit me, but he seemed to think himself above that. My father was a gentleman. The next minute he was at my bedroom door.

'Jacqueline, now you better listen to me,' he said in a dangerously soft voice. 'I don't ever want to catch you disrespecting me like that again. You tape over that VHS right now or I swear to God if you so much as – '

'Dad, I'm really sorry, I didn't mean to upset you.'

He turned his back on me and made to leave my room, but turned around again. Had my father been an actor, he would have been one who always insisted on having the last line in every scene.

'You love causing trouble, love making us all miserable with your constant questions and your fucking defiance! Nothing's ever good enough for you.'

'That's not true, Dad, I don't want to make you miserable!'

'Liar! You hate it here, you hate Ladysmith, so why don't you go? No one would miss you, *no one*, so go – and leave me to look after this family. I've got sons who love me, they fucking adore me.'

'I'm sorry, I'm sorry, I'm sorry,' I said, wishing I could say it more, say it faster, say it so that he would stop speaking.

He turned away from me, breathing heavily. The back of his neck was red and his fists were clenched.

'Want to know what I'm sorry for?'

I shook my head dumbly.

'I'm sorry I didn't make sure your mother brought the right baby home from the hospital when you were born, because fuck, there are times when I can't believe you are my daughter.'

I stared. When I was little, he'd tease me that my mother had wanted a daughter so badly, she'd swopped her fourth son out at the hospital for a girl. I had found it funny. But he wasn't joking now.

I found myself crouched on the floor beside my bed. I was seeing him as if through the wrong end of a telescope, hearing his voice, but not hearing it. I wished I was a different person. The room had tilted and I felt dizzy, ice cold and he was looming over me, his finger pointing, pointing, pointing. Everything was too close, too hot.

And then he was gone, slamming my bedroom door behind him. A fly buzzed lazily around my head. I smashed it against the wall with the flat of my hand, leaving a small smear of blood and guts on the white paint.

Two weeks later, my father spoke to me again for the first time and I was so grateful I could have cried with joy. He came to my room one evening with a cup of tea that he put down on my desk. I was studying for an Afrikaans test the next day and I didn't really have time to talk. But no one told my father they didn't have time for him. It was his world and he was the only one who was allowed to draw boundaries. It was a case of: *If you want to live in my house, you abide by my rules and do as I say.*

'Jacqueline, I've been tense lately. That's why I didn't appreciate you videoing me. I know moving to Ladysmith hasn't been great, but it's been hardest on me. I've had to start everything from scratch to make sure that you get the education and the lifestyle you deserve.'

'I know, Dad. It was completely my fault. I'm really sorry.'

'I need your support for our life here to work out. You're my girl, Jacqueline. You and I share things that your brothers don't even know about. You've got to step up to the plate for me, okay?'

A voice inside of me wanted to tell him then that I didn't want to keep our little secret anymore, that I was done, but the part of me that wanted to be his favourite girl was too strong.

'I'm sorry for upsetting you, Dad. You don't deserve it,' I heard myself saying.

'So you'll never disrespect me again?'

'No Dad, never.'

He hugged me tightly, so tightly that my back twinged.

'Dad,' I said breathlessly, 'Can I ask you a favour?'

'Anything, Jacqueline.'

'Can I go and see a doctor about my back? I mean,' I hesitated, 'I know it's expensive and all that, but I really think it's getting worse, and maybe –'

'Of course, I'll take you to the doctor,' he said, and gave me one of his warmest and most generous smiles.

It made me feel as if I was looking directly into the sun but without any of the harshness.

CHAPTER EIGHT

Your beliefs become your thoughts, your thoughts become your words, your words become your actions, your actions become your habits, your habits become your values, your values become your destiny. – Mahatma Gandhi

I WAS DIAGNOSED WITH ANKYLOSING SPONDYLITIS shortly after my 15th birthday. No one would tell me exactly what this meant, but through overhearing whispered conversations, I knew it was bad. I went to the library and searched an encyclopaedia for information on my disease. I kept on reading and paging until a picture started to emerge, made of words like severe deformity of the spine; erosion of joints; no current cure; exercise worsens the condition; leads to significant disability; limits mobility and quality of life; neurologic and lung defects. There was a drumming in my ears, but I kept reading, knowing exactly what I was looking for. I found it – one cold, black-and-white sentence. 'In patients who are diagnosed when younger than 16 years old, life expectancy is reduced by 60%; furthermore, patients can expect to be severely disabled by their early 20s'.

I wrote this down and was sitting outside as I re-read it. Surely someone was playing a trick on me. Not God, but maybe David who carried the title of little brother proudly and couldn't resist teasing me until I was half-mad with irritation. I looked around the garden, hoping that David would appear with a grin and tell me that it had all been a big joke, but he didn't come. Bee-eaters and bush shrikes sang in the trees. Dying didn't worry me as much as the idea of being confined to a wheelchair with my Olympic dreams crushed.

My parents seemed to know the moment I stepped inside that I had found out more.

'We're going to get you well again,' my mother said. 'We'll pray to God that He heals you, Jacqueline. I know how important your faith is to you.'

'It's a test,' I said. 'It's a test from God. I'm not going to take this lying down. I'm going to fight it – I'm going to live.'

I didn't know where this sudden confidence had come from. Perhaps God had made me that way. Although a little part of me wanted to be held by my parents, I crushed it. Nothing was allowed to scare *me*. God must have meant for me to rise up and conquer it.

'That's my Jacqueline,' said my father and he sounded almost tearful. 'Always a fighter.'

I didn't tell anyone at school about my back because I didn't want their pity. While I waited for my parents to organise a trip to Johannesburg where I would see a specialist, I focussed my energy on being positive.

Around this time I met Alison, a girl in my grade. Alison was half my size and had soft brown hair, a round bum and duck feet. She didn't play any sports and she preferred History and English to Accountancy and Economics, so I wasn't sure what we would have in common but I liked her.

'So, listen,' said Alison one day in the school quad, 'I heard through the grapevine that you've gotten drunk before.'

'Ja, maybe,' I said casually, not wanting to admit that I'd only been drunk once, that time I threw up on Nicole's shoes.

'I can hook you up with some booze if you like,' said Jason, a friend of ours who had a crush on Alison.

'What do you think, Jackie? You in?' Alison asked.

'Of course I'm in.'

'Let's meet at the building site by the old convent on Friday afternoon? We can have a party of our own,' said Jason.

That Friday Alison and I stood in the building site in the gathering darkness for an hour before we decided that Jason wasn't coming.

'What a flake,' Alison grumbled. 'I really wanted to get drunk.'

'We can go to my house. My folks are away for the weekend and Alan is supposed to be in charge, but he's cool,' I said casually.

'Oh my god, is your brother Alan, like *the cool Alan?*'

'I get that a lot,' I said, as we walked. 'He's actually totally chilled.'

When we arrived home to an empty house, I poured half a bottle of liqueur, some brandy and two beers into a large jug. Alison looked at it doubtfully.

'You sure we should be mixing it?'

'Course! That's how you drink booze. Now we need to add juice and then we're good to go.'

An hour later Alison was giggling feebly, flat on the pantry floor. I'd decided not to drink because I'd promised Alison I would look after her. I found a box of bacon-flavoured crackers and a tin of smoked mussels in the pantry and managed to feed most of this to Alison while she poured out her life story. She was born in January and loved winning, she played the piano and it annoyed her that at home no one did the dishes or cut the lawn – and she couldn't catch a ball. I confessed that I was going to die young and that I was scared of being in a wheelchair and that I had been praying that, when I went to see the specialist in two weeks' time, I would be miraculously healed. She produced garbled words of sympathy and we embraced. Alison crawled to my room and I tucked her into my bed and put a bucket beside it before she passed out.

I woke the next morning to the pungent scent of alcohol and

vomit. Alison had vomited all over my floor, but by then we were best friends, so I didn't mind cleaning it up in the slightest.

———◆———

A fortnight after Alison and I had consecrated our friendship in secrets, alcohol and vomit, I travelled to Johannesburg with my mother to get a second opinion on my back. The doctor performed a lumbar dorsal myelogram, which required sticking a thick needle into my spine to fill it with fluid for the X-ray projections. I had passed out from the pain as the anaesthetist had tried and failed to give me a nerve block. I woke up much later.

'What happened?'

'You became unconscious,' said my mother. 'When the nurse came in to measure you for a brace, you started screaming that you weren't ready to die.'

I vaguely remembered images of the nurse measuring me for what I thought was my coffin.

'Jacqueline, it's not ankylosing spondylitis: it's only chronic scoliosis.'

I hung onto *only* and thanked God for answering my prayers.

'It is, however, severe as you've got a 47 degree curvature. There's a 90 per cent chance that it will get worse and if it does, they will consider a spinal fusion.'

I had no idea what any of this meant.

'But I'm not going to be in a wheelchair, right?'

'No, you're not. You'll have to wear a brace, though, and sleep in a corset.'

'At least I'm not going to die young!'

'You won't be able to play sports, Jacqueline. You'll have to be gentle with yourself.'

No bad news could bring me down now. On the drive back to Ladysmith I couldn't stop smiling as I silently thanked God a thousand times. By the time we arrived home, I'd devised a plan that would allow me to be involved in sports even if I couldn't play. I would become the scorer for the cricket A team and I'd aim to be house captain of athletics and swimming. I knew I was in line to be a prefect — maybe even head girl — in a few years' time, so being involved in school activities was important. God made me with a curved spine and if He wanted me to be a sports leader instead of a sports player, I would follow Him. I vowed that nothing would stand in the way of God's will.

We continued travelling to Johannesburg regularly for medical check-ups and Mom never once complained about the four hours there and the four hours back. After that first visit, Dad stopped coming with us and I was enjoying the time away from him.

Late on Sunday afternoon we arrived at Mom's cousin's house in Johannesburg, where we stayed before my appointments. Auntie Anne welcomed us inside and made a fuss.

'Oh, look at you, Jacqueline! You've grown a lot in the last few months! How old are you now?'

'She'll be 16 in April,' said my mother.

'Your mother tells me you're preparing for confirmation later this year?'

'Yes, Auntie Anne.'

'Jacqueline is very devoted, Anne,' said my mother. 'She went to the Presbyterian Church once with her friend Alison and so enjoyed Reverend Jones that she convinced us to move churches!'

'Jacqueline,' said my aunt. 'Why don't you join me this evening at the Assembly of God Church? They are doing prayer faith healings this evening. You know well that your Mom was faith healed after being told that she would never be able to carry a pregnancy. Maybe they can lay hands on you and pray for you, Jacqueline. What do you think?'

'Yes, I would love to be faith healed like Mom!'

We drove to the Assembly of God church, which was the biggest church I had ever seen. Auntie Anne walked me towards the group of people near the altar and introduced me to the pastor.

He had me sit on a chair in the centre of the group and they prayed, the pastor leading us. I closed my eyes and I felt six pairs of hands placed on my shoulders and upper back. The prayers continued. I focussed on God's love and opened my heart and mind to whatever was out there. My eyes were closed, but suddenly, out of the blackness, a bolt of white light came at me, straight to my chest. The heat of it melted through me and the white light turned to a soft gold. I felt warm, golden oil dripping over me. It was slippery and slid down my shoulders and down through the centre of my spine. A bar of warmth pulsed where my spine was.

'Amen,' said the preacher.

There were tears in my eyes when I opened them. There was no need to say out loud what we all knew already: God had spoken *directly* to me. I was healed.

The next morning at my doctor's appointment, I sat perched on the edge of the bed beaming.

'Doctor, I don't know if my mother told you, but I've been cured.'

'Well, we'll see. If you could stand up again, please?'

'My spine is straight again. I've been faith healed.'

'I'm glad you're feeling so positive,' he said kindly. 'In fact my wife and I prayed for you last night. We're praying you won't have to have your spine fused.'

'Yes, I know. You prayed at 6.30 last night.'

'How do you know we prayed at exactly that time?' he asked, surprised.

'That's the time I was faith healed. I could feel you with me in my prayers, as if you were right there.'

Although my doctor was a man of God, he was also a medical man. He performed every test he could think of, including a full body X-ray. What this revealed was that, despite my never having had an operation, I had a perfectly straight spine. I now believed my purpose was to share my story by writing about God's greatness and preach

His message to the world.

Upon returning to Ladysmith, I joined the Assembly of God Church as well.

CHAPTER NINE

*After climbing a great hill, one only finds that there are
many more hills to climb. – Nelson Mandela*

I THINK I'M GOING TO get my ears pierced,' Hannah announced
suddenly one day.

We had taken a three-day holiday job at the Makro wholesale
warehouse freezers as stock takers. Her announcement shocked me
so much that I nearly dropped the frozen chicken I was holding.

'Pierce your ears? But aren't you worried about looking easy?'

Hannah burst out laughing.

'They're only *earrings*, Jackie. You should get yours done, too.
We can go together.'

'I don't know,' I said hesitantly. 'My dad says that if God wanted
us to have holes in our ears we would have been born with them.'

'What is this, the 16th century? Maybe you should stand up to
your dad a bit, Jackie.'

'It's not worth it. The earrings thing will make him mad. But – I
guess that's silly, to be mad about earrings, right?'

'Ja, it is. Everyone has earrings. You just turned 16. You can do
what you want now.'

'I s'pose.'

'So are you in, or are you *in*? I want to go this afternoon.'

'I'm in!'

When I got home from the warehouse later that day, I told my mother about it while she was trimming roses in the garden. She said I should do whatever felt right to me. Within minutes of me leaving her in the garden, she'd told my father. I was already at the garden gate when he called out to me to stop and walked down the path to where I was standing.

'I hear you want to pierce your ears, Jacqueline.'

'Ja, I'm meeting Hannah at the pharmacy,' I said, cursing my mother.

I always stood up for her when Dad was bringing her down, so why couldn't she have my back this once? All I wanted was someone to talk to and she had to go and tell him.

'Let me drive you,' he said.

My palms had started to sweat and I rubbed them on my shorts. We got into his new car, his pride and joy, and drove off. I tried to slow my breathing. He could start screaming at any moment.

'Are you sure you want to go through with this? It's very permanent.'

'I think so,' I said in a small voice. 'Hannah and I wanted to do it together. We're the only ones in our year who haven't had our ears pierced.'

'I'm not sure Lord Jesus would want you to do this. It's your choice, but in Peter it does say that your beauty should come from your inner self. If God wanted you to have holes in your ears, you'd have been born with them.'

'I didn't think of that.'

My resolve started to crumble. Ever since my faith healing, I had become even closer to Jesus. I was devoted to Bible study, had joined a Christian Youth Group on Fridays and even went to church twice on Sundays so that I didn't have to choose between the two churches that I loved. I still had scores of unanswered questions about the way

Christianity worked in society and I wanted to know more. Since my faith healing, I felt I had a direct line to God and I believed He would answer all my unheard prayers now. I was even busy working on the outline of my book where I would write about how God had personally revealed Himself to me and healed me. In my emptiest moments, this connection was what kept me going and I was terrified of being without it.

'You could always hold it off until you're a bit older,' my father said. 'It's natural to want to try things the other teenagers do, but remember: if it doesn't come from faith, it is a sin. I'm not telling you what to do, but I do think the answer lies in the Bible and you know it.'

'I know,' I sighed.

Now I'd have to let Hannah down and she would call me a coward. There was a long silence. We were almost at the pharmacy.

'It's completely your choice, Jacqueline,' he said, and reached over and patted my thigh.

He wouldn't scream at me, not today. Today he was Reasonable Dad, Affectionate Dad, and even though I hated how he touched me at times and the mean things he said to me, I loved him and he loved me. It made such a change to be spoken to rationally that I had no choice but to obey him.

'Can you wait for me? I want to tell Hannah that I don't want to do it anymore.'

When I got back in the car he smiled at me, but I didn't experience the usual thrill. I wanted to please him, but I also wanted to make my own decisions. It was impossible to reconcile the two. I leaned my head against the passenger window and watched the people walking down the main street – 'aimless, hopeless, useless people' – as he stroked the inside of my thigh, stopping as the outside of his hand brushed up against my crotch. The autumn wind blew dead leaves back and forth across the pavement, taking them nowhere.

Hannah had gotten a head cold from working in the freezers at Makro and the only person at work that Sunday morning that I knew was Vinesh, an Indian boy who had been working alongside us. I didn't know Indians could be handsome or that I could feel attracted to anyone who wasn't white, but I did.

'You know Vinesh? Don't you think he's... I don't know... *hot?*' I'd said to Hannah the night before.

She'd blown her nose and then looked at me, eyebrows raised.

'No. He's Indian.'

'But he's so tall – and those eyes!'

'Jackie, don't even go there, okay? He's Indian and it's against the law!'

That had been the end of my attempt to talk to Hannah about the confusing mess of feelings that Vinesh was causing.

'Phew. Pretty boring work, hey?' I said, trying to start a conversation with Vinesh.

'Let's take a break,' he said, smiling at me from across a mountain of frozen peas.

We stood outside in the sunshine and made nervous small talk while he smoked. Since we had met, I had only ever seen him wearing golf shirts and jeans. He was preppy enough to look like he'd stepped out of a British boarding school. I didn't think to ask him if he went to school in Lesotho or Swaziland, where apartheid didn't exist and you could send your child to any school you wanted.

'So, what do you do for fun, Jackie?'

'I dunno,' I said, kicking a Coke can across the parking lot. 'I play a lot of sports.'

'I bet you play hockey, don't you?'

'No,' I laughed, 'My parents wish. I play netball, I run and I do modern dancing.'

I wanted to tell him about my love of cricket, but there was a chance that he was the only Indian I had ever heard of who *didn't* like cricket and that he would think I was stereotyping him.

'And if you can't play sports, what do you do?'

'I like scrapbooking, sewing things, you know. And –'

I broke off, blushing. He looked right at me.

'What is it, Jackie?'

'I write poetry and I am writing a book.'

I'd never told anyone about my writing. If it got to my father, he'd go berserk. Even though my mother had gone to university to study Fine Art, I knew well that no child of his would ever be some 'fucking mentally ill layabout artist type.'

'I knew there was something different about you,' Vinesh said.

'We'd better get back inside,' I said, and then wanted to kick myself, because it was our last day together.

I spent the rest of the afternoon lifting and packing in a rhythm, but my attention was on Vinesh. It felt as if there were threads tying my consciousness to him. I was so drawn to him that I didn't notice a shelf in the giant walk-in freezer toppling forward. The next thing I knew I had been knocked to the ground, bags of frozen peas covering me.

'Jackie! Jackie!'

'I'm okay!' I shouted, my voice muffled by the peas.

It was a miracle that it hadn't been worse. I heard Vinesh scrambling over the peas and then saw him appear above me.

'Whoops,' I said, and we both burst out laughing.

We started pushing the peas off me and when I was almost free, we were face-to-face between the freezer and the wall. I shivered. He was so close I could count his eyelashes. My heart was beating hard, but in a good way. His eyes were on my mouth and then we were kissing. We broke apart after a few seconds.

'Wow, you people kiss the same as us,' I blurted out.

'I was thinking the same thing,' he said.

When I left, there was no exchange of addresses or telephone numbers. We knew we would never see one another again. As I walked, I remembered how I'd wanted to become a sniper only the year before so that I could kill every non-white in Ladysmith to make my father happy. I was dazed and kept seeing Vinesh's eyelashes before me – and then a heat would rise through my body. I'd kissed boys before, but I'd never felt thrills like that. But he was Indian. I couldn't tell anyone. My father would have either died from the public shame or have killed him with his bare hands and hung him up in our garden for everyone to see, if he knew that I'd been kissing a 'coolie'. Not only that, it was against the Immorality Act.

The Republic of South Africa said that it was God's will that white and non-white mustn't mix, but that couldn't be right, because in my heart it *felt* wrong. I should've spoken against the system in whatever small way I could, but I kept my silence out of fear. I was only 16, and a girl, I told myself. No one cared what I thought. Nothing I did would make a difference. If I was too weak to stand up to my own father, how would I ever make a difference in the world? I started to run, desperate to get home so that I could pray – not for forgiveness, but for answers.

A few weeks later the school term was well under way, but I was still struggling to force Vinesh out of my mind. I needed a distraction and my fights with my father weren't helping. He'd even called me a fucking bitch in front of Alison.

So, I decided I would try and pierce my ears and see what God's response would be. This time I wasn't stupid enough to tell my mother. It was a Friday afternoon and Alison agreed to accompany me to the pharmacy before we went to our youth group. My ears had been wiped with rubbing alcohol and I was about to go through with it.

'Hang on! Can I use the phone?'

Alison groaned and spat out her chewing gum. She chewed gum all the time for weight loss. I'd gotten fat too and would've loved a quick fix, but my father would never have let me chew gum.

'Please don't tell me you're going to call and ask for permission.'

'My dad said I could do it if it was an informed decision, so I want to show him respect and let him know.'

Alison looked at me strangely and I realised that she pitied me. I had always thought it would be the other way around. Alison was poor and my family had overcome our difficulties and could buy nice things again. Alison was terrible at sports, her mother had let herself and her home go, while my mother was the picture of poise and our house was *Stepford Wives* tidy. But when I looked at myself from Alison's perspective, I didn't like it. So much had changed in the last two years. I had been in a back brace, although now I was cured. I wore baggy clothes and looked ugly so that the boys wouldn't notice me. My marks at school were starting to slip. My father's fluctuating moods left a frostiness that didn't exist at Alison's messy-but-happy house. I wasn't cute, or petite, or sassy like Alison. All the teachers liked her. I, on the other hand, arrived late to class, was snappy and some of them hated me, especially my English teacher. I didn't care to impress any of them anymore.

The real reason I wanted to call him was that I wanted to check whether he'd meant it when he said it was my decision. I wanted his respect. I went to the pay phone and dialled the home number and Mark, at home on military pass, answered the phone.

'Hi, Mark? Listen, can you tell Dad I've pierced my ears?' I lied.

'Dad, Jacqueline got her ears pierced,' he said.

'*YOU TELL YOUR FUCKING SISTER I'LL PUT FIFTY STITCHES IN EACH FUCKING HOLE WHEN SHE GETS HOME!*'

'I guess you can hear him.'

'Jacqueline?' said my father.

He started screaming so that I held the receiver away from my ear. I was stammering so much I couldn't say I hadn't done it yet. I was sobbing when at last he hung up with a reminder that he was ashamed to call me his child.

'What happened?' asked Alison, but I couldn't answer.

Alison called her mother, who drove me home because she didn't think I could walk. They dropped me off in the driveway and I tried to gather myself and focus on what he would say or do to me once I was inside. I hesitated for a second at the garden gate, deciding what to do, and then stepped forward.

'*I HAVEN'T PIERCED MY EARS, I HAVEN'T PIERCED MY EARS, I HAVEN'T PIERCED MY EARS!*' I screamed, over and over again, as I walked down the driveway holding onto my earlobes.

I didn't care who heard me. The only thing that mattered was that my father heard before he saw me.

'*I HAVEN'T PIERCED MY EARS! I HAVEN'T PIERCED THEM!*

I concentrated on what would hurt the most, praying that whatever he said wouldn't be worse than my imagination. But somehow it was. He didn't care that I hadn't pierced them. As he howled his anger, something seemed to drift out of me.

'*YOU LIAR, YOU FUCKING LIED TO ME: I CAN'T BELIEVE YOU'RE MY CHILD! I BET IT'S FUCKING ALISON THAT'S PUTTING THESE CRAZY FUCKING IDEAS INTO YOUR HEAD!*' he screamed.

I knew he didn't like Alison because he said her family was poor.

'Be careful of that girl, Jacqueline. She'll take the shirt off your back one day,' he'd once said.

I imagined him bursting a blood vessel if I told him it was Hannah that first suggested I have my ears pierced.

Instead, I looked into his watery blue eyes and realised I felt nothing. No terror, no love, no hope.

'I *hate* you. I wish you were *dead.*'

This time it was me who turned my back on him after these final words.

I realised as soon as I got to my room that God didn't give a damn about my ears.

CHAPTER TEN

*As far as we can discern, the sole purpose of human existence
is to kindle a light in the darkness of mere being. – Carl Jung*

I FOUND MYSELF BATTLING TO concentrate in my confirmation
classes with Reverend Jones. I was dejected, performing badly in
school, I couldn't sleep and nothing I did made a difference. Reverend
Jones must have sensed the change in me, because after class one
evening he stopped me on my way out.

'Jackie, something is troubling you. If you can't speak to me
about it, have you asked God for advice? Ask and the answer will be
given to you.'

So that evening, before bed, I decided to ask God for help.

'God, I haven't been okay since – well, since the fire. I feel like
my life is already over and I'm only 16.'

I heard His voice in my head, as clearly as if He were sitting
beside me on my bedroom floor, asking me what was causing this.

'It's my father,' I said at last. 'He's ruining my life, all of our lives.
I hate the way he speaks to me, Mom and to David, too. I know it's
my fault, but then sometimes I think it's not me and that he's just a
bad person. But he's my Dad and I love him. And then sometimes this
feeling comes up in me and I want to hurt him back. Lord, can't you

let him die? Can't you have him killed in a car accident or something? I want him gone. I want him dead so badly, Lord.'

A weight had been lifted. I didn't know how I hadn't realised what I wanted before – or perhaps I had, but to feel something vaguely is not the same as to acknowledge it out loud. I wanted him dead. I heard God speak again, telling me that killing is a sin and asking me if I felt I was at war with my father.

'Yes, God. I'm at war with him and I'm tired.'

'Then you know what you must do. You must kill your enemy, but you mustn't kill with malice. You mustn't gloat when he falls; you mustn't let your heart rejoice. This is my command.'

'But I don't want to sin against you.'

'Did I not appear to Joshua as the commander of the army of the Lord? And did I not command King David to destroy the Philistines? Come now! When soldiers came to John the Baptist, did I not tell them to be content?'

Could this be real? Was this really happening? I questioned it, but truly, there was no doubt in my mind that God was speaking to me the way he had the day that I was faith-healed.

'And they are all my sons, as you are my daughter. And now I'm telling you to free your family.'

'But, Lord, if my father dies, will he go to heaven?'

'Yes, child. He believes and for that reason he will never truly die.'

'Good. And – and me? I'll get the death penalty?'

'Have faith and trust in me.'

'I trust you, but how do I do it? I've never killed anyone before.'

But no one answered and I was alone in my darkened bedroom. My father was snoring in his room across the passage, so I stood up to go and roll him over. My mother had gotten used to it after so many years of marriage, but I hadn't and hated it. Soon my sleep would no longer be disturbed by him. Soon he would be dead. I slept properly that night for the first time in months.

———◆———

There was only one death row in South Africa at Pretoria Central Prison and the death penalty was by hanging. South Africa was a hanging factory. I knew this. Although cases of white people getting the death penalty were few and far between, I thought that should be my punishment. No one would miss me if I went. I wasn't even good at athletics anymore.

Dad and I had a formula to our fights now. We would scream the worst things we could think. I'd tell him to admit what he did. He'd shout that the Lord Jesus had forgiven him. I'd say I wished he were dead. What I didn't tell him was that I'd been planning how it would happen.

That night it was storming outside my window as I waited for my father's snores to start. For weeks, I had been visiting his room every night at midnight, poking him and prodding him, tugging at his pillow, and he never woke up. Finally, I heard his snores. At midnight, I got up and pulled my running *takkies* (sports shoes) on. I wanted to be properly dressed when they came to take me away.

I stood beside his bed for a few moments, watching his belly heave with snores. He looked peaceful under the shaft of moonlight that fell across their bed. I wondered how it was possible for him to be a loving father and a monster all at once. I glanced over at my mother. I believed she would be grateful when it was all over. I stared at Dad. His pillow was shifted away from his head and in the shadows I could make out his gun, which he kept under his pillow every night lest the blacks rose up and tried to kill us all. Now was the moment. I lifted the pillow and reached for the gun. Before I knew what was happening the gun was cold on my skin and being held to my forehead. My father's eyes were wide with terror and in a split-second the back of my skull could have been plastered all over the floor: he had been taught to act first, think later. But as he recognised me, his eyes narrowed. He didn't lower the gun. We glared at one another. I didn't look away, wanting him to know that I was not done. He turned his head briefly to check that my mother was still fast asleep. Even in cases of life and death, appearances were everything. Then he lowered the gun, tucked it under his pillow and lay down again turning his back to me.

In shock, I returned to my room, lay down on my bed and started to cry. But then I felt something warm, a light comforting me. 'God, was this a test? Did you send an angel to protect us from each other?' I knew that it was so, but still, I couldn't stop the tears. I wished that my father had killed me and then been hanged for it. That would've taken care of the both of us. Maybe after I was dead people would read my journals and understand how unhappy I was.

The next morning, I woke late and stumbled to the kitchen for a cup of coffee. My parents were sitting at the breakfast table eating cereal. My mother greeted me, but my father didn't look up.

'Sweetie, I've been thinking,' he said to my mother in a carrying voice, 'It would be safer if I locked the gun away at night.'

'But you've slept with it under your pillow for years.'

'Are you questioning me?'

He looked up at me and smirked. If I'd had a knife, I would have stuck it in his neck.

Winter had arrived and I was sitting alone in the family room, trying to concentrate on my economics textbook, but it was futile. How could I have wanted to kill my Dad? Sometimes it seemed like he did love me. Just last week he implied that he might let me pierce my ears and it wasn't even a year since the idea made him so mad.

'Whatcha doing?'

It was David, who had recently become more annoying than ever, or maybe it was me who'd become snappy.

'Trying to study.'

'What subject?'

'David, I'm trying to concentrate, okay?'

'I thought you were s'posed to be the big brainiac. You don't need to study.'

'Yes, I do!'

'So, what you studying then?'

'Economics,' I said shortly.

'Huh. Sounds boring. But you're boring, so it's a perfect fit.'

'David, not today, okay? Stop teasing me. Just go away.'

'Make me.'

'You're so freaking immature!'

'And *you're* so mature, asking Alison all your stupid questions the other night!'

I froze. I knew which night he meant. We had filled the bath with bubbles and Alison had been telling me about her relationship with Jason. They'd had sex – made love, in Alison's words. She didn't talk about sex the way the gang did. I didn't hang out with them anymore. Alison spoke about it as if it were an out-of-body experience, something surreal and indescribably beautiful.

'I heard you talking about *sex*.'

'You were listening at the door.'

'You were talking loudly,' David said, defensive.

'Leave me alone, okay? Please, David!'

'What if Karl wants to do stuff I don't wanna do, Alison? What do I do when his hands are all over me when we're kissing, Ali? What do I do, Ali, Ali, Ali!'

'Shut up!'

'Alison, Karl thinks I've had sex before with Andrew, but I didn't, but Karl doesn't believe me and says we should have sex, because that's what boyfriend and girlfriend do, Ali. Oh, Ali, Ali, what do I do?' he said in a sing-song voice.

'That's rubbish,' I said, trying to keep calm.

'If you have sex with Karl, Dad's not going to like that.'

'David, I am warning you, shut up,' I said, getting up and taking my book to the *stoep* outside.

It had been a cold winter, but the *stoep* was warm. I sat down on a bench and tried to continue reading, but David followed me.

'What'll you do if I tell him all about it?'

I slowly closed my book, my hand shaking. Blood rushed up my neck.

'You wouldn't.'

'You might as well stop studying for your test now, because when I tell Dad, he'll kill you.'

'You wouldn't dare.'

My breath was coming quickly and my nails were cutting into my palm.

'Why not? You'd tell if I was stupid enough to talk about that in the house.'

I wanted to hurt him.

'You don't know what you're talking about.'

'If you have sex, Dad will kill you,' he said again.

My hands were shaking.

'I heard him call you a fucking whore.'

Suddenly I was smashing David against the wall and was punching every inch of him that I could reach. He was screaming for me to stop. I'd thrown him onto the ground and I was on top of him, slamming my fists into him, wanting to break him, wanting to make him bleed.

'*FUCK YOU, YOU PIECE OF SHIT, I'LL FUCKING KILL YOU. I SWEAR TO GOD I'M GONNA FUCKING KILL YOU!*'

I heard the words in the air and for a split-second didn't know who had screamed them. Then, as my fist made contact with David's nose, I knew it was me. I seized his head in both my hands and started smashing it into the wall.

'Jacqueline! Jesus Christ, someone come – '

My brother Steve was the only one home. He had heard David's screams and had run outside to help. He pulled me off David, but I kept lashing out.

'*STOP IT, STOP IT!*' Steve bellowed.

I was hitting David all over with all my strength.

'JACQUELINE, STOP!'

It was the fear in Steve's eyes that brought me back. That was how I must have looked whenever my father went berserk on me.

'I – I don't know what happened,' I whispered.

David was lying in a heap on the floor, his hands covering his face. I felt like I could've gone on until I killed him. What had I become?

'Get out of here, I'll deal with it,' said Steve.

I stared at myself in the mirror in my bedroom. Where was the feisty girl who loved her brothers and was happy if only she could run, go to church, write and see friends? Gone were the days of me being proud of being athletics captain, or cricket scorer, or top in my economics class. I didn't care about any of that shit anymore. It was childish rubbish and anyone who thought different wasn't living in the real world. Nothing you could do could stop things from turning to chaos. I hit out at the mirror but it didn't break. I hated my reflection and the reminder of my existence that came with it. It was irrefutable proof that I was nothing more than a fucking whore, a dumb bitch and a stupid little girl who would never achieve anything. Except I had almost achieved something: I could've killed. Twice. It seemed impossible when I thought of it now, my breath still coming hard. I loved David. My cheeks were still flushed and my eyes were wet from shame.

'You need to leave,' I said to the girl in the mirror. 'You need to leave before you hurt someone properly.'

I started packing my things and then stopped at the sight of a photograph of my mother and I. What would happen to her? I tried to protect her when he belittled her, which only saw him turning on me. She was so gentle, so blind to my father's faults. With me gone, who would protect her from his humiliation, his disregard of her opinions, his constant control of what she did, who she saw, what she thought? With me gone, he would blame her even more. But I couldn't stay; it was too risky. I zipped up my bag and tiptoed to the kitchen. My parents weren't back from work yet and I could hear Steve calming down David in the living room. I'd have to be quick, because if my parents found out what I had done, they would go ballistic.

My plan was simple. I called Hayley, who I hadn't seen in over a year as my father said I wasn't allowed to be friends with her anymore. She had left school and moved in with her boyfriend. My parents wouldn't think to check there. Hayley agreed at once to help me out. I'd lay low at Hayley's house and then go to my boyfriend Karl's mom's farm in Winterton. Once things settled down, I'd make my way back to the Cape. I only had a few minutes before my father would come home and all hell would break loose.

———◆———

Hayley and her boyfriend smuggled me into their house without the neighbours noticing and agreed to drive me to Winterton after dark. It started to rain as we sped along Harrismith Road, which led out of town. A slow blue flash in the distance made my breath catch.

'Stop, it's the police. Quick, do a U-turn before they notice the car.'

'They've got to be for you,' said Hayley. 'Your dad must have called the cops.'

Hayley's boyfriend turned the car and drove off in the opposite direction.

'It can't be a coincidence,' I said, panic bubbling inside me. 'We have to wait them out. If they don't catch us now, my dad might think that I'm not trying to leave town. Let's wait at the drive-in. No one will look for me there. I mean, who runs away from home and goes to the movies?'

We drove to the drive-in, bought three tickets and settled down. I couldn't concentrate on the film and was glad when it ended. When we pulled up outside Hayley's house again, there he was. Standing there stock still, hands on his hips. I threw myself down onto the floor of the car. He would kill me this time. Hayley and her boyfriend got out, shut their doors and greeted my father but he didn't reply. The back door of the car opened and I squeezed my eyes shut, pressing my face into the carpeted floor.

'I thought I'd find you here,' he said, his voice hard and thin. 'Get out of the car.'

We drove home in silence. A police car was parked outside of our house.

'I've found her, officer,' said my father. 'I appreciate all of your efforts tonight.'

'Any time, sir,' said the cop.

He looked at me briefly, but didn't seem to see me. I wanted to shout at him, 'Don't you think there's a *reason* I tried to run? *Isn't it your job to ask?*

My mother and brothers weren't waiting at the front door when we came in.

My father marched me to my bedroom. The bedroom door slammed behind him and his finger was an inch from my face when he started screaming.

'*HOW DARE YOU TRY AND RUN AWAY AFTER ALL THAT I'VE DONE FOR YOU? AND THEN YOU RUN OFF TO THAT LITTLE SLUT? YOU DISRESPECTFUL FUCKING BITCH, HOW COULD YOU DO THIS TO ME AND BRING SHAME ON OUR FAMILY LIKE THIS?*'

He howled the last sentence as the spit flew out of his mouth onto my skin. I stared at him and found to my surprise that I was unaffected by his words. I was stuck in a parody fight, where the actor was passionate but the script unoriginal.

'Where the fuck did you think you were gonna go, huh? In fact, I don't fucking care. All these years I've never raised a hand to you, but tonight your mother and I've decided you need a hiding, just like your brothers, and I swear I'm going to give you the hiding of your fucking life in the hope that you will start to fucking listen!'

He stripped his belt from his waist and told me to bend over. I shook my head and looked at him defiantly.

'*Bend!*'

I smirked and cocked my head back. I wanted him to hit me. He screamed at me to bend over again.

'If you want to hit me, then you're going to have to hit me standing up.'

'Fuck, you are impossible!'

'Come on. Hit me,' I said.

He hurled his belt to the floor and screamed.

'*YOU WON'T GET ME TO HIT A WOMAN TODAY, NOT EVER. YOU WON'T MAKE ME DO THIS, YOU LITTLE BITCH!*'

'That's right dad, just like I *make* you call me a bitch and a fucking whore. For your information, I'm a fucking virgin.'

'Don't push me.'

'How about we talk about the fire?'

He turned his back to me and made as if he were about to leave the room. I knew he'd turn around and pass one last comment.

'Fuck you, Jacqueline!'

'I should've killed you.'

'The Lord Jesus have mercy on your soul, you twisted bitch! You think you can push me around, well, you've got another thing coming! You can threaten to expose me, you can run away, you can wish me dead, but I'll tell you one thing straight, you little shit – you'll never get rid of me. No matter what you do, I'll be here, because I'm your father and I'm not going anywhere.'

'You're not my father. You're a liar and a fraud and I'll make sure everybody knows it.'

I was almost serene as I said the words. I laughed as he opened the door, the fight having gone out of him.

'I can't hit her. You deal with her, I'm done,' he said to my mother, who was now standing outside the room.

'Well then I will, she needs to be punished,' I heard her say, as she stepped inside.

Fury marked every line of her face and my laughter died in my throat.

'*How dare you,*' she whispered. 'How *dare* you humiliate us like this!'

She was whispering and looked half-mad.

'Your father may be a gentleman and would never raise a hand to you, but that won't stop me! *That won't stop me, do you hear?*'

'Do whatever you want. I don't care.'

She picked up the belt and wrapped it around her hand as if it were something she did every day. We looked at each other for a moment and then she started lashing me. Blow after blow bore down on my backside and the backs of my legs. She was grunting with the effort of it, her breath coming hard. I didn't cry out. The belt was twisting and whirling through the air, now one side would hit me, now the other. It went on and on, like my life, on and on, useless, pointless, violent, painful. I wanted it all to be over.

Later that night Steve snuck into my room. We didn't speak, but he held me gently and told me it would all be okay. I didn't believe him.

'I love you,' he mumbled.

I knew that Steve would soon be finishing high school and going to the army. It would only be a couple of months before he would be gone. David would be going off to boarding school and I would be alone. I wouldn't survive without them. Maybe I had misunderstood God and he was actually telling me to kill the enemy within. I promised myself that by the time Steve left home, I'd either have run away for good or I'd be dead. Those were my only two choices.

Chapter Eleven

Three things cannot be long hidden: the sun, the moon, and the truth. – Buddha

I WAS TRYING TO FOLLOW MY dance teacher's instruction. 'Kick ball change, attitude turn and hold! Good work girls. Time for a break. Jackie, great characterisation but remember to point that outward-turning foot, okay?'

The group of girls broke apart and started chatting to one another immediately. I stood in the middle of the dance studio. Everything was hazy. Was it soon going to be over, here, like this, in the middle of a dance studio on a normal afternoon? Is that how people died? Bile rose in my mouth. I didn't want to vomit up the bottle of painkillers I'd swallowed before my dancing lesson. I needed this to work. Alison, who was fixing her hair in the mirror, turned to me and smiled. She thought I was coping better now, because I'd told her my fantasy that everything had changed since I'd tried to run away. It was easy to smile back at her now, when I knew that soon I would stop acting for good.

'Okey dokey, everyone in position? Let's take it from "Now go, cat, go!"'

I tried to leap into the step like everyone else but stumbled.

'Focus, Jackie!'

The room was spinning and my vision was blurring. It was happening, now, and I didn't want to die in front of my dance class. I stumbled to the bathroom and started vomiting hard. No, keep it in. But I couldn't; the bitter vomit forced itself out of me.

'Jackie, you poor thing,' said my dance teacher from behind me.

She waited until I had finished vomiting and then helped me to my feet and took me to the office to telephone my mother. Fifteen minutes later I was in the car on the way to the doctor.

'Have you been feeling off-colour lately?' the doctor asked. 'Any muscle aches, headaches, cramps or fever?'

'I swallowed a bottle of Panado.'

'Ah,' said the doctor, looking at the ceiling and scratching a spot on his chin. 'Well, too many painkillers would do that, wouldn't they?'

My mother gave a tinkling laugh.

'Silly Jacqueline. You shouldn't take more than two. Kids!' she said to the doctor, shaking her head.

'It wasn't a mistake: I did it on purpose,' I said, but it came out a weak mumble.

'Well, there will be no lasting damage,' said the doctor. 'So you can go home and get some rest. I recommend nice bland foods.'

My mother led me back to the car without saying a word. What did she think of me? As we drove home, I imagined her mind at work, snipping 12 August 1982 out of her memory and carefully shredding it into tiny pieces. Until it was permanent, until I was properly dead – preferably in a way that couldn't be described as an accident, such as hanging myself, slitting my wrists or shooting myself in the mouth, she wouldn't believe that I wanted to die. It was too inconvenient a fact and what would the neighbours say? Only white trash actually killed themselves.

She parked the car in the driveway and we got out. It was a white station wagon with wood panelling on the sides, just like Sue Ellen owned in *Dallas*. We loved watching *Dallas* on the television, but my father didn't approve of it. I always hoped it was because the main character, a dirty businessman and manipulative egomaniac, must have reminded my father of himself, but this was unlikely because my father was the least self-aware person on the planet. Had our surname been Ewing, I still doubt he would have drawn the parallel.

'Come on. What are you staring at the car for? I want you to try on your confirmation dress.'

Ten minutes later she had me standing on the coffee table in my confirmation dress as if nothing had happened.

'Okay, you can get down and take it off now. I'm just going to get a garment bag,' she said, and left me standing there alone.

Just as I'd pulled the dress off over my head, I heard my father walk into the room.

'That's a pretty dress,' he said, looking at it in my hands.

He smiled as he walked over to me and put his hand around my waist, resting it uncomfortably close to my right breast. I froze and stared straight ahead. I didn't want to be held like this. I heard my mother's footsteps returning. Then, slowly, just before she stepped back into the room, he removed his hand and patted my bum.

'You will be the prettiest girl at your confirmation,' he said.

He left the room.

'Jacqueline, put the dress back on for one last alteration while I've got you here,' said my mother.

I stood mute while she fidgeted with the pins.

The dress was white and lacy, with a straight neckline and puffy sleeves that came in at the wrists. My mother had been making it for weeks. I was sorry I wouldn't get a chance to wear it and make her happy. I so wanted to be there for Reverend Jones and for the rest of my confirmation group, but I'd be dead by then.

It was the Friday before my confirmation and spring was in full bloom. Orange clivias had burst open in every garden and weeping boer-bean trees dripped blood-coloured flowers onto the pavement.

Hedges of hot pink bougainvillea lined the roads while red and orange poppies forced themselves out of every crack in the tar and each gap in the paving. I saw none of it, because I was in a panic about my father finding out what had happened that afternoon.

I had befriended a kid called Connor a few months before when I had found him crying at school. Connor was three years younger than me and a boarder. Connor was crying because when he phoned his drunkard father to ask for something, his father screamed at him, saying he was a selfish, stupid little idiot. I told him I knew how he felt and promised to be his friend. Now I had betrayed him. He had come to our house after school and I said he could ride my scooter up and down the driveway. Connor was only thirteen and didn't have a licence, but he took my scooter and drove it down the road, without a helmet or anything. I tried to chase after him, but he'd disappeared, leaving me standing in the road, terrified of my father finding out that he'd taken my scooter.

A policeman walked up the drive, holding Connor by the shoulder.

'Sir, I'm so sorry,' I said. 'Please forgive me. It was my fault. I shouldn't have let him ride the scooter.'

'It was very irresponsible of you, young lady. Where are your parents?'

'They're at work. But please, officer, I promise I will never, ever let this happen again. I'm truly sorry.'

I was petrified that he would tell my father and was ready to spend a week in jail rather than have him find out.

'I'll give you a warning,' the policeman said. 'But I'm going to come back later and report this to your parents.'

'No, please – please, I beg you, don't!'

I almost said, 'He'll kill me!' but bit my tongue.

'I'll be back later,' he said, and then left me standing with Connor in the driveway.

'What were you thinking, Connor?'

'Aw, come on Jackie. I just went around the corner.'

'Just around the corner? Just around the corner? Are you *stupid*?'

'Please, Jackie, don't say that. I'm really sorry, please forgive me!'

'I don't give a shit and I *won't* forgive you! My Dad is going to kill me!'

'Please forgive me, you're my only friend,' he said, and started to cry.

'I said *NO!*'

He looked up at me, shocked. I'd never screamed at him before. *'AREN'T YOU ASHAMED OF WHAT YOU DID?* I yelled, *'WHY DON'T YOU JUST QUIT FOLLOWING ME AROUND AND GET A FUCKING LIFE?*

'I just wanted to ride your –'

'LIFE'S NOT A GAME, YOU IDIOT! WHY DON'T YOU JUST GO? NO ONE WOULD MISS YOU, NO ONE, SO WHY DON'T YOU JUST GO!

I watched my words, his words, cut Connor as if from a long way off. We stared at each other for a shattered moment and then he left. What have I done? Oh, Lord, what have I done? My words rang in my ears. These were my words, not my Dad's words. Connor would never forget them.

My father was still at work, but when he found out he would scream at me the way I screamed at Connor, but worse. The air hung with the overpowering scent of magnolias, sickly sweet and heady. I tried to imagine what my father would do, but as my terror rose I couldn't. I didn't know what he would say that would make my life even more unbearable. I could picture him facing me, turning away, facing me, pointing in my face. I could picture the spit flying, picture his lips drawn back over his teeth, picture the veins pumping in his neck and forehead. This time I wouldn't recover. This time he wouldn't come to sweet-talk me twenty-four hours later with an uncomfortable cuddle. This time he would make the life I lived completely worthless. I had no choice but to beat him to it.

I picked a single Dutch Iris from the garden and placed it in a glass vase on the dining room table before setting about killing myself. Our medicine cabinet was well-stocked and I took everything I found in it – painkillers, muscle relaxants, anti-nausea pills, cough syrup, unfinished antibiotics, anti-diarrhoea pills, allergy pills, cold and flu meds, all of it. After twenty pills I thought I wouldn't be able to swallow another pill without gagging, but I kept on going. Thirty pills, forty, fifty. Once there was not a single pill or drop of syrup left, I left the house.

The tar of the road took on a weird shimmer as I crossed the road to school. I didn't know where I was going until I found myself at the cricket nets where Mr Collins, the coach and maths teacher, was instructing the boys.

'Jackie, what are you doing back at school?'

His voice came at me through an echoing tunnel. I replied something and he laughed. I wasn't sure if it was him or some other teacher.

'So true. Have a great weekend, then. And good luck with your confirmation!'

I said something else and the man smiled and waved at me as I stumbled away, his arm twisting weirdly in the sunshine. It wasn't Mr Collins.

'Jackie, do you have any last-minute questions?'

I blinked heavily. It was Reverend Jones, sitting at his desk opposite me. I didn't know how I'd made it all the way to church.

'I would have thought you didn't have a single doubt in your mind. What's troubling you?'

I had that uncanny feeling that someone had asked me this before, somewhere. What's troubling you? What's troubling me? Troubling? But no one asked – no one cared – no one.

'Jackie, are you feeling all right?'

I saw him through a heat wave, his kind face, his white collar. Reverend Jones, oh, I loved him. I loved him even more than I loved

Mr Collins. If they were my fathers, if they were, if. But I loved him, I did love him, Daddy, my daddy.

'S'all my fault, mine.'

'What's your fault? Jackie? What's your fault?'

Daughter, whore, not a boy, liar, bitch. All darkness, not like Heidi. Heidi died in a fire. Sinner. Girl. Cow. Coward. My fault, mine. He deserved better, they all deserved better than me. Not me, anything but me. But hatred, shouting voices, sadness. No more. None of that. A sharp pain sliced through my head. I had toppled forward and hit the desk.

Chapter Twelve

There is no easy walk to freedom anywhere, and many of us will have to pass through the valley of the shadow of death again and again before we reach the mountaintop of our desires. – *Nelson Mandela*

WE WERE DRIVING. THE RING of blackness was so close, only two pricks of light left. The ring closed.

I felt a lurch as the car went over a bump. That bump always felt the same, the bump was in our driveway, the bump meant the house, the house meant my father, the house meant my mother, no no *no* –

'*Not here please not, please, please, please!*'

'Stay calm Jackie, we're almost home, your parents will take care of you –'

'Reverend Jones, please don't leave me with them, don't leave me, I hate them, please help me –'

'Jackie, stay calm!'

'Please help me,' I said, but my words had grown thin and he didn't hear.

Why was he doing this? Why? They were all the same, they didn't care, they didn't listen. *Why would no one listen?* The blackness crept in again and I was gone – and when I woke, I didn't know where I was. I heard my father yelling somewhere and tried to block it out.

'*JESUS FUCKING CHRIST, MY OWN FUCKING DAUGHTER, DOES SHE HAVE NO SHAME? HOW DARE SHE DO THIS TO ME AND MY WIFE?*

'Please, sir, this is a hospital. Someone take him away!'

The lights were too bright and I was gagging on the tube in my throat. My mother's expressionless face swam at the end of my bed and I saw my father being ushered from the room. I tried to pull on the tube with my teeth, not wanting it to suck out the pills I'd taken.

'Easy now, we're pumping your stomach. Just lie still, Jacqueline, you'll be okay.'

I didn't want to be okay. I wanted to be dead, but here I was: the ultimate failure. I had failed to kill myself twice and was now nothing more than a desperate, attention-seeking loser.

'Can you tell us what happened, ma'am?' someone asked my mother.

'She got in trouble today and was too afraid to face the consequences. We will deal with this at home. It's just typical teenager stuff, doctor. Attention seeking, you know.'

'Do you know what she ingested?' he asked. 'It's important.'

'Oh, I don't know. It appears it was everything in the medicine chest.'

'We'll have to keep her here for a few days. Rather safe than sorry.'

'Absolutely impossible. She has her confirmation tomorrow. And look – she's fine now.'

They both looked at me. I was still struggling to clench my stomach and hold in whatever I could, but it was futile. The syringe was slowly pulling everything out.

'I must insist that we keep her here for a couple of days,' the doctor said. 'It's standard procedure after a suicide attempt.'

My mother's words drifted through me. She had her own standard procedure for revising an embarrassing scene like this. I hadn't tried to kill myself, I was just a troubled teen, or seeking attention, or faking.

A few hours later I was back home as if nothing had happened.

———◆———

I stared at myself in the mirror of the church bathroom. My skin was damp and pallid and my hair looked ridiculous, fluffed into a round bowl cut around my head. I forced a smile, imagining how I would pose for the photograph with Reverend Jones afterwards. My face was warped, bloated, disgusting. All I had wanted to do was to write my book and spread God's word. It had seemed so easy with Him by my side. He had filled my meaningless life and now He was gone. Had I imagined it all?

'Jackie, it's time!' someone called.

I joined the rest of the group who were waiting for me in the vestibule. The air in the church was stale and I breathed in deep lungfuls, filling myself with it. I walked out towards the sound of the organ and followed the group dumbly down the aisle, keeping my eyes on the floor so that I wouldn't have to see my family or Reverend Jones. My throat hurt as I repeated Reverend Jones's words. It was all an act. I was speaking words that affirmed my faith in some God, swearing never to forsake Him while knowing that I was forsaken. God was nowhere. He had not just left me: he had never existed. My confirmation had come too late.

My brain commanded my heart to pump blood and my lungs to breathe – and for me to live, live, live. But everything else was dead inside of me. No one could save me now. 16 years of devotion – all for nothing. I had thought that my love for God was a diamond, unbreakable and brilliant, but it was cheap glass and the shards cut me. I stood there in a white lace dress, smiling for a photograph, stretching my mouth open to show the world my teeth, to signify that I was happy, I was whole, I was a good young Christian. But I was none of those things. I braced myself for another flash of the camera and grinned. I was theirs to do with what they wanted.

CHAPTER THIRTEEN

In all chaos there is a cosmos, in all disorder a secret order. – Carl Jung

THE NEXT YEAR PASSED IN a grey haze and before I knew it my school life was over. I had wanted to repeat my penultimate year at a different high school, as I wanted to put my life back together again as well as get better grades, but my parents had refused. It wouldn't have looked right, they said. But nothing about me did look right. My parents were ashamed of me, teachers loathed my disruptive presence and while I still had some friends, Alison was pulling away from me because I bore no resemblance to the person she had become friends with at 14. In a last-ditch attempt to try and reconnect with her, I bought her a camera for Christmas as I knew she desperately wanted one. I also hoped that when we moved to different cities for university that January – she to Pietermaritzburg, me to Cape Town – we would stay in touch and send one another photographs. We had always exchanged gifts for birthdays and Christmas and I couldn't wait to see the look on her face when she opened the box and found a Kodak camera inside. When I went to her house and through to her bedroom, she didn't meet my eyes.

'Hey! Merry Christmas!' I said, sounding falsely bright, even to myself.

'Hi Jackie, merry Christmas,' she said. 'It's been a while.'

'Ja, it has, hey? I haven't seen you since the end of exams. That's, like, the longest we've ever gone without seeing each other.'

'Ja. Have you had a good holiday at your Ouma in the Strand?'

She sounded as if she was forcing herself to stay in the room with me.

'I had a great time. I met a really cool guy, Jack. We're actually going out. And I've been working at Trust Bank in Somerset West, but I've got off for Christmas.'

'Cool.'

Usually she wouldn't stop talking until she found out every single detail about a love affair, but Jack didn't seem to interest her.

'I've got your present here.'

'Oh, gee, thanks Jackie. I – I actually haven't got you anything yet. I –'

Even though we'd been drifting apart, it had never crossed my mind that we wouldn't exchange presents like we always did.

'Don't worry about it. Here,' I said, passing the carefully wrapped box to her.

'Wow! A camera,' she said, smiling genuinely for the first time.

There was an aching silence as we stared at one another.

'Thanks, this is great.'

'I thought maybe,' I said, willing my chin to stop shaking, 'I thought we could send each other photos when we're at university.'

She hugged me hard then and I tried to put a lot of unsaid things into the hug. I wanted to ask her to remember me like I used to be. I wanted to tell her I was sorry for becoming this other person. I knew I had changed and that neither of us liked the unhappy version of me, but there was nothing I could do about it. I wasn't sure if she understood.

Six months later I had flunked out of my B.Com at the University of Cape Town and was living with my grandparents in the Strand. Ouma was still the same Jesus-loving Christian that she always was and now that I no longer believed in God, it was really annoying, but she and Oupa Bunny had huge hearts and always had space for their grandchildren, so they gave me a room in their house while I looked for a job. I felt lighter than I had in years and although it grated my nerves when Ouma pronounced my name Jak-ka-*leen* as opposed to Jac-kwa-leen, I was happy to be with them.

Soon my days were divided up into slots of working at the Allied Building Society as a teller, smoking with my grandparents' maid Maria in her tiny back room and seeing Jack. We were drunk in love and I would sit at my Ouma's dining room table and practise signing my name with his surname for the day that we got married.

'I think you should change the spelling of your name from Jackie to Jacqui,' he said one day. 'We don't want people getting confused when we have the same surname.' Wives honoured their husband and so that day I became Jacqui.

I'd already had sex with Karl, so I figured that there was no point in not letting my future husband have his fun too, if you could call it fun. Sex involved me lying on my back with my eyes squeezed shut and waiting desperately for the shudder that meant it was finally over and we could lie side by side and smoke. It was an ordeal, but I knew enough from the Ladysmith gang that men expected sex and without it the relationship would go nowhere. Jack was the love of my life and there was no way I was going to break up with him over something stupid like not putting out. I took my contraception advice from one of the gang back in Ladysmith, who said it was safe to have sex the week before your period. It proved to be excellent advice – until I got pregnant.

It was raining hard outside and I had just vomited for the eighth time that week, this time on the side of the road. Jack put his arm around me in the back seat of his Ford Escort.

'Shit! Shit! Shit! Jacqui, what are we going to do?'

'We'll have to get married.'

'My parents will disown me if they find out!'

'But we're going to get married anyway, we might as well —'

'No we can't. You don't understand, my dad will disinherit me, Jacqui!'

'Trust me, I understand fathers' threats. We'll work something out, all right?'

I wanted to snap at him to keep it together, to remember his training. But he hadn't had any: Jack's parents doted on him and gave him everything his heart desired.

'How are you so calm, Jacqui?'

I stared at him for a moment and didn't answer. This is nothing, I wanted to say. I'd take pregnant at eighteen over a fight with my father any day. But we'd never spoken about my father or my attempted suicides. There was not a chance that Jack would love me if he knew. We spoke and laughed about the good things only. When I became disconnected and despondent, he would give me my space, perhaps send me a bunch of flowers and happily chalk it up to my time of the month.

'I'm pregnant and we'll have to get married. That's that.'

'We will get married when we're older, but we can't now! What are we going to do, oh God, what are we going to *do*?'

'But if we don't get married, and I have a baby, my dad will kill me.'

'But he'll kill you anyway if he finds out that you're getting married because you're pregnant. We've only got one option.'

'What do you mean?'

'I'm going to call my brother. I'll ask him if he knows of anyone who can, you know, help us out.'

'I don't want to do that. Jack, it's illegal.'

'It'll be fine. I mean, didn't your dad burn your house down when you were a kid? And he got away with it.'

'Who told you that?' I snapped, sounding just like my mother.

'Everyone in town knows your father did it.'

'Oh, so you have no evidence, you just heard a rumour,' I said sarcastically. 'Anyway, I don't think getting rid of it is a good idea.'

'It's our only choice. I know we'll get married later and as long as we're together, nothing can hurt us.'

He pleaded with me until I agreed. What choice did I have? Little as I wanted to break the law, I wanted to be an unmarried mother even less. Jack's brother Charles, after much raging about irresponsibility, found a doctor who would be able to help us with our problem.

I told my grandparents that I was going away for the night with a couple of girlfriends and the next Friday Jack and I drove to the Holiday Inn in Cape Town to meet the doctor. As we waited, Jack paced the length of the cramped hotel room. At last we heard a light knock on the door and I opened it. Jack froze when he saw his dark skin and looked at me with terror. An Indian doctor. I smiled and greeted him. He was soft-spoken, dressed in a smart suit and smelled faintly of lavender. He gave me a gown to change into and then seated me on the bed on a large plastic sheet. Jack stared out of the window at the city, unable to watch.

'This is going to be safe and quick,' he said, 'But I'm afraid it may hurt a little.'

'That's okay. I don't mind pain.'

'You will have to stay completely silent. We can't have anyone hearing you.'

'I'll be quiet. What's your name?' I asked, trying to distract myself.

'I can't tell you that,' he said with a sad smile.

Jack decided it was all too much for him and left, saying that he would wait outside. The doctor slipped on a pair of plastic gloves, pushed my legs apart and began to examine me. I felt hot and humiliated.

'Are you sure this is what you want?'

He asked me gently and, in that moment, I realised how lucky I was to have him and not someone else, someone with a hanger or a knife, or someone who might molest me afterwards. He seemed like a good man.

'I'm sure.'

Later, when we were older, Jack and I would have another baby and we would love her unconditionally. I held on to that thought as he began unpacking his medical bag. A speculum, a collection of what looked like dental tools and a thin tube attached to a pump.

'It'll be over in ten minutes. I'm going to insert this tube into you and pump fluid into your uterus. You'll feel bloated. Afterwards you can expect some cramping and then you will miscarry. The cramping might be quite painful, so stay the whole weekend.'

'But we've only booked to stay one night. That should be fine, right?'

'Yes, if everything goes according to plan, you'll miscarry early tomorrow morning and then you can go home. Okay now, are you ready?'

'Ready.'

'Try to relax. Knees up and apart, please,' he said, and gently pushed my legs apart with his gloved hand. 'Good. Try and relax now. I'm going to give you some painkillers to drink afterwards.'

I lay flat on my back and tried to focus on the light fixture on the ceiling. It was filled with dead midges. I gasped as he pushed the speculum inside of me.

'That's okay, that's okay. Just the speculum. Perfectly normal.'

I started to pant and sweat. It was cold inside of me and I knew that pain was coming. It felt as though the very heart of me was being stabbed and pulled wide open. The pump made a wheezing sound and I started convulsing.

'Breathe, Jacqui. We're almost done. You're doing so well.'

I was crying silently.

'All right now, it's all over.'

He took off his gloves and clasped my hand for a moment.

'You're going to be just fine.'

I was covered in cold sweat and didn't even have the strength to raise my eyes and look at him. I felt the sheet being pulled out from under me and I clumsily tried to get my panties back on over my knees. The door opened and I heard him talking to Jack. The door then closed again.

'He says you've got to try and rest now,' Jack said, giving me two painkillers, the kind you'd take for a headache, and a glass of water.

I drank them and he lay down next to me and kissed the side of my face. It felt as if there was a balloon full of water inside of me and soon it started to hurt. I sucked my breath over my teeth.

'It's just the cramps,' he said.

Just cramps? What did he know about cramps? It felt as though I had been split open.

'Just try and sleep. I'll look after you.'

I closed my eyes, but white hot pain shot through me and I bit down on my pillow so that I wouldn't scream out. Hours passed as I slipped in and out of sleep.

'You're bleeding, Jacqui. That's a good thing. It's working,' he said at some point in the night.

The pain mounted as the night went on and I watched from above as an anxious boy held a pale girl's hand. Her back was arched and body shaking. I saw her blonde hair sticking to her head with sweat. I was above it all. The hotel room was baked with sun when I came to.

'Jack?'

'I'm here, can you see me? Can you see me?'

'Yes,' I whispered, struggling for breath.

'You've been … strange. You've been talking. Laughing. How do you feel?'

'Is it Saturday?'

'It's Sunday afternoon. I think we should stay another night.'

'W-what? I was supposed to be home yesterday!'

I pushed myself up onto my elbows and looked down.

'Oh, God, Jack, I'm still bleeding. I'm still bleeding!'

'The doctor said it's normal, bleeding and cramping is normal,' he said, sounding panicked.

'No, it's too much, I'm bleeding too much.'

Dark blood had pooled into the towel Jack had placed under me. My thighs were wet with it. Frantically Jack held a second towel between my legs, his hands shaking. I felt very cold and every few seconds my body would seize up. Soon the blood soaked through the second towel, big dark clots of it sticking to my thighs.

'Call him,' I said feebly.

'I can't, I don't have his number, I don't know his name. Jesus Christ, what are we going to do?'

'Jack, listen to me. I'm going to bleed to death. I'm dying and you need to do something, now.'

He clasped his hands and started to pray.

'Stop fucking praying,' I gasped. 'I need a hospital!'

I had never sworn in front of him before and it seemed to help.

He carried me to the bath, perhaps hoping that if he could wash the blood away it would be okay. But fresh scarlet streams mixed with the running water, twirling down the plug. Jack had started to sob drily.

'Call my doctor, now, or I'll die,' I said, before passing out.

I came to on the highway. My thighs and the seat were wet and warm. It wouldn't be so bad, to go like this. I would slip from the back seat of a sports car into infinite nothing. It would be like how it was before I was born: zero.

The next thing I knew, I was lying on a cold floor, Jack's arms wrapped around me.

'I brought her to you as fast as I could, doctor. Help me lift her so we can get her inside.'

'Jesus help us. I can't do anything for her: she needs the hospital,' said a man's voice, vaguely familiar from somewhere.

What would my father think when he heard that I had died from a botched abortion? My mother would craft an alternative story, but not my father. I hoped it wouldn't give him a heart attack. I hoped he would make it through this. He had such lovely blue eyes. I loved him. I didn't want him to be sad. And then everything went black.

'What in God's name persuades these girls to do this? Jesus have mercy on her,' a voice whispered.

'She needs a transfusion or she'll die.'

Other sounds started filtering into the picture. A machine bleeped and wheels rolled across a smooth floor. A curtain was drawn closed and someone was being admonished in the distance. A heavy door swept shut, swept open, swept shut again on its own rhythm. With a stab of dread, I realised I was in a hospital ward. I blinked and tried to focus my eyes on the clouded room. Whose voice was whispering? Who was he? How did I know him?

'Get Jacqueline ready for theatre, now,' he said, and the memories snapped into place at last.

I was two years old and he was listening to my breathing with a stethoscope. I was eight and he was dropping liquid into my eye, holding my lids open. I was twelve and he was setting my broken foot. The memories came faster and faster, muddling into one another. The dread turned to horror as I realised that my childhood family doctor, Dr Matthews, was trying to save my life. What was he doing here? If only I could bleed to death.

'Please,' I whispered, as he adjusted the drip in my arm. 'Please. It was an accident.'

Shame on you, shame on you, shame on you. That's what they will all say.

'Jacqueline, you're going to be okay,' he whispered, stroking my forehead.

CHAPTER FOURTEEN

Where there is love there is life. – Mahatma Gandhi

TWO WEEKS LATER I SAT wrapped in a blanket on a bench at the Strand beach, watching the sunset. I was still weak from my time in hospital and all alone. My only friend, Maria, was not allowed to join me at the beach, as she was coloured. Jack had dumped me without giving a reason and was already fucking some other girl. I hoped she enjoyed it more than I ever had. In the days after my abortion, all I had been able to do was lie in bed, hide out in Maria's room and cry on her shoulder or smoke with her until my lungs hurt. Ouma never asked why I came home two days late and I didn't bother to offer any explanation. Oupa Bunny seemed to notice that I needed some unquestioning comfort.

One morning he came into my bedroom while Ouma was out doing her daily grocery shopping.

'Give me a cigarette,' he said bluntly.

'What! I don't smoke, Oupa.'

'Jacqueline, I've been taking three of your cigarettes every day since you moved in here. Now let's have a smoke together, but don't you dare tell your Ouma.'

I needed someone to laugh with.

We sat side by side on the bed smoking while Ouma was out. This was to become our daily ritual. If you'd said to me that one day I'd have an abortion, I might have believed you, but smoking with Oupa Bunny in my bedroom? No ways. But then again, everything was upside-down in my life. For years I had held on to the dream that if only I could get back to Somerset West or the Strand, everything would go back to how it was before the fire. Somehow if I could get back home, time would be reversed. Even though in the months that followed I'd made an effort to make new friends, like Jenny, Dean and Marco, it was a strange place to me now.

A month later I was watching the waves again, waiting for it to be time to go to the restaurant. Alison had come down from Pietermaritzburg with my parents for a visit.

'Won't that be lovely?' asked my mother in her brightest voice. 'I've even organised for the two of you to have a little dinner.'

Alison and I sat at a table in the corner. We covered all the basics first – how was varsity, who was dating whom, what the gossip in Ladysmith was – before we got to the real reason that she had come. She chewed her piece of rubbery steak slowly and then spoke.

'I'm worried about you, Jacqui.'

'Oh?'

'There's a rumour that you, uh, that you had an abortion.'

She flicked her hair off her forehead and leaned back in an invitation for me to tell her everything. After not answering months of letters and not calling me once, she was here on a trip with my parents to pry into my life. It was their idea, I was sure of it, but she didn't seem to mind: this was just one more piece of juicy gossip to share with our old friends and she'd gotten a free trip to the Cape to sweeten the deal.

'An abortion? Who told you that?'

Didn't my parents know that the days of me trusting Alison, or anyone, had died a long time ago?

'Gee, I can't think now.'

'Funny. You'd think you'd remember who told you something like that.'

'Dr Matthews told your parents, okay? I said I'm just worried about you, you know.'

I wanted to laugh in her face.

'So, is it true?' She was relentless. 'Did you have an abortion?'

'Not that I know of. If I ever do have an abortion, I'll make a note of it and call you up,' I said coldly, and waved to our waiter. 'Bill, please.'

CHAPTER FIFTEEN

Holding onto anger is like drinking poison and
expecting the other person to die. – Buddha

ALISON WENT BACK TO PIETERMARITZBURG AND I spent more time with my friends, especially Jenny, Dean and Marco. It was the first week of November, a Wednesday, and I had bunked work so that the we could spend the day at the beach. I was driving my car, a yellow Opel Kadett, a gift from my father. When he'd heard that I'd bought a rusty old VW Beetle with the help of Oupa Bunny, he said no daughter of his would drive a hippy car. The road to Cool Bay had been cut into the cliff face and the sea sparkled a hundred and fifty metres below. It was a turquoise day, but the sea was never flat in False Bay. The swell rushed and crashed around the granite boulders. Marco, who was sitting in the passenger seat, turned on the cassette player. *Sugarman* by Rodriguez came on and Dean put his feet up between our two seats. It was good to be outside in the summer sun, without a worry in the world. Something made me think of a similar day a fortnight previously, when Jenny and I were musing about all the deaths that had happened on that road.

'The only way to save yourself is to get out of the car before it hits the water,' she'd said. 'If you don't, you're dead.'

'Pity Jenny couldn't join us today,' Marco said.

'Jacqui, pass me a smoke?' asked Dean from the back seat.

I reached down between the seats to get my cigarette box. In that split-second of distraction, the car drifted and one wheel hit gravel on the mountain side of the road. I slammed on the brakes and tried to turn the wheel but it was too late. The car spun in an arc, wheels slamming into a boulder before the car went over the cliff. We were tossed into the air. Everything happened slowly: Marco's head hit the dashboard and his eyes closed shut. *Sugar man, won't you hurry* – the song stopped playing and the cassette floated out of the tape deck and then we smashed down onto the cliffside and everything sped up again. We hurtled towards the water and the world turned upside down as the car hit another boulder and flipped again, landing on its roof, the windows shattering. I reached out of my driver's window, trying desperately to grab hold of anything and get out. I heard Jenny's voice. 'If you don't get out of the car before the car hits the water, you're dead.' I had seconds before the car was going to hit the water. The car jerked sideways and in that instant I grabbed onto something and held onto it as the car swung away from my body. I watched the smashed-up yellow car with Dean and Marco still inside hit a ledge and slam roof-first into the water.

I had to save them.

Something took control of me as I careered down the cliffside towards the water, my legs spinning out of control. I tripped over a rock, flew forwards. The car was sinking.

I needed to get the car out of the water before my father killed me!

My legs were bleeding when I found myself on a rocky ledge.

If I jumped down onto those rocks, I'd die.

The cliff had become a sheer drop. I could risk the jump or waste minutes trying to find a safer way. I felt a powerful presence with me, a light, and someone told me that it would be okay. I could do it. I turned, closed my eyes and threw my body down the cliff side, onto solid rock. My body bounced on the rock surface. I thought my bones must have shattered, but there was no pain. I stood up, took a breath and jumped into the water.

I reached the exposed wheel of the car and dived into the cloud of bubbles. I pushed out at the water to force myself deeper. Pressure throbbed all around me, forcing itself against my eardrums. I needed to breathe. The car was hazy in the water. I grabbed a window frame and pulled myself down through the back window to look for Dean.

Dean! Where the fuck was Dean?

I pushed myself back out of the car, glass scraping my skin in the cold water. I needed to breathe. I kicked but my legs were aching. My clothes dragged at me, but I kept kicking, slower and slower until cold air broke over my mouth and nose and I was gasping air. I dove again and this time found Marco's hand looming through the haze. I tugged his forearm, hard, harder, but he was stuck. My lungs ached. I grabbed his shirt and tried to turn him but he just swayed, his eyes closed. If he wasn't dead already… I pulled, but I was growing weak again. I let go and forced myself to the surface. I blinked water from my eyes, kicking to stay afloat and then noticed Dean. He was coughing hard, sitting on a rock a few metres away.

'*DEAN!*' I screamed. '*HELP ME! MARCO'S DOWN THERE!*'

Dean looked at me blankly. He was in shock.

'Come *ON!*'

Dean blinked and didn't seem to know who I was. His leg was bent sideways at a funny angle. But then he shook his head and came to himself and we dove down. I forced myself into the car through the side window, while Dean made his way through the back window. I kept pulling, while Dean pushed and suddenly Marco came free. We were almost out of the car when it swayed dangerously in the water. A wave of swell knocked us backwards, and before I knew what was happening I was pinned down by the car. It landed on my legs in slow motion. Just as I thought I'd die down there, the swell lifted the car back onto its nose and we heaved Marco to the surface.

'Oh God, Dean, he's dead, Marco's dead!'

Marco's lips were blue and swollen, his eyes unseeing. We pulled Marco towards a rock, but it was too steep to lift his body on to it.

'Hold his head, we'll have to resuscitate him here.'

Dean took breath after breath and blew as hard as he could into Marco's mouth, but there was no response. He was dead. We pushed him against the rock as we kicked to keep ourselves afloat. I held him in place with one hand while Dean breathed into his mouth and I beat at his chest with my free fist.

'Come on Marco,' I cried, *COME ON!'*

Dean blew a giant breath into his mouth and I pumped his chest with my last ounce of strength and he retched back to life, water dribbling from his mouth. We continued to resuscitate him until he looked stable and then Dean and I pulled him by the arm half onto the rock. We didn't know it at the time, but that arm was shattered.

'Dean, hold onto Marco while I get help.'

I swam to the water's edge and began to scramble up the cliff side to the road. My heel was hanging in a bloody flap from my foot, but at last I got up to the road. I stood on the hot tar with my arms stretched wide, hoping for a car. All I could think was that no one would stop for a girl in a black denim mini skirt and a Mickey Mouse t-shirt. But in minutes a car pulled over and the driver and his friend rushed out towards me. I couldn't speak.

'Did you crash?' asked the driver.

'Yes.'

'Into the sea?'

'Yes.'

'How many are with you?'

'Two. Two guys.'

'Are they still under water?'

'No, on a rock.'

'Are they alive?'

'We just got Marco breathing. He – he was dead.'

'You,' he said to his friend. 'You've got the information, take the car and *go,* I'm staying here. Get the paramedics. *Go!'*

———

The three of us survived, but the paramedics told me it was a miracle. I was fetched from hospital by my Auntie Lilly. She told me we weren't going back to Ouma and Oupa Bunny's house, but to her house.

'Why aren't we going to Pop Inn?' I asked.

'Your father is pissed off, Jacqueline. You're going to need someone on your side today.'

She asked my Uncle John, who was driving, to double park outside a corner café. When she got back in, she tossed me a carton of cigarettes.

'You're going to need a lot of those!'

Auntie Lilly struggled with my father almost as much as I did, but the cigarettes made me think that I'd be dealing with a whole new level of angry. I thought of my Granny who, when she found out that I was a smoker, said 'Smoke until you're forty and then give it up. That's how we did it in the forties.' In stark contrast, my Ouma had told me she was ashamed of me for smoking. She did, however, promise to pray for me to be cured at church that Sunday. I wished Granny was with me. I still felt shaky. When we got to Auntie Lilly's house, I lay on her bed listening to her answering and hanging up the phone over and over. I could hear my father screaming and swearing through the receiver.

'No I will *not* let you talk to her. You should be grateful your daughter is alive and not worry about the fucking car. When you've calmed down and stopped shouting, I'll pass her the phone.'

In the outside world, the accident even made international news. I was hailed a hero.

But in here I lay sobbing as I counted the calls, one, two, three, four... fifteen. Why couldn't he just love me?

———

Eight months later, the accident was back in the news. My parents had moved to the Strand and were now also living with Ouma and Oupa Bunny at Pop Inn. Rumour had it that my father had been fired again for doing something illegal. I hadn't cared enough to ask. I'd left my job at the bank, gone back to university and flunked out again within six months. I had taken a job at an ad agency in Stellenbosch in the hope that I would soon have enough money to get my own apartment so that I didn't have to be near my parents. My boss was a cocaine head and my salary pitiful, but I was loving it.

I had just finished a jog along the beachfront before getting ready to go to the Hottentots Holland Publicity Association awards evening, where I had been nominated for an award for bravery for saving Marco and Dean. The telephone rang and I went to answer it. It was a representative of the Publicity Association, phoning in a panic to check that I didn't have any special dietary requirements.

'No, none at all,' I said.

'Thank goodness. Well, that's all I called to ask about,' said the woman. 'Congratulations again on your nomination for tonight and well done on your Red Cross gold medal that you were awarded for bravery last year.'

'Pardon. What medal?'

'Your medal from last year. The Red Cross gold class medal for bravery. That's a great honour, you know. Apparently they haven't awarded one of those since World War Two.'

'I'm sorry, I'm not sure what you're talking about. I only know about the award nomination for tonight.'

I slammed the receiver down after polite goodbyes and went straight to my father's bedside drawer. I pulled it open and started digging for evidence. There were books and old papers, his wallet, a packet of Rennie's antacid and there, suddenly, an open envelope addressed to me. It was a letter from the South African Red Cross Society. I slipped the letter out and began to read.

Dear Jacqueline,

On behalf of the Regional Council of The South African Red Cross Society, I have pleasure in enclosing the Conspicuous Service Medal in the Gold Class, as the Society's recognition of your extremely courageous act on 7 November 1984.

This medal is the highest form of recognition awarded by Red Cross for acts of bravery.

We extend our sincere congratulations.

> With kind regards,
> Yours sincerely,
> Mrs B. Blackwood-Murray
> Regional Director

Stunned, I turned the letter over, but the back was blank. There was no explanation. I looked inside the envelope and found a second sheet of paper had been stuffed inside. I uncrumpled it. It was a letter addressed to my father from the South African Red Cross Society. I read.

Dear Sir,

On behalf of the Society I do want to apologise for any problems which may have arisen from our recognition of Jacqueline's conduct after the unfortunate accident had occurred.

As parents of four robust and independently-minded children, who have grown into fine adults, my wife and I experienced many of the problems that young people go through on their way to maturity, resentment towards discipline, etc., so I can assure you that you have my full understanding. Let us hope that this accident has had a sobering effect on Jacqueline.

Her actions after the accident certainly displayed a great deal of courage and control under severe conditions and, again from personal wartime experience, I know that personal control is necessary for anyone to act in this manner immediately after suffering the trauma of such an accident.

We do hope that in time you will be able to regard this medal as the honour it is meant to bestow.

Yours sincerely,
Norman H Patterson
Regional Chairman

I was breathing hard. Fucking son of a bitch! I wasn't a rebellious child. I was a child with a lying criminal of a father! I wanted to scream and I wanted to cry. Instead, I placed the letters neatly side-by-side on my father's pillow, straightened my skirt and went to the awards evening with a smile hitched onto my face and a bubble of hatred swelling in my heart. Once again, all I did was smile for the camera.

When I asked him about it the next morning, he sighed.

'Jacqueline, why do you always have to be so sensitive? I never had this kind of trouble with your brothers.'

'That's because my brothers haven't had to keep your secrets.'

'There's a lot of things that your brothers haven't done that you have, which you should be ashamed of!'

We were veering dangerously close to forbidden territory and he knew it.

'Besides, you didn't deserve the award. You caused an accident that could have killed your two friends: you should have been ashamed of yourself and not rewarded in any way.'

'Dad, it was a fucking accident. I didn't do it on purpose! Why can't I just make my own decisions in life now?'

I was seething. The paramedics had told me that from where I left the car it would have been physically impossible to save Marco in the amount of time I had, yet Marco was alive and well. I couldn't exactly tell them that a great light had allowed me to land safely on that rock.

'Because you're still a child, Jacqueline.'

'I'm nineteen. I'm not a child anymore,' I snapped, sounding immature even to myself.

He seemed to think so too. He smirked and when he spoke again it was very slowly and clearly, as if I were stupid.

'No matter how old you are, I'm your father, and since you live under my roof, you will abide by my rules.'

'It's not your roof. We all live under Oupa Bunny's roof, which you have to live under because you're broke and got fired *again*, just like that time when you burnt our home down, or have you forgotten? You're so stupid, everyone in this town knows you did it and to think I defend you when they talk about it. You're the one who should be ashamed.'

It was stupid. I shouldn't have said it, but I was unable to control myself around him. There was a moment of shocked silence before he exploded – the way he always did. He went berserk, carrying on about how he knew he had sinned against Jesus, but that he had re-devoted his life to Him, been forgiven and now I needed to do the same.

I laughed in his face, turned and left the room, knowing I could not go another year living under the same roof as that man. It was time for me to get away from him forever.

CHAPTER SIXTEEN

No problem can be solved from the same level of
consciousness that created it. – Albert Einstein

I GOT A JOB AT a bigger agency and moved to Cape Town in the summer before my twentieth birthday. I was a city girl and lived in a bachelor flat with nothing but a microwave and a mattress on the floor. My days were spent at work and my evenings were spent numbing my pain practising Kyokushin, full contact karate. My bruises were now my medal.

I was happy, if a little lonely, so when Alison told me that she was moving to Cape Town after finishing her degree, I offered to let her crash on my floor. Alison was the closest thing I had to a sister. I was ready to put our history behind us and excited to have her close by again.

'Okay, I'll be home tomorrow,' I said to Alison one afternoon from the door of our flat. 'I'm going to the Strand for the night.'

'Please don't tell me you're going to see your parents.'

'Come on, they're my parents, Ali. I love them.'

'You know what's going to happen. You'll go there, you'll say something normal and your dad will lose his shit about it for no reason.'

'I can handle it. Why don't you come with me? We're having steak.'

'Tempting, but I'll pass. Have a good time.'

I don't know why I always defended him, but, like my mother, I didn't seem to be able to help it. I'd even gotten into a shouting match with Ouma over the way she continually bad-mouthed my father to the whole country. I met my parents at a restaurant in the Strand and we started catching up.

'How's living with Alison going? After visiting you at your flat, I was telling your mother how untidy she is. How do you put up with her? You know I don't trust that girl.'

I ignored him. It wasn't as if Alison liked or trusted him either. I took another gulp of my brandy and coke.

'I just got back from Johannesburg, actually. I was on a business trip with my boss.'

'Wow, that's quite something!'

My father puffed his chest out and I could've sworn he looked proud of me. I started bragging and the next thing I knew my father was talking with me – talking with me, not at me as he usually did – about his new business. We bragged and drank like two old buddies and my heart nearly jumped out of my chest when he said, 'You know Jacqueline. I always expected my boys to take on careers in the city, and now you're the one doing it. If I didn't know any better, I'd swear you were my only son.'

It was the closest to 'I'm proud of you' that I'd ever get and it was enough. All of that hell we'd lived through was erased in an instant.

After a year at the advertising agency, I was retrenched and took a full-time job as a waitress at an all-night restaurant, Naughty's Moonlight Grill. This outraged my father, which took us back to our cycle of fighting. I didn't want to spend the rest of my life as a waitress, but I was a little lost and confused. I knew I wanted to travel the world and so I sought advice from the only person who had ever been honest with me, my grandmother. Granny reminded me that my father would not approve of his only daughter travelling alone through Europe. I didn't care what he thought.

Granny had always been clear with me that she loved my father, but that she often found it hard, if not close to impossible, to like or respect her son's actions.

'Your grandfather, may he rest in peace, always had a different view. He used to say that no matter what our son did, even if he killed a man, he would hold his hand on the way to the gallows. But maybe he would think differently if he had lived to see what your father has done to me.'

I assumed she was referring to the fact that I had heard that my father had refinanced her house and lost the money, which had forced her to rent a tiny place in her old age.

'Jacqueline, all I know for sure is this. When God made you, He was determined to piss your father off and He did a fine job of it.'

We both burst out laughing.

'My advice to you is that at almost twenty-two you need to get out from under your father's thumb. Go see the world.'

'Do you think it is okay if I travel alone?'

'Oh come, I know you aren't scared. You're adventurous like me,' she said proudly. 'You've been working at that awful all-night restaurant for nearly a whole year now.'

'Where should I go?'

'London! Paris! Milan! Go to the continent, Jacqueline: you'll never regret it. Experience the world and open your mind. There is so much out there to learn.'

'But I won't be able to work legally.'

'That never stopped your father,' she said drily. 'Take a leaf out of his book, but only this once.'

We laughed again.

'Take a year to be young and free and to not worry about anything. I always thought you had to grow up too fast,' she said. 'But there is nothing we can do about that now but try and enjoy ourselves in the time we have on this earth. Don't you agree?'

I did, so I took all my savings, ignored my father's threats to blow up the aeroplane should I attempt to embark on this venture and bought a cheap ticket to Luxembourg that offered a free bus ride to London. I also blocked out his shame story about how 'his only daughter travelling alone would look like some tramp'.

I returned home a year later, three months before my 23rd birthday, after working in England and travelling through parts of Europe. With a mind broadened from meeting different people with different beliefs and reading books that were banned in South Africa, I returned to Cape Town with a pair of fur-lined gloves from Harrods just like my grandmother's (even though I had had to go without food for a week to afford them) and a new-found shame. I was ashamed of my flag and my country.

It had been a whirlwind year and I wasn't the same woman when I returned. In between travelling, I worked as an au pair, a carer for the elderly and a cleaner. It was exquisitely freeing to be able to do what I wanted without anyone judging me. I had a year of spending time with people who had no preconceived ideas about me and it gave me the energy and confidence to start living properly when I came home, something I realised I had not been doing since I was 16. I wanted to build a career for myself, one that would keep challenging me the way my year abroad had. My writer's dream was reawakened and I had millions of ideas floating around in my head, but once I was back in the city, it didn't seem like a good time because I needed money to pay rent and support myself. My plan was to get into business and then hopefully work for an NGO to bring about change in my country: the much-needed change that I had learned about abroad. Although my father never tired of telling anyone who would listen what a great businessman he was, I wanted to be nothing like him. I was going to go back to university so that I could develop myself professionally. As for my personal life, after a year away from my family I felt I was finally getting some perspective – a perspective other than theirs. I wanted to see a therapist to talk about the verbal and emotional abuse I had experienced, as well as the disturbing way my Dad used to touch me. It had been drilled into my head that therapy was for wackos, but at last I decided I had no choice, if I didn't want to turn out like my father. Alison and I had moved in together again and she encouraged me to get professional help. I hated how out of control and unkind I could become and sometimes, in my darkest moments, when he and I were screaming at one another, it was like we were each other's mirrors. On top of that, no matter how I tried, I couldn't convince myself that everything that had happened – the fire, my father's screaming, my wanting to kill him, beating up David, running away, trying to commit suicide, having an abortion, the car accident, getting retrenched – was all my fault. Whenever my father and I fought, my mother would say to him that I was not stable and that he should try to remember it. 'Jacqueline is not well'. I wanted a therapist to help me find out if this were true and I wanted to find out how to heal all the negativity that I carried deep within me. The shame that the fire caused me was as acute as if I were still 13 years old and was a sticking point in every fight with my father. I was sick of how this lie made me feel disconnected and sick of hating myself for keeping it. I still never looked at myself in the mirror, not even when I was brushing my teeth.

And then one day, something changed. My father offered me a job. He actually thought I was the best person for the position. Stranger still was the fact that I turned him down. It was my mother's clothing manufacturing and retail business, Bettina, and he was helping her with the accounts while he worked on some huge business deal that was apparently going to make him millions. I told my father that his salary offer was lower than anything I'd been offered in the city and I think he was shocked – and maybe impressed – that I hadn't come running. I was stronger now. But when my father matched the highest offer I'd received in Cape Town and offered me five per cent of the company, I couldn't say no. I figured as it was my mother's business, he wouldn't be around too much and besides, he seemed to have turned over a new leaf. While I was away, he'd written me a letter telling me that he'd changed and that he'd opened his heart to the Lord Jesus once more and had been forgiven by his Lord and Saviour. This was probably the hundredth time this had happened. I didn't believe him, but I had faith in myself that no matter what happened, I could stand up to him now. Therapy was helping. I was starting to live on my own terms.

I agreed to join Bettina on two conditions. First, I'd stay in Cape Town. Second, I'd study part-time while working and I enrolled to do a B.Com. My studies had to work out this time, because my mother didn't have formal business training and I wanted to do right by the trust she had placed in me by bringing me into her business. I wanted to make Bettina grow so I needed to upskill as quickly as possible. Studying wasn't a bid to impress him – I was done with that – but even I was surprised by his total lack of acknowledgment of me going back to university.

'Why do you think Dad doesn't care about my results?' I asked my mother on our lunch break one day, shortly after I'd found out I'd done well in my first-year exams. 'He doesn't even wish me good luck before I have to take an exam?'

'Well, I think it's because your father doesn't believe you're going to finish.'

'He what?'

'He says you don't finish anything you start.'

But it wasn't all about him anymore.

CHAPTER SEVENTEEN

A man who has not passed through the inferno of his
passions has never overcome them. – Carl Jung

FOR FOUR YEARS I CONTINUED to work for Bettina. Alison cheated on her boyfriend with a guy I had a crush on, so within a year we went our separate ways. I first moved into a digs and a year after that I moved in with my boyfriend Greg. My parents were horrified that I was living in sin and insisted that I tell both my grandmothers. I wasn't surprised by Ouma's response.

'Dear Lord!' she said. 'This is going to bring shame on the family. Jakkaleen, I'm going to have to pray and ask for your sins to be forgiven.'

Granny was always a bit of a dark horse, but even so I was taken aback by her candour.

'Jacqueline, it makes such sense in the modern world. You've got to try it out first, if you know what I mean,' she said, winking. 'I loved your grandfather, but I think we got married as soon as we did because we were horny.'

With that out of the way, I only had one more hurdle to face: Bettina was in financial trouble. The economy was depressed and, at the same time, large retailers were expanding all over the country. Small clothing boutiques were under pressure. I was determined to find a solution. I'd been promoted to office manager and could now access the accounts. I took a look at them and discovered that my father was running expenses through Bettina that had nothing to do with the business. I didn't want to do anything drastic about the issue in case there was a reason behind it. My father had been on the straight and narrow for a couple of years, or so I thought, so I gave him the benefit of the doubt and called him over to the computer one morning at work.

'Dad, could you please run through the expenses with me?'

'Jacqueline, what are you doing behind that computer? Get away from there!'

'Could you just explain these purchases?'

'Explain myself to you?' he grunted, before going off at me.

I was learning from therapy not to stoop to his level and get into an argument – and most of the time I managed to keep it together. He stormed out of the room, slamming the door. I kept scrolling through the files. None of it added up and there was cash coming in from an unknown source. It didn't take me long to find out where the money was coming from. He was refinancing Ouma's house, Pop Inn. I couldn't believe it, not after he had lost his own mother's house the same way. I went to Pop Inn, which was as loud and floral and Jesus-infested as ever, to try and convince Ouma to stand her ground, but she was resolute.

'Listen, Jakkaleen. My daughter made her choices and the Lord knows – goodness, everyone in this town knows – that they weren't always good ones. But that's that. Bettina is my own daughter's business. You think I can sit by and watch her business fail when it's the one thing in her life that brings her any kind of joy? She's my daughter.'

I was silent. A plastic Jesus eyed me from the top of the television set. 'Heartless!' he seemed to cry. Before I could come up with a way to stop it all, my father approached me with a solution.

———◆———

My parents and I were sitting in the small lounge area of the Bettina offices.

'Bettina is in trouble,' he said. 'Your cash flow has literally stopped, but I've found a solution. The Department of Trade and Industry (DTI) has introduced a funding programme for businesses like yours that are looking to expand. It's perfect timing, because there's a material measuring machine that your mother and I believe would be essential for the business.'

There was a short pause. What in the hell did we need a measuring machine for? We wanted to do the opposite of expand.

'The DTI will fund the machine, which will improve our margins and sort out our cash flow problems.'

'Have you researched this, Dad?'

'Of course! You're not the only one looking out for the business, all right? Let's focus on getting the DTI on board.'

My father said he had our application fast-tracked and within days two men from the DTI arrived for our interview. We exchanged niceties and I couldn't help but notice that my father was being more charming than usual. The men explained that the process included an inspection of the financials, interviews with the shareholders – my mother and I – and each shareholder signing off on the application. They had already met with my parents and now they wanted to interview me. We went to my office and one of them asked me a hundred questions about Bettina, my parents, the measuring machine and our business strategy.

'Finally, and most important of all, are you up to speed with your company's accounts?'

'Kind of,' I said quickly; too quickly.

'It's important that you examine all of the financial statements over the past years that have been submitted to us. If there's anything you feel I should know, be sure to contact me.'

'No, there's nothing,' I said, thinking of the unrelated expenses I'd seen on the computer.

'All righty then. My colleague and I will leave documents for you and your mother to sign.'

The men left and I explained to my parents the necessity of me studying the financial statements from the very beginning of the business until now.

'Ag, there's nothing new in there,' said my father. 'I've had Monica prepare and check it.'

Monica was our part-time accountant.

'I still need to see it all.'

'Why can't you just take my word for it? Jesus Christ, Jacqueline, why do you always have to be so difficult?'

'I'm not being difficult, Dad. The man from the DTI said it's a requirement that I examine them.'

'Well just sign the forms they left and you can look over all of that another day, okay? I want to get this done so that I can get back to my own work. I'm busy working on an extremely important deal worth millions. I don't have time to keep helping you women with every single bloody thing.'

My father spread the documents across the coffee table and my mother dutifully signed and then handed me her pen. I baulked, staring at them both.

'Your mother and I have a lunch date. Can you hurry up and sign?'

'Here, take the pen, Jacqueline,' said my mother.

I took it and signed the documents and my father put them back into his briefcase.

'Come on, Sweetie, let's go.'

My parents left and I resolved to get a copy of the accounts submitted to the DTI. Monica printed them out for me and I skipped lunch to study them. As I paged through the documents, I grew cold.

There wasn't a single final balance that matched with the original statements I had remembered seeing on the computer. He'd created figures out of thin air.

I heard my mother laughing as my parents came back in. I hated that I felt so confused. I got up from my desk and went to my father, who was standing over the computer. He spun around to face me.

'Dad, I've been looking at the statements you prepared to give the DTI tomorrow and I'm confused.'

If I had flat-out accused him of fraud, he would have lost his mind and then I would have made no progress.

'Who in the hell gave them to you?'

'Monica.'

He swore softly under his breath.

'Walk with me to my car, I'm having a busy day and need to hurry,' he said, steering me out of the office.

'I'm not sure we should give the DTI the application –'

'Goddammit Jacqueline, I dropped the signed documents off at their offices after lunch. Just forget about it, okay?'

'You *what?*' I bit down on my anger and tried to focus. I could not lose it with him.

'Respectfully, Dad, I do understand. I appreciate that I don't have the years of experience that you do, but things aren't adding up and I'm afraid there might be an error.'

'There's no fucking error, okay? Just trust me.'

'I really think there is a mistake, Dad. The expenses, for instance –'

'Enough! Your whole bloody life you've been harassing me with questions and I'm done. You're 26: just accept the fact that I know what I'm doing. We need that money from the DTI if we want to keep this company going. Don't you want that?'

'Of course I do, I just –'

'I swear, as soon as we get that machine, I can't wait to leave your mother and you to run this business alone. I don't have time to keep helping you out here, but I guess that's what happens when two women run a business. I mean, why in the hell does your mother even want this goddamn measuring machine? It beats me.'

I was filled with relief. If we didn't need the machine, we didn't need the loan and if we didn't need the loan, I could go over to their offices, retract the application and we could all forget about the fraudulent statements.

'Dad, that's exactly what I've been thinking. We don't need a measuring machine, seriously. The business is struggling and I don't know how we're going to make enough money to repay such a big loan. I'm going to tell Mom right now.'

'Wait! No!'

I turned slowly.

'Just — just wait. I don't want to upset your mother. Let me answer your questions. Come, let's go back to my office. I was rushed before; my other business can wait. Let me see if I can't help you understand things first.'

'Okay,' I said slowly and followed him back to his office.

We had barely sat down when the phone at the desk started ringing.

'Please take a message,' he called to our receptionist. 'My daughter and I have important business to attend to.'

He only called me his daughter when he wanted me on his side.

'So, what are you concerned about, Jacqueline?'

'Sir, the message is urgent,' said the receptionist.

'I'm very busy,' he called again, not taking his eyes off me.

'He says his name is André and that it's extremely urgent.'

At the mention of the name André, my father's face went white, but he kept on smiling.

'Ah, okay then,' he said with an affected sigh. 'I apologise, Jacqueline. Won't you give me a moment?'

'No problem.'

'Er, could you give me some privacy?'

'Oh, sorry,' I said, jumping up.

I stepped outside, but could still hear him speaking in a low voice.

'Please, André. I promise I'll have it sorted soon. I beg you, I need more time.'

'I'm working on something right now with the DTI. I swear on my life! By Monday, I'll have the money.'

'Yes, I'll pick up right away. I swear to God I won't avoid your call again.'

'Thank you.'

I was frozen just outside the office door and heard him push his chair back and it toppled over.

'What the fuck are you doing lurking outside my door! You fucking little bitch! I asked you to give me some privacy and you listen at the goddamn door!'

'I didn't mean to listen, I was just standing –'

'Stop fucking lying to me and get out of my way!'

He stormed off to find my mother.

———

I had to stop the DTI application. Whatever my father had gotten into, requesting a loan based on fraudulent documents would only make things worse, so I called the DTI and asked to postpone the processing of our application.

'I'm calling a meeting,' I said to my parents, as they were leaving the office that afternoon. 'I've asked the DTI not to process the application right away. I want to meet with both of you on Saturday morning to discuss something important.'

'Jesus fucking Christ, you told them not to fast-track it,' my father moaned.

Fear seemed to cancel out his rage. On Saturday morning, I was the first to arrive. I sat on the couch for a few moments and then on the chair. I crossed my legs, uncrossed them, got up and sat on the other couch. I ran to the bathroom and retched, but I'd had the foresight not to eat breakfast. My parents arrived and sat down side by side on a couch. My father played a smile across his lips and leaned back, acting casual. My mother clutched her handbag in her lap. I would have to say it all in one go and leave no time for them to interrupt me. I took a deep breath, looked straight at my father and began.

'I cannot allow Bettina to apply for that loan. I refuse. I know that the financial statements are fraudulent, because I saw the originals. We all know that there's no point in getting that machine and that the loan is just a cover. I know that you refinanced Ouma's house, where we spent every single Christmas holiday, and that she's going to lose it because of you.'

'You fucking –'

'Don't interrupt me. Dad, after accidently overhearing your call I suspect you're in debt to someone, but you can't commit another crime. I won't let you.'

'Oh, God, Jacqueline,' my mother cried out.

She covered her face in her hands and started sobbing.

'I'm so s-sorry, Jacqueline, I didn't want you to be involved. Your father – he –'

She was choking on the tears and shaking.

'He took a R100 000 loan from a loan shark and he says he'll kill him if we don't pay now. Please, Jacqueline, please – you can't tell anyone, you've got to help us!'

Her mascara started sliding down her face in black stripes.

'And – Monica's client –' she choked and my father rounded on her.

'Don't say another word!'

'What about Monica's client, Mom? Tell me!'

'Monica's other client, she's an old lady, and Monica was entrusted to look after her money. Monica gave Dad access to the money and he lost all the money –'

'How could you do that, Dad? How could you do that to an old lady, to Monica, to Mom, to me?'

'This has nothing to do with you, Jacqueline. What's done is done.'

'Dad, this has *everything* to do with me. You made me sign my name to those documents. I'm a shareholder!'

Suddenly we were both on our feet facing one another, with my mother still sobbing into her hands.

'Oh, for fuck's sake Jacqueline, you don't know what you're talking about! This has nothing to do with you.'

'Dad, stop!' I said, losing my temper. 'You've been lying for years and it's the end. All of this has got to stop, now! You burnt our house down, you've taken an innocent elderly lady's money, Ouma's money, Granny's house and now you want to get us all neck-deep in fraud only to pay back a loan shark – no! We're putting an end to this today. We aren't going to go down with you.'

He leaned in closer and the look in his eyes – I knew I'd never forget it. His pale eyes were filled with gloating evil and he started to laugh like an insane person.

'You'll never be able to prove it,' he laughed, 'because I got your mother to sign off on every single statement. She's the one who'll face criminal charges and I am sure you want to protect her.'

Something within me snapped. I'd been challenging him for years, but in that moment I lost any semblance of a filter – or anything that therapy had taught me.

'*YOU DISGUST ME, YOU MISOGYNISTIC, ABUSIVE PIECE OF SHIT. HOW COULD YOU DO THIS TO HER?*

Still screaming, I turned to my mother.

'*MOM, WHY HAVE YOU STOOD BY HIM ALL THESE YEARS? DAD SPEAKS TO YOU LIKE YOU ARE A PIECE OF SHIT AND THIS IS HOW HE REPAYS YOU? I'M SICK AND TIRED OF HIS CONSTANT LIES AND ABUSE. HE'S BEEN CONTROLLING US ALL OUR LIVES AND I'M TELLING YOU*

NOW, LOUD AND CLEAR, THAT I'M DONE WITH HIM TREATING ME THIS WAY. ALL HE DOES IS BLAME OTHER PEOPLE FOR HIS FUCK-UPS. AND WHEN I TRY AND TALK TO YOU ABOUT THE THINGS HE HAS DONE TO ME, YOU CALL ME A LIAR OR TURN IT AROUND ON ME. MOM, WHY DON'T YOU EVER BELIEVE ME?. PLEASE LEAVE HIM!!!

My father grabbed me by the shoulders and spun me around to face him.

'SHUT THE FUCK UP! YOU SHUT THE FUCK UP RIGHT NOW OR I'LL FUCKING KILL YOU!'

'ALL THESE YEARS, ALL YOU'VE WANTED TO DO IS HIT ME – YOU'VE BEEN SCREAMING AT ME, CALLING ME A SLUT, A BITCH, A FUCKING WHORE, A DISAPPOINTMENT, YOU NAME IT, SO WHY DON'T YOU JUST DO IT THEN? OR ARE YOU TOO SCARED TO RUIN YOUR FUCKING GENTLEMAN'S IMAGE? PLUCK UP THE COURAGE AND HIT ME, YOU FUCKING LOSER!'

Before I knew what had happened I was flying across the room. I smashed into the wall and slid to the ground. I felt nothing. I was delirious with rage and at the same time couldn't stop laughing.

'You think you can hurt me? You know what, just like your version of Jesus Christ, I'm going to turn the other cheek. Here, why don't you hit me on this side now?'

My mother buried her head in her hands and pleaded for us to stop, to please for the love of God stop, but there was no stopping either of us and there was no love of God there.

'How dare you make me hit you, you fucking bitch –'

But I didn't hear his insults anymore. I got up from the floor and went straight up to him, turning my left cheek to his face.

'Come on, Dad. I dare you.'

He said nothing and I laughed in his face.

I went straight to my office and packed the contents of my desk into a box, grabbed my car keys and walked out. He was waiting for me next to my car. When he saw my face, which must have looked terrible, he started crying.

'Please, Jacqueline, you've got to help me, I'm so sorry.'

He clasped his hands in a prayer position.

'Please, forgive me. You don't understand what it's been like, the pressure I've been under –'

'Always the same fucking story. Get out of my way.'

'No, please, you've got to support me, you've got to help me. You've got to help me and Mom. We're a team, remember Jacqueline, we're a team.'

I opened the car door, but paused before getting in. I was determined to have the last word. I looked up at his tear-streaked face.

'All of these years you've been calling me a fucking whore. Well, for what it's worth, by your standards I am. I've slept with more than three men and you know what? I just lie back and let them fuck me.'

All the air seemed to go out of him and he sank to the ground. It was the worst thing I could've said to him. He kneeled in the dusty car park and sobbed.

'Your words can't touch me anymore. I'm done with this fucked-up relationship. I never want to see you again.'

I got into the car, slammed the door and drove off, a sense of ugly power surging through me.

Less than three months later, I married Greg. My father walked me down the aisle and together we smiled for the cameras. When I came back from my honeymoon, there was another letter from him, explaining how he'd given his life over to the Lord Jesus yet again and that it was my duty to forgive him, as Jesus had. I added it to the steadily growing pile of Jesus letters from him. Forgiveness was no longer an option.

PART TWO

BURNING BRIDGES

For My Mother

no will to live
i do confess
a wish to die today

lost in hell
i'm in distress
i cannot find a way

the screaming truth
of this desire
to end it all i see

is in the shadow of my Self
and not in truth
me

CHAPTER EIGHTEEN

Beware the barrenness of a busy life. – Socrates

THE SNOW MELTS AS IT touches my skin and I wish it would pile up and cover me, a white hand covering my mouth and nose so that I don't feel angry anymore. I'm hiking alone in the Rocky Mountains, in Colorado. I hike for answers but the mountains look on impassively. Granny would say I must work it out myself. What else would she say if she were here, hiking beside me? She would be hard and straight with me as she always was.

Twenty years have passed since the day my father hit me. My marriage to Greg didn't last long. Even so, I've been happy – gloriously so, at times. But now I am totally lost and, to be honest, somewhat terrified. You'd think I'd have had it all figured out by now, but I feel like a bat flying around a kitchen while someone swats at me with a dishcloth. From the outside, things look simply marvellous. I'd always thought adults had it all figured out, but the older I get, the more I realise that no one really has a clue what's going on. Sure, my mother's business went insolvent and Ouma lost her house and my dad is as crazy as ever, but apartheid had fallen and I'd done well.

I'd completed my undergraduate degree, gone on to get an MBA and had had a ball studying in the Netherlands for a semester. I had fallen in love with my country again, made money and had a great career. I had built up a business from an insolvent mess to something worth millions. I had created jobs, salvaged failing businesses, made friends, travelled to many corners of the world and learned more than I ever could've foreseen. I had fallen in love with people, places, work and life – and I believed that, in my own small way, I had made a difference in the world where I could. I had helped people access better education and work opportunities and I had even adopted and fostered abandoned animals.

I'd cut ties with my father and made an effort to get closer to my mother – when my father allowed it, that is. I had learned that Dad had kept many secrets from Mom and noted that Mom forgot distressing events as her way of managing life. She'd even erased whole parts of my life from her memory. I had observed how painful this was for me. Although I missed my family, the status quo was best for all of us. Best of all, I had met the perfect man, fallen in love, got married and moved into a gorgeous house in one of the world's most beautiful cities. Michael was everything I could've wanted.

And still everything fell apart.

'Jacqueline, you're not the young woman I used to know,' Granny would have said. 'And quite frankly, dear, I don't like what I see.'

I don't like what I see either. I'm exhausted and angry, but I have no idea how the hell I'm going to change. I feel trapped in my anger towards Michael, his business and the last decade of my life. I am even angry and ashamed of my country again. I also don't much like the fact that I'm talking to my dead grandmother in my head on a mountaintop.

'You've achieved so much on the outside, but what about all that stuff going on inside you?'

Well, what about it? I've been to so many therapy sessions I practically have a PhD in psychology and even though I've made progress on the outside in terms of achieving goals, my grandmother is right. I'm an angry mess.

'Focus, Jacqueline. For once just cut out all the noise and think. Do you continue being this angry person that you have become or do you change?'

I know what I should do, but divorce is too painful. I don't even want to think about it practically.

'Oh, stop whining. You're strong. You'll make it through this.'

I've been strong for other people for too many years and now I don't have anything left for myself. I want to collapse in the snow and stay on this mountain forever. They will find my bones and my wedding ring one hundred years from now.

'I see you've developed quite a flair for dramatic self-pity, Jacqueline.'

Oh, for God's sake, just tell me what to do!

'This is your choice to make. You have to work this out for yourself.'

That's what she would say. She was always telling us as kids to solve our own problems and be independent. It was typical of her to tell me that everything in life is a choice. I know I need to change, but I can't.

'Michael, I can't do this anymore. I just can't.'

My voice had broken as I'd spoken the words months ago back in Cape Town. Michael and I had spent the best part of a decade bringing a court case against Deloitte over the valuation of Michael's business. Their valuation had in essence assessed a piece of costume jewellery at the price of a Tiffany diamond. They had appeared to finally be ashamed of trying to defend their valuation. So they had settled. But at what cost to us? Despite being annoyed that they had forgotten to silence me from sharing the horror story of what they had done, they had, in fact, won. We were broken. I had put my life on hold to fight for Michael, whose breakdown a decade earlier meant that he could neither run his business, nor fight against the bullies who were trying to destroy us. That had fallen to me and I resented him for it.

'I want to be in the mountains. I want to write.'

'I know you do,' he said.

'If only we –'

I always came back to this: if we'd only emigrated to North America a decade ago as planned, none of this would have happened. If Michael hadn't backed out then, we wouldn't be in this situation. 'This situation' was his business, now in financial trouble again, the Deloitte case and me, exhausted. 'This situation' was me in tears, writing him letters about how heartbroken I felt over everything I'd sacrificed, begging him to notice that I existed, pleading for support from him when I was consumed by chronic fatigue yet again. Worse yet, 'this situation' was now my unkindness and our constant fighting. It was who I had become. My dear friend Jill encouraged me to talk to Michael and impress upon him how important my writing was to me.

'Jacqui, I promise it's going to be okay,' he'd told me.

But I didn't have faith in us anymore. His promises to support me seemed empty. Nothing had changed. I no longer believed in the dream that we would be able to love one another through anything that life threw at us and then walk triumphantly into the sunset. I wasn't even walking anymore; I was crawling through my life, knees bruised and palms bleeding.

'I know you're angry. But we're going to get past this. You can go to the mountains, you can do nothing but write and I will fix the business this time. We can work on our marriage when you get back from America.'

But I just shook my head, our marriage lying shattered all around us. All I had to hold onto was the idea of making Deloitte pay for what they'd done to us.

'You don't need to bring criminal charges against Deloitte. The commercial case is over now. It's over, Jacqui.'

But I believed a criminal investigation was the right thing to do. Michael was the one who had wanted the commercial case against them, but what about what I wanted? They had destroyed documents to hide what they had done and I thought they should be in jail for it.

I was wishing I could've drawn the curtain down on my life years ago, when I was happy and successful and excited about my life and my marriage. But life isn't a play; shit just keeps happening and suddenly, at 45, I find I don't have the strength to keep the act going.

'Just leave Deloitte alone,' Michael had said. 'We won our case; they settled because they didn't want the truth to come out in court. You can achieve this through your book.'

But in the process we had lost everything that mattered. Did he not see that? We had lost one another. I shook my head as I remembered, blinking back tears.

I didn't believe we had won anything; they had settled to shut us up. They needed to be exposed for what they had done. While they had bought Michael's silence, mine wasn't for sale and I was going to tell those stories. I didn't like who I'd become and maybe if I could tell the stories… I didn't know. All I knew was that I no longer recognised myself. All of this unkindness, this negativity, this anger inside of me.

Neither of us liked who I was with him anymore either, so we had agreed that I would go to Colorado for two months, to live in a cabin in Columbine Lake, organised by my friend Amanda, and finish writing my book. It was Amanda's shoulder I cried on a decade earlier. 'Amanda I don't want to run Michael's business.' I cried.

'You don't have to Jacqui.'

'But Amanda, my father in law says it is my duty as Michael's wife. Micheal is broken, I cannot abandon him in his time of need.'

And so a decade later with my tears suppressed and anger in my heart, it was Amanda I was running towards yet again. At the airport in Cape Town Michael and I had hugged briefly but couldn't look at one another.

'I know things are in trouble and I hope that this will bring our marriage back together again. But Jacqui, what happens in America stays in America.'

The wind comes up and I concentrate on the murmurs of pines rustling far below and try to put Michael out of my mind, but it's impossible. The things that hide in me come out again in the snow. I think of what my friends and family back home would say if they saw me now, totally alone in the snow. They would think that I'd lost it – what happy 45-year-old woman leaves her husband at home and travels halfway across the world to go hiking alone in the snow? It's not as if she's got anything to complain about, but there she goes, trying to find herself. They probably think my life is perfect and that I've gotten past all the unpleasantness of my teens and twenties. My family must think I've finally realised that there is no such thing as emotional abuse and that at last I've put to bed the lie I always told about how creepy it felt the way my father touched me. Well, it turns out I'm apparently not the only one whose skin he made crawl when no one was watching.

They probably think that now that our court case is over, I can focus on my wonderful husband. They think I should be happy, but it isn't that simple. The memory of Michael emerges again from the blinding white surrounding me. With every step I take in the snow, he steps alongside me.

I met Michael in my late 20s through work and, after dating for a year, I knew he was it. I realised that for him I'd be able to become the woman people wanted me to be. I would be able to support him and adore him. I would be able to host dinner parties with him and travel with him, share all my days with him and love him until it hurt. I would be able to pour my soul into this man and he would pour his soul into me and at last I would be whole again. He was a weird mix of parts, unlike any man I'd been with before. He was both soft and abrasive, naïve and intelligent, quirky and traditional, sensitive and arrogant. I loved how peaceful he looked when he slept, his curls dark against the white pillow, half-light on his pale skin. It was the only time he was ever peaceful. Awake, he was a constant bustle of sound and activity. I loved the fact that he had no filter and blurted the first thing that came into his head, even if it was often downright offensive. He couldn't help being incurably honest and Lord knows I hated lies more than anything. He had a bizarre creative side that splashed out often and I cherished it. He made me laugh until I cried and when we started working together, the office joke became that while I thought out of the box, Michael flew right over the box. We made fun of the fact that I, as the boss, needed to put him inside a glass container where he wouldn't be able to disrupt business or say something he shouldn't, but could slip his brilliant ideas out to us and leave his imagination free to roam.

'Jacqueline, why aren't you enjoying this magnificent hike?' Granny would say, if she were here.

Instead my mind wanders back to Michael.

Michael and I were both outsiders and in the early years of our marriage I hoped that together we would wash away that particular pain. He struggled with severe ADHD, which had always forced him away from the centre of things. It was finally diagnosed after we'd been married for five years. His disruptive personality had caused his mother great shame, although she would never admit it. We shared that, too – mothers who wished more than anything that their children were as perfect as they had dreamed them to be while still in the womb. But we had been born with quirks that were then warped by life and there was nothing our mothers could do but deny, deny, deny. For Michael and me, life was like constantly walking with your shoes on the wrong feet: doable but difficult. We thought that together we might change that. But two wrongs don't make a right and no matter how much we tried to love one another through it all, I remained hamstrung by my past and Michael, too, was unable to stop feeling that he had let himself down for not doing more with his vast capabilities. The little digs that had been piled onto him for decades – pay attention, Michael; you're lazy, Michael; you could have been great, Michael, with that brain of yours, Michael; imagine what you could do, Michael – grew into a mountain that even I couldn't shift. He didn't expect me to and I didn't blame him for not being able to understand everything about me either. I just wished that after fourteen years of marriage, he knew me better than he did.

Maybe it was I who didn't really know myself?

'You're weird,' he once said. 'It's like you don't even see people. You just look right through them.'

I wanted to say to him that the bodies weren't important, that it was the spirit of the individual that I was looking at, the part of me that he used to see when we were younger, the part that knows nothing but love. Although I know it now, I didn't realise at the time that I had dissociated from my body, and from the bodies of those around me, when I was 16. When I left a room, I would not remember if the person I was speaking to was skinny or fat, tall, short, dark or fair. But I would have seen other parts, parts that made them who they were in ways other than the physical, and it hurt me that Michael could not see who I had become and what I wanted: a man I could lean on and feel safe with when I was falling apart. But Michael had lost this part of himself after his breakdown. Maybe I'd made him lose it.

I desperately wanted to be a good wife and a good person. I had this idea that if I only followed the right steps – a great career, a wonderful husband – I would be catapulted into a life of bliss and contentment.

In our first year of marriage Michael told me a lie and it hit me like a freight train. I snapped three days later when I uncovered the truth after his multiple denials. I screamed at him and slapped him through the face, then threw him out of the house, and yet we managed to get past it. I hated myself afterwards and somehow, since then, I had managed to keep this angry part of myself silent for most of our marriage. But recently, the part of me that was mean like my father had started raising its ugly head again. I had become vicious and malicious. I found Michael's weak spots and pressed them. I victimised him in our own home, snapped at him in public and hated myself for it.

A decade before, Michael had bought a business that turned out to be insolvent. An arbitration case was brought against the previous owner and Deloitte was asked to value it so that the matter could be settled. The Deloitte evaluation was irresponsible and full of calculation errors. It also appeared that they had broken the law in the process. It led to Michael having a breakdown. I was already running the business and now I had to manage the legal battle with Deloitte on Michael's behalf. It lasted almost nine years. All the while, I was struggling with chronic fatigue.

I'd come to the mountains for two months to finish my book. A tell-all story about my father and about what Deloitte had done. Michael must be relieved at the thought that we are spending two months apart. I sure would've been happy if my dark side had announced that it wanted to go on holiday overseas, but unfortunately we're stuck together. And as for writing, that's not exactly going according to plan either. The manuscript lies in the cabin far below, untouched. Do I really want to write about my father's abuse, as well as the manipulations of a massive corporation, or should I rather bring criminal charges against Deloitte so that the truth can be publicly exposed?

But being stuck in a legal battle for another decade, always angry, always trying to win – that isn't what I want for myself. All I had ever wanted was to be a writer, work in a non-profit and live in North America. I have to keep reminding myself of why I am here, because my mind is a stuck record playing, 'Why me', 'I wish' and 'If only' again and again. Why did Deloitte do this to us? I wish my father hadn't become so mean. If only Michael hadn't changed his mind about moving to North America.

'We haven't received our visas because I haven't applied for them yet. I want to stay in South Africa,' he had said, and so I stayed and pushed my dream aside.

Why had I done that? Not another fucking question, I groan, my lungs burning as I hike. I've been bumping my way through life, responding only in a way that I think will make others happy, in the hope that they will love and accept me. It probably all boils down to Daddy issues – who knows, maybe every decision I've made has been part of my plan to numb out my father's conditional love by making others love me and feel grateful to me.

As I hike onwards, my goggles fogging up, other people I've known and loved pop into my mind. Memories of Greg, my first husband, make me laugh out loud. We started dating in my 20s. He was a surfer boy who played the guitar and handsome as hell. We'd been dating for a few years when he proposed to me at 27. I had burst out laughing.

'Greg, are you kidding me?'

'No. All of our friends are getting married and we keep trying to break up and we haven't yet. My mom is dying, Jacqui, and I want her at my wedding.'

He was my best friend and my parents would be overjoyed if I settled down and got married, so we went ahead and did it. On the fourth day of our honeymoon, after a massive wedding where my parents and I pretended we liked each other, we decided to stay together until his mother died, which sadly happened two years later. It was a beautiful marriage, if a strange one.

I take my goggles off and wipe my face and look around. I blink at the white glare and sit down to drink it all in. It dawns on me that I haven't felt this free since I was 13. I haven't had a moment to myself to do nothing but take life in. Instead, I have been performing non-stop like a furious marionette, with God knows who pulling the strings. Michael knows as well as I do that we are putting on a show of happiness and success for our friends, families and colleagues. Have

I become obsessed with all the outward markers of success?

And then it hits me: I am alone. I am up here, in the snow, with no one expecting anything of me and I am bloody loving it. I am loving being alone, without the person I've become in our marriage. The important thing, I tell myself as I hike uphill, is to remember that I'm here in the snowy mountains now, like I always wanted.

I came here to Colorado to write, but that hasn't been as easy as I thought it would be. Ever since I arrived Michael's been emailing me, wanting this, needing that. And when he isn't emailing me, he's stalking through my very thoughts. I came to America to carve out a small space for myself and I'm getting elbowed out of my own life. On my hikes I'm followed by Michael, Deloitte and my father through the snowy woods and onto the mountains.

'Leave me alone,' I whisper.

My voice falls softly onto the snow without an echo. Who am I talking to? Myself? Am I really that insane? Or is it my father? Or Michael?

'Leave me alone,' I say, louder.

I wonder if I'm speaking to Michael now. Although I've only been in Colorado for two weeks, already the mountains are more used to my anger and confusion than Michael is.

'*LEAVE ME ALONE,*' I scream, loud enough to start an avalanche.

I want the mountains to force Michael to listen to what I need to say but cannot bring myself to say.

I scream and scream, but the avalanche doesn't come. It's oddly exhilarating, if a little nuts. Michael is probably also thinking that he is happy to be free from me. Just that morning, I'd screamed at him on the phone again.

'*WHY THE FUCK ARE YOU CONTACTING ME ABOUT WHAT TO DO IN THE BUSINESS? I HANDED OVER A SUCCESSFUL BUSINESS TO YOU THREE YEARS AGO AND I DON'T WORK THERE ANYMORE. I DIDN'T FUCK UP THE*

BUSINESS: YOU DID! I CAN'T RESCUE YOU ANYMORE! DO WHATEVER THE FUCK YOU WANT AND WHILE YOU'RE AT IT, DRAW UP THE DIVORCE PAPERS.'

That is the heart of what I screamed, but there was an entire monologue of blame. After the phone call, my cruelty hung around me like gun smoke. I've screamed for a divorce a few times over the last year, but I still haven't left him, perhaps because I love him more than anything. The only person I hate is myself. I didn't want to leave Michael, but I didn't know how to stay. We had both tried changing but we kept failing.

No matter what I threw at Michael, there was always a warm bed to crawl into, shamefaced, at the end of the day. If I leave him, the only person I'll have to put up with is myself and frankly, that sounds worse than anything. I am running from his loving arms into a cold, empty hell full of ready-meals and my own jokes: it makes no sense. I'll have to make small talk with strangers, decisions that have an impact on no one but myself and reservations for one. I will probably drink too much whiskey. There will be no more drama. I'll be left in the silence, perhaps with the television playing some inane show in the background, probably with a couple of cats for good measure. My life will become a backdrop to other happier lives. And people will talk about me. It's not the 19th century, but still, the gossip about me and my two divorces will wear me down. My days without Michael will pass heavily and slowly until I find myself wandering around town in a tracksuit and Ugg boots and cursing at children and the elderly. It's not as if I have a bountiful future awaiting me: a lover, a marvellous new career or any of those wonderfully romantic reasons for which people leave their partners. There's nothing in front of me. I've become an angry woman but at least I have a beautiful home, money and someone to talk to (and scream at). How do I know that if I do this, I won't become a lonely angry woman with no home, no money and no one to talk to?

I thought that giving up what I wanted for Michael was a brave sacrifice that would finally make me happy. But it didn't work. I thought that working for my mother at Bettina would make me happy because I was supporting her. But it didn't work. When my parents got into financial trouble again, I put their house in my name and helped them through it just because my Mom looked happy. She'd even started painting again, but it didn't last. I go on, thinking of all the times that I have sacrificed myself to make someone else happy, and I keep circling back to my father. I gave up on my life at 16 because I knew that everything about me angered him. I gave up on as much as I possibly could without killing myself so that he would love and accept me. Surprise, surprise, Jacqui. It didn't work.

People always say that women become their mothers and I never believed it, but maybe they're right, right about me at least. My mother never stopped sacrificing herself. There was always one more heartbreak, one more humiliation, one more task for her to do for my father. Once, I almost thought she would leave him. I was 26 or so, just before I stopped working at Bettina, and I went to dinner at my parents' house. My father was calling my mother 'fucking stupid' over some trivial thing and I was shouting back at him in her defence. I guess something flared up in my mother and she snapped.

'I'm done with this. I'm leaving you!'

I could hardly believe my ears.

My mother ran to their bedroom and my father followed screaming.

'YOU THINK YOU CAN LEAVE ME? YOU HAVE NO RIGHT TO LEAVE ME, YOU'LL NEVER LAST A DAY WITHOUT ME!'

I pushed past him to get between them, shouting at her to pack quickly. My mother sat on the edge of the bed, rocking back and forth. With her head in her hands, she started to sob.

'Jacqueline, I can't leave. I made my vows in front of God and I need to stay.'

'Are you kidding me? Where the fuck is God for you right now?

What has God ever done to help you?'

Something broke inside me that day. I hated her for staying, but now I wonder if I'm not becoming her in sacrificing everything that matters to me until I'm trapped with no exits. I can't let what happened to her happen to me.

Every muscle twinges as I hike on and abruptly I find it: the silence. I step into that sublime nothingness that I've come here to find and my thoughts grow thin and fade away. The Rockies go on forever and I have them all to myself. I breathe in and out but hear nothing. The silence is so deafening it knocks the wind out of me.

I do all that I can to hang on to the silence but my emotions roar inside of me. Despite everything, I'm ecstatic. I've freed myself from the business. I'm writing (or procrastinating, whatever you want to call it) full time and I'm in America, in the mountains and solo hiking in the snow. I try to focus on the view and on the nothingness and for a moment I catch it again – and it's sheer joy.

I glance at my watch and see that it's getting late in the day. I've got to keep going. Not just along this trail, but always. If I want to be happy, I need to find a way to express my true self and screw the consequences. Before I start hiking again in earnest, I look over the Continental Divide stretched out as far as I can see, taking in the trees far below and the mountain peaks yearning towards the sky way above me. Soon, I tell myself. Soon I will have peace, but for now, this is my moment.

CHAPTER NINETEEN

Every moment of light and dark is a miracle. – Walt Whitman

I'VE DECIDED THAT I'M just not going to think about the last ten years. No, make it the last thirty years. I'm going to pretend they didn't happen and bloody well enjoy my time in Colorado while it lasts. This is what I've been telling myself all week, until I realised with a thrill of horror that that's exactly what my mother has been doing all her life. The truth is I can't simply block it all out.

I'm hiking again. This time I'm doing the Snow Mountain Shore and the Ranger Meadow Loop trail – and it's below freezing. I woke up late this morning, but if I keep up a good pace, I'll still be home an hour before sunset. I forgot my gloves and my frozen fingers are stuffed inside my pockets, feeling like they might snap off. There's none of the harsh brilliance of a sunny snow day. It's moody out, with clouds billowing on a distant peak, but luckily most of the trail winds through the woods along the side of the lake. Icy wind shakes the trees and I tramp along, getting lost in the meditative crunching of my snowshoes. Occasionally I stop and drink and look around to make sure I'm on the right path. The trail starts taking me higher and it's steeper than I expected. When I stop and take another drink of water, I realise that I'm running low. At least I'll soon reach the trail's highest point and then start my descent, loop around Ranger Meadow and head back to my car. My snowshoes keep sinking and getting caught up in hidden branches. There shouldn't be branches on the trail. I stop to eat the snack bar I brought along with me and push on, waiting to see a trail marker that will tell me how much further I've got to go.

I can no longer see the lake through the trees. At last I break through into a clearing, my heart hammering in my chest, and look around me. I see Ranger Meadow – or something that looks like a meadow, but it isn't in the right place. I battle to shake open my map with stiff fingers and blink at it, wishing my body would stop shivering so I can focus. Fear billows inside me as I study the map and realise that I've wandered off the trail. I study the landscape but all I can see is the storm coming in. If the meadow below me is Ranger Meadow, all I need to do is walk to the far corner of it and my car will be there somewhere. I take a small sip of water and hear the remaining inch slosh at the bottom of the bottle.

I plough down the mountain side and stumble. I get up and stumble again, checking my phone every few minutes to see if I can get signal to call for help, but there's none. There's a weird drumming in my ears and every sound makes me jump. At last I give up on calling and simply try not to get caught up in the branches hiding below the snow, but I can't see anything. Everything is white and starting to blur. I take off my goggles to see more clearly. Stupid. I'm blinded and the objects near to me start warping. I put them back on with hands that barely function and trudge on, slower and slower.

My vision is coming in flashes. The wind is howling. I'm in the meadow, I think, or I'm going uphill, or down – I don't know. I must keep moving. It's getting harder and harder. It's impossible.

I see a woman, once myself, fold slowly. Her knees hit the ground, her body slumps sideways. Snowflakes land one by one on her exposed hands and face. I see her blinking hard. She wants to get up and keep going but she can't. Her trail is covered by heavily falling snow and there's no going back. She doesn't know where she is. Her eyes close. Hours pass.

I don't want to die.

I want to live.

This time around, I'm going to live.

I wake with a start and everything is darker. It's past sunset. I'm shivering so hard I think someone has been shaking me. I've passed out and if I don't move, I'll freeze to death. There is ice in my veins as I drag myself to my feet and stumble onwards, not knowing where I'm going, but compelled to keep on living. I have spent decades existing in a half-life and it has to stop. I won't die, not without living first. Strength from nowhere comes surging into me and I strike out against the snow. I'm coming home to myself.

The deep snow drags at my ankles and I'm pulled back into the chilly bosom of despair. It's comforting and familiar. It would be so easy to slip back into that life, to call Michael and tell him I'll come home and that we'll wade on through our marriage until the end. But I refuse. If we are meant to be together, we need to change how we treat each other, but we can't do it while living together. I'm going to get through this storm. I'm going to find my car, drive home and change everything.

I limp on in the dark and the snow tries to confuse me and to lead me in circles, but I concentrate as hard as I can on getting through the woods. As I warm up, the clouds that fill my mind are driven away. At last the woods expel me onto a pathway next to a lake. I must keep the lake on my right and keep walking. Through the haze of the snowstorm, love for my life sparks a light inside me. I've thought for many years that there's much more out there than the Christian God I grew up with and, as I walk, that powerful light surrounds me once again. It's the same light that drew me back to my father's arms when I was two and almost drowned in our swimming pool. It's the light that comforted me when I was 15 and thought I would die in hospital when I was being treated for my back pain. The presence that is with me now is the one that stood between my father and me as he held the gun to my head when I was 16. It also saved me when I tried to kill myself that same year. It is the warmth that cradled my body when I was bleeding to death in a hotel room after the abortion. It is the power that rose inside of me when I saved Dean and Marco from the car accident when I was 19. This same light held my bleeding head on a ski slope when I was 42 and waiting for the helicopter to arrive to help me.

It is with me now. I'm blinded by the knowledge that I will make it out of this storm and through the storms that are to come. I've refused death's offer again and now there is nothing for it but to do whatever I need to do to get back to the life I was meant to live. That includes staring hard at what repels me more than anything: myself.

I find my car at nine that night and I've never been so overjoyed to see anything as I was to see that rental car. When at last I get back to my cabin, I'm on a high of relief and grateful for everything I see. I lie in a hot bath for two hours until I finally stop shivering and can pull on my pyjamas and sit by the fire.

The flames hypnotise me. I've been in denial about what I want, but coming through that storm has made it clear. Suddenly I don't want to wait for my life to start. A few days ago, I thought death would be easier than the pain and humiliation of going through a divorce, but I was wrong. I have to break everything apart and tear myself to pieces if I am to save myself from the person I have become. I don't want to hurt the one person I truly love. But I do. Why can I protect Michael from the world, but not from my own temper? I will have to leave Michael, for good. Not another separation, not another threat, but a divorce this time. It must be final. No matter how much I love him and no matter the terror I feel at the idea of being without him, it isn't enough to still the infinite ache inside of me. I want to rip the Band Aid off. I need to speak to Michael as soon as possible and tell him, firmly and calmly, that I am serious about getting a divorce.

His voice crackles on the other end of the line. There's the painful small talk. I tell him about the weather, about driving on the wrong side of the road. I don't tell him about surviving the storm. Then my courage comes back to me.

'I'm not coming back to South Africa. I'm not coming back to our marriage.'

I tell him I've realised how each time I attacked him it was tied up with my past. I tell him none of it is his fault, but he doesn't hear me.

'I'm staying in America until I figure myself out. I hate this person I've become. Screaming at you, always feeling angry. We can't go on this way -'

I didn't think it would be easy but this – this is torture.

'You can move there now while I sell the business and then I can join you,' he says. 'Take your time. I'll support you. You know I will.'

'I love you, Michael. I love you more than I ever thought one person could love someone else. But I need to be away from you because I don't know how to be myself without feeling like I'm responsible for you in every single way.'

'I know the court case and running the business has been hardest on you, Jacqui, but please –'

'It's not just that. It's everything. I need to figure out who I am and to stop defining myself in relation to you, to anyone.'

'Jacqui, what are you saying?'

My voice is thick with tears.

'Michael this time I am serious. I want a divorce.'

CHAPTER TWENTY

Insanity: doing the same thing over and over again and
expecting different results. – Albert Einstein

AMANDA TELLS ME THE ONLY way to get past this is by going to Vegas, baby. I don't have the strength to tell her that all I want to do is lie on the rug in front of the fire and cry. I want to indulge myself. I want to scream and cry with unbridled misery until the woods are filled with it, because I haven't done enough crying in my life. Michael and I are getting divorced. It's what I now believe is right as we can't seem to fix ourselves in the marriage. Even though it's agony, I need to put on a brave face.

It doesn't go well. Amanda organises the trip of a lifetime, complete with burlesque and Cirque du Soleil shows, five-star hotels, limo rides, breakfasts in bed and a helicopter ride to the Grand Canyon, while ensuring I have a dress and high heels for the trip. But it's all futile.

'Jacqui, you're determined to be miserable,' she says, but she's teasing... I think!

Mostly. It's just hard knowing that Michael and I won't be married anymore. People say marriage is forever, but really, it's just about how long you can keep it up. Divorce – now that's forever. At least I'm getting my sense of humour back, if only in small flashes. At the Grand Canyon a couple gets engaged and they might as well have stabbed me in the heart, right there and then. A part of me wants to shout, 'Enjoy it while you can, you naïve lunatics, before you know it your life will be in shreds!' I restrain myself and settle for a smile and a quiet 'Congratulations.'

On our last night in Vegas, Amanda loses her temper with me.

'I think I'm going mad,' I say, tears gushing out of me. 'I can't take this. It hurts so badly.'

Perhaps it's because I tried never to cry throughout my childhood, but I now seem to have an infinite supply of tears. The sight of a man with brown hair like Michael's sends me almost into hysterics.

'Jacqui, for God's sake, pull yourself together! I don't know you like this.'

'Of course you don't,' I wail. 'I don't know myself like this. That's the whole problem.'

I want to go into all the gritty details and tell her how my whole life has been an endless one-foot-in-front-of-the-other-and-for-god's-sake-don't-let-your-true-emotions-show nightmare, but she has already heard it a thousand times and it will only send me into further fits of crying. I feel completely ridiculous.

Amanda reminds me that I am a go-getter, a doer, a mover and a shaker and that whining isn't going to help me.

My grief is so acute it's almost comical. Why can't I just bloody well cry and enjoy it instead of judging my every tear and grimace? I knew that changing my life would be humiliating, but had I really known the full extent of it, maybe I would never have made that phone call.

'I've become a horrible person. I know it sounds dramatic, but you don't even know the half of it. I scream at Michael when I am mad at him and God, the things I say to him. And that thing with Trevor.'

I don't even want to think about what I did with Trevor, let alone say it in words.

'Jacqui, stop it. You're a good person and what you did with

Trevor was just dumb, not evil. Stop dwelling on it.'

She glares at me from across our swanky hotel room, her arms folded across her chest.

'You're wallowing. You've asked Michael for a divorce because you believe it's right for both of you. You should pat yourself on the back, because it was a hard thing you did.'

Amanda is right, I suppose. Instead of commiserating with people who announce their plans to divorce, why don't we congratulate them on taking a difficult step or at least wish them luck?

'I know,' I say. 'I've got to get a handle on this. We're in Vegas, after all.'

'Exactly, we're in Vegas. I get that you're angry at yourself, your life, your choices, but just get the fuck on with your life, okay?'

Amanda's tough love is having a sobering effect on me. She reminds me of my grandmother when she is like this, except that Granny didn't swear. She leaves and the door bangs closed behind her. I jump, thinking of my father. Then I wipe my tears, put on the pink dress she took out of her wardrobe for me and follow her down to the hotel bar in a pair of her high heels that are a size too small.

———◆———

When I get back to the cabin in Columbine Lake, I write a long and enthusiastic email to 37 very close, personal friends and tell them how fantastic everything is. My life is fantastic. Vegas is fantastic. Hiking is fantastic. Can they tell that I've used too many positive adjectives? Is anyone reading this in Cape Town thinking, 'Oh please, Jacqui, I see right through this. Stop the act and get back to your actual writing.' I know Michael must be.

Time passes slowly in the mountains and I hike every day. At night, I lie under the covers with tissues, my favourite chocolate and my manuscript next to me on the bed. I'm a little lonely in the cabin and I've started talking to myself in my head. I wonder what it would be like to go out... but that would require telling people that I'm getting divorced. Everyone in Columbine Lake and the adjoining village, Grand Lake, thinks I'm happily married and on a writing retreat and I don't plan on telling them different. If no one knows that your life is falling apart, is it really falling apart? I cling to the last moments of being married.

Soon it will all be out in the open. *Twice divorced.* People will whisper the words to one another with wide eyes, raised eyebrows and pursed lips over canapés. And my poor family! My first divorce was hard enough. My father had nearly given himself an aneurism when I moved in with Michael after Greg and I got divorced. I was thirty years old and Michael asked me to move to Johannesburg so that we could be together. It would be a fresh start for us, away from my father. The sad fact of the matter is that I loved him and still wanted his approval. The day before the big move, my parents hosted a family farewell lunch at their house for me. Alison, with whom I had reconciled yet again, was also there. It should've been bitter-sweet, but my father had a dark cloud over his head. His misery pulsed through the lunch party until I could practically see the potato salad sticking in Alison's throat. He was cursing under his breath and glaring at anyone who dared to make eye contact with him. My mother went to fetch the dessert.

'I can't wait to explore the big city,' I said, in a feeble attempt to make light conversation.

He shook his head at me in disgust. No one spoke.

'Who wants dessert?' my mother said brightly.

'Don't want,' he snapped. 'Going to watch TV.'

He shoved his chair backwards.

'Dad, don't you want to stay for dessert? It's your favourite and I'm leaving tomorrow.'

He exploded in front of everyone. It was always the same, but this time there were added threats about hell and me not being a child of God anymore.

'Dad, please don't speak to me like that.'

'You're a divorcee, no better than a whore, I don't want you in my home, and I never want to hear a word about that loser of a man that you call your boyfriend. What self-respecting man would date a divorcee? I have only one son-in-law and that's Greg!'

We fought; he left. There was a stunned silence, broken by the sound of my father's car starting and driving away. The next day I called him from Alison's house before she drove me to the airport. I tried to talk to him and apologise for screaming back at him the day before. He screamed all his old favourites as I sobbed and begged him to stop. At last, with a final roar of 'Go to hell, you fucking bitch,' he hung up the phone. Alison witnessed it all and hugged me.

'Jacs, I've watched his abuse since we were teenagers. You are keeping yourself stuck in this abusive relationship. You've got a choice. You can stop this.'

'I've tried everything. Nothing works. I've tried talking, I've tried walking away, I've even written him letters. I feel sorry for my mom and want a relationship with my dad, but he just says either I must become a different person or I can go to hell. And a week after each fight or lie I catch him out on, I get a letter from him telling me he's confessed to Jesus Christ and that I must submit to Him as my Lord and Saviour and ask for forgiveness or he'll have nothing to do with me. It's like he's got this massive list of conditions that I have to fulfil for him to love me. Why can't he just love me as I am?'

'If you get one more letter about how Jesus has saved him, I might have a stroke,' said Alison and we both started to laugh. 'Seriously though, Jacqui, it's a choice and only you can make the change for yourself,' she repeated.

'I don't get it.'

'Jacqui, it is as if you keep trying to save your dad. You can't change him, but you can look after yourself. You can stop this if you're no longer present to receive it.'

It was some of the best advice I've ever received. Yet despite not seeing my father in over a decade, he was still everywhere – in my heart, in my thoughts, in my manuscript. I pick it up from the bed and page through it. His shouts, his pointing finger is on every page. Here and there are the moments where his warm, spontaneous side shone through. I don't want to see him again, but I miss those blue eyes, that smile. I miss how it felt when I was a little girl and I had my awesome Dad to turn to. I'd like to send him a message and tell him I love him despite it all, but he wouldn't understand. Every letter I wrote would just start another fight. I couldn't even get that right.

It hurts to read it all. It hurts to read between the lines and feel the old hot shame from my past rise from the pages.

I must have fallen asleep reading, because when I wake it's almost dawn. I unroll my yoga mat in my bedroom and begin with mountain pose, my hands at my heart. I breathe deeply. Yoga has always helped me to relax and to stay with my feelings instead of avoiding them, something at which I've become an expert like my mother. I avoided my feelings for years by keeping busy, first with my MBA and then with building a life and a career. But avoiding my feelings backfired – I was so busy it nearly killed me.

At 33 I was diagnosed with chronic fatigue syndrome and the Epstein Barr virus. Oh please, chronic fatigue, that's not a real illness, I told myself, and I ignored it despite suffering chronic pain, diagnosed as fibromyalgia. It got worse and worse, until my doctor told me I'd be dead in six months. I didn't listen and my doctor fired me.

I realised it was serious when I woke up one day lying on the floor of a toilet cubicle at work. I'd snuck in there thinking that all I needed was a ten-minute power nap before I got back to work and instead I'd passed out and woke up three hours later. I went straight to my boss to tell him I needed to go to and visit Michael, who was in New York on a week's break from his studies at Duke University in North Carolina. I needed to tell Michael what had happened and ask him to come home to help me. Michael didn't even hesitate. He stopped his studies in America, came home, booked a doctor's appointment under his name and convinced my doctor to take me back.

Despite the doctor's grim prediction, I didn't die. I took her advice and was on the road to recovery when Michael and I moved to Cape Town for a quieter lifestyle. We planned to start a family when my health improved and I was on the brink of taking a job at a non-profit when Michael bought a business, the business that broke him, me and us. I eventually collapsed again at 42. Years of pain had been locked away and one day in my office the lock broke. The chronic fatigue had gotten worse with the addition of the court case. I was about to step into a board meeting but instead I slid from my office chair and cowered under my desk, sobbing. As managing director I was meant to announce a year of outstanding results, but instead I was paralysed. The only part of my life that was not in ruins was my bank account. I was richer than ever; I was poorer than ever. On advice from my therapist, I went home and forced myself to do the unthinkable. I studied my face in the mirror and what I saw shocked me. The pain in every line of my face was clear. How had no one stopped to ask if I was okay? But it was there, that hard line around the mouth, the confident glint in the blue eyes – I hid it well. I looked strong and capable. I acted as if I was tough, but buried inside of me was just a scared child. Within weeks I dragged Michael to a meeting with my two business mentors and they begged him to notice the decline in my health and well-being. I then informed the board that I needed to leave the business. I had turned the business into a success and they no longer needed me. Despite Michael's mother's protest at my decision, saying that Michael would destroy the business without me at his side, I left. I vowed to strip myself of all of the meaningless bravado with which I filled my life and to start studying and writing again. Instead I committed to the court case full time and eventually started consulting again as the business had started to struggle under Michael's management.

Just thinking of that time makes my breathing shallow and quick. I focus on my mantra. I breathe slowly. Yoga, Jacqui. Yoga!

But seriously, how the fuck did that happen? Sure, I had to step in because Michael's health fell apart. Why did no one worry about my health? And then both of my grandmothers died in the same year. In thinking of it all I'm practically hyperventilating, rushing my way through the poses. Isn't yoga supposed to calm me down?

It's no wonder I'm sick with chronic fatigue again. I haven't exactly changed much since the day I flew to New York a decade earlier to tell Michael I needed him. If anything, I pushed myself harder and became addicted to saving him.

Focus now, I tell myself. Stop thinking about all of that and just be.

I flow slowly through the poses into a back bend that opens my chest up and relieves my anxiety. I then settle into Supta Baddha Konasana, lying flat on my back, arms loose by my side, knees open and the soles of my feet drawn up and pressed together. Yoga tells me to be still in the moment yet not ignore my deeper issues, but it's hard for me to listen. Perhaps yoga was invented for people less messed up than me, I think, and then snort with laughter.

At last I manage to still my mind. I get up and wash my face and as I unzip my toiletry bag to get my face lotion, I notice them.

Seven boxes of sleeping pills.

I've been slowly accumulating them, apparently without thinking about it. Telling my doctor I wasn't sleeping well was true. Telling my doctor I would be flying to America was true. I can't remember all of the reasons why I needed those pills. All I know is that half of them weren't true and that it looks like I've been meticulously planning to kill the screaming bitch in me. Is that why I came here? To kill myself? I know the answer. I know my shadow and what it wants, what it has wanted since I was 16.

I keep my eyes on the pills, avoiding the mirror as ever. Slowly I start flushing them down the toilet. They bob in the water, refusing to disappear. At last they are all gone and I'm sitting on the bathroom floor, staring at my feet. My toenails are chipped cherry red. I painted them for the first time ever before going to Vegas and seeing them like that sends a tickle of excitement down my spine. It's slow, and it hurts, but I'm changing. And it's also really scary.

I'm scared of the shame of being a two-time divorcee. Now that I'm writing full time, I'm scared of the guilt that comes from forcing the scores of other people who depend on me – factory workers, my charitable endeavours, family members, friends, my pets – to cope alone, without help. And I'm scared my writing is bad and that I'll never get the book finished.

The thought of the book snaps me out of my reverie. I get up from the bathroom floor and gather the manuscript and notes off my bed. I lay them neatly on the kitchen table. It is a pile of hundreds of sentences that all boil down to the same essentials: Why me? If only I'd had a different father? I wish Deloitte had not made the calculation errors? This book is an angry tell-all that wants to see the perpetrators burn in the face of public shame. This is not the book I want to write.

I decide to take a walk to clear my head.

'That's not me,' I say out loud. 'And now I'm speaking to myself. Fabulous. Man, I need to get out and see people!'

As I walk along a lane heavy with snow, I wonder: 'If this is not me, then *who am I?*'

The sun is rising and there is a slow play of golden light on the snow. Snowflakes fall and balance on the strands of my hair and on my shoulders. I wonder how I will silence my secret shames? How will I silence my internal doubt? How am I going to change?

A great hush hangs from the trees as if they are waiting for the answers.

CHAPTER TWENTY-ONE

The meeting of two personalities is like the contact of two chemical substances: if there is any reaction, both are transformed. – Carl Jung

AMANDA KEEPS TELLING ME TO let loose and have some fun instead of lying around the cabin sobbing my eyes out, but I can't imagine anyone wanting to party with me. Nevertheless, I dutifully go to a small bar in Grand Lake once a week, order a meal and a club soda and get to know the locals.

I've just returned from dinner with a new friend Sean and his son, who is visiting for the night. I left them at the restaurant after making Sean promise to spend quality time with his son instead of drinking the night away at the local bar. Sean drinks too much and, like me, he's going through a divorce. As I struggle to unlock the door to the cabin, I see Sean's SUV drive past. His son is driving and Sean is nowhere in sight. Motherfucker! I bet he's sent his son home while he gets wasted at The Sage Brush again. Not my problem. I'm not going to get involved. I keep telling myself this, until I find myself driving back to Grand Lake to find Sean.

The bar is packed with a group of guys that I assume are from out of town when I arrive. As I push through them to get to where

Sean is sitting, they try to strike up a conversation with me – the usual 'What's your name? Where are you from?' I see Sean at the bar, laughing madly over what looks like a double vodka. At last I reach him and tell him to finish his drink so that I can take him home. He laughs me off, but I'm not giving up. I settle his check and tell him I'll wait in the car. I push back through the group of men.

'Hey, are you really from South Africa?' one of them calls.

'What are you doing here in the middle of nowhere?' another asks.

'We are visiting from the Midwest, come join us for a drink,' another suggests.

The last thing in the world I want is a drink with a bunch of rowdy men. As I struggle to get to the door again, I catch the eye of one of the men. He's smiling to himself and slowly stirring his drink.

'Leaving already?'

'Just trying to pick up my friend there and take him home.'

He laughs and shakes his head, as if to say it's a lost cause. There's a niceness about him, but I don't want to stop and chat. I smile and go and wait in the car. Five minutes pass. Ten. After twenty minutes I decide to go back and fetch Sean. The man raises his eyebrows when he sees me enter again. You again, he seems to say.

'Are you really just here to take your friend home?'

'Yes, I really am,' I say ruefully, already feeling like an idiot for trying to act the saviour.

'That's really nice of you. Sorry if my friends are harassing you.'

'That's okay, they seem like they are having fun,' I say, and make my way back over to Sean. 'Sean, come on! It's not cool that you're making me wait outside for you while you finish your drink.'

'But Jacqui,' he whines, 'This here is a new drink.'

'Five minutes, Sean. I mean it.'

Ray, a local, tells me not to worry: he'll bring Sean out in five.

I thank him and promise to come back and buy him a drink if he does.

I leave again and on the way out the same man stops me.

'Seriously, is that man *really* only your friend and not your boyfriend?'

'Honestly, I don't know him that well, but what I do know is that he loves his son and they're supposed to have breakfast together before he leaves. For some reason I've made it my job to make sure that breakfast happens.' I don't tell him that unless someone drags Sean out of here, he'll only leave at closing time and then be passed out until tomorrow afternoon.

There's a small pause and the man smiles again. He looks right into my eyes and that look seems familiar.

'Hi, my name is Dan. You seem very kind. Why don't you join me for a drink once you've dropped your friend off?'

Amanda's instructions to have a little fun hang over me, but I stick to my guns. I just don't do drinks in bars with strangers. I barely drink, period, so I thank him and decline his invitation.

At last Ray brings Sean out to the car. I drop him off at his place and then drive myself home. There are no lights on inside the cabin and I don't feel like going in.

'Go out, have fun, let loose!' Amanda seems to whisper in my ear. They seemed like a wild bunch, but that guy Dan seemed sincere in his offer. Plus, I could buy Ray that drink I promised him.

The moment I step back into the bar I regret it. I could be curled up on the couch drinking hot chocolate and reading a book and yet here I am in a noisy bar. I sit down on the only empty bar stool, which just so happens to be between Dan and Ray. I buy Ray his promised drink and I buy myself a club soda. Ray thanks me and we try and fail to make small talk for a while. It's unbearably awkward.

I feel Dan's eyes on me, but don't look up. I watch the bartender and count the bottles lined up behind the bar. After a moment, I glance at him. We acknowledge the awkwardness and then slide into ease.

'Hi again,' he says. 'So tell me, what do you do for a living?'

I don't want to tell him my sob story or hear about his whole life. I want to remain anonymous amongst a group of strangers. I lean back, take a deep breath and stick out my hand.

'I guess I didn't introduce myself earlier. Hi, my name is Jacqui and if you don't mind keeping it to yourself, I'm actually a hired assassin.'

He starts to shake with laughter, but I keep a straight face.

'How strange,' he says. 'So am I.'

'But what are you doing in the mountains?'

'I guess I could ask you the same question.'

'I asked you first.'

'Well, I'm here to do one hit for the weekend. A quick job, in and out. You?'

'I'm here for three months of solo training in isolation. I need to train in extreme conditions for a big hit.'

'Of course, that's assuming that you'll make it through this weekend.'

There's electricity in the air. We can't take our eyes off one another.

'Are you threatening me?'

'Well, you don't know who my hit is, do you?'

'Good luck, then. You wouldn't be the first to try and just know: none of the others made it out of this town alive.'

We're bantering, but I want to stop and say that I feel like I've known him forever. The noise disappears and I'm with him and he is staring straight into my soul.

Dan is from Detroit and can't believe I am from South Africa. He wants to know what I am doing such a long way from home. I tell him that I love the mountains, the snow and hiking and that I've recently committed to life as a writer. I share that I have come here to feel inspired, but that it's all sort of unfolding differently to what I expected.

I don't say that my whole life has unravelled and I'm trying to slowly strip myself of my obsessions and change my life, but I feel like if I did he wouldn't bat an eyelash.

'So, you're just out here, hiking on your own? Just like that?'

'I like to hike above the tree line and chase the silence. It's the biggest rush I've ever felt. I love it.'

'You're an adrenaline junkie?'

'I sure am. And you?'

'Me too,' he says, smiling again.

'I love speed – racing cars, parachute jumping, you name it – and I'm addicted to adrenaline, but I think my biggest rush is solo hiking above the tree line in the snow. It's incredible; it's intoxicating. You can hear everything that you're meant to hear, including yourself, and something out there speaks to you. If I didn't know better, I would say it is God. The silence is so pure, so deafening. Sometimes you might only find it for a second or two, in the middle of winter without a breath of wind. But even that is enough of a fix for me. It's unreal.'

I'm rambling.

'Fascinating,' he says. 'And a bit weird.'

'But I love weird. We're all completely weird and we've got to celebrate that. Who wants to be normal anyway? It's just a mask that hides the magic in each of us. So anyway, tell me one thing about you.'

'Hmm. One thing. Okay, I'm actually a ditch digger.'

This time it's my turn to burst out laughing. I don't know what's so funny about it – he's probably a builder or a blue-collar worker of some sort – but something about Dan cracks me up.

We talk about everything and when he tells me about his daughter, Kelly, his face lights up. The hours pass without noticing until we realise that the bar has gone quiet; his friends have gone down to play pool and dance at a place called Grumpies and I offer to give him a lift there before I go home.

'Join me for one drink at Grumpies?' he says, as he climbs into my car.

'Just one,' I say.

It's freezing in my car as we drive to the next bar and he has his hands between his legs to warm them up. Before I can get out, he stops me with a hand on my arm.

'Can I ask you something?'

I shut the car door again to keep the warmth inside.

'Can I kiss you?'

'What?'

I'm a teenage girl again and my heart is racing, my palms sweating. When have I ever been asked for permission? I can't take my eyes off his mouth, but I'm nervous.

'Can I kiss you?' he says again.

Our lips meet and it tastes like life and knowledge and it leaves me speechless. There is nothing like a man who knows how to kiss, but this was something else. This is a kiss I've had before. The bite of vodka is still on his tongue and shivers run through my core as he kisses me, hard and gentle at the same time. We stare at one another in the darkness of the car, his lips slightly parted still, the shock of the intensity of my feelings painted on his face.

'Thank you,' he says, and I understand.

The moment we step into Grumpies a solid wall of sex and country music hits me. Although it's out of season, the bar is filled with a crowd of bodies rubbing against one another, twisting and dancing, pawing and kissing and drinking and shooting pool. His friends wear wedding rings, but their bodies grind up against the local girls, who are rumoured to be desperate to catch a nice city boy and 'get outta here'. I'm chillingly sober compared to this crowd and Dan buys me a drink. I realise he's had a few too many when he leans in towards me. His breath tickles my ear.

'So, now that I've had a kiss, do you think you would come back to my hotel?'

'Are you insane?' I laugh out loud.

'Come on, that kiss was amazing: why not?'

'Dan, it's been so great spending time with you, but it's not gonna happen.'

'Well, can I kiss you again?'

'That sounds great, but do you see this ring?' I say, holding up my left hand to show my wedding ring. 'The reason I wear this is because I don't want anyone hitting on me. I don't want any complications, I don't want any drama and I want everyone in this town to continue thinking I'm happily married, even though I told you I am getting divorced. So the answer to your question is no.'

But the flirting continues and the air is clouded with blatant desire.

'So, I've been thinking,' Dan says later. 'I want to make a proposition. I promise to give you the night of your life.'

He can't continue because we're both laughing too hard. It's ridiculous and deadly serious at the same time. I'm almost in tears laughing over my drink. God, it feels good to laugh. I feel it right through to my toes and fingertips. He hiccups back into seriousness.

'No, listen. I promise to give you three orgasms before I even have one.'

'Not gonna happen. Sorry!'

'Come on, you like me, I like you, the kiss was great – better than great – so let's do it.'

'Are you married? I see that your friends are wearing wedding bands.'

He lifts his left hand to my face and wiggles a bare ring finger at me.

'That means nothing. Dan, are you married?'

'No, I'm not married.'

'Are you divorced?'

'Yes, I am.'

'Do you have a girlfriend?'

'No.'

'Fine. You need to understand that I'm *not* going home with a married man. That's where I draw the line.'

'Well, we are good to go on that score then, sweetheart.'

'Now, this may sound very bizarre to you, but my friend has been telling me for a long time that I should have a one-night stand

and that I should go to a bar, meet a man, not ask his name and just shag his brains out. So, this might just be your lucky night, excepting, mmm, it can't be you because I know your name.'

What am I doing? Who has taken over my body and is saying these things? Hell, this is even more crazy than the way something took control and got me out of that snowstorm. This is downright nuts. It must be the third drink I'm having. Dan's grinning stupidly again: he cannot believe his luck, so he continues to flirt with me for another hour as we sit at the bar sharing stories and cracking each other up, until I can no longer resist him.

'Dan, I'm game for this, but these are the rules. I'm not coming to your hotel. You can come back to my cabin with me and when it's over, it's done. No more than that. I don't want any complications.'

'Are you telling me not to fall for you?'

'Exactly.'

'It's a tall order, sweetheart, but I think we'll be just fine.'

We drive back to the cabin and as soon as I turn the bright kitchen lights on, I realise I'm dealing with a very drunk man. I think I should sober him up and so I pour him an organic cranberry juice – an acquired taste, but it's all I've got.

'This is disgusting. Don't you have any vodka?'

I tell him I don't but he's already forgotten all about the vodka. He's pulling me towards him, pressing me against him and kissing me hard and I'm leaning into him and kissing him back. Panic strikes me. What the fuck am I doing? What about Michael? What happens in America stays in America, he said – well, screw that, this just doesn't feel right. Michael and I are getting divorced, so that's not the problem. The problem is that I don't even know this guy. For all I know, he could be an axe murderer or –

'Who the hell are you?'

'I – what?'

'I don't even know who you are. Show me your driver's licence!'

He shows me his licence and I choke with laughter at his

surname. Biscotti.

'What's so funny?'

'Biscotti! Your surname is Biscotti!'

'Yeah, so?'

But Dan isn't listening to me describe the different kinds of biscotti I love – almond, chocolate, orange and hazelnut – because he's running his hands over me, down my back, over my hips and arms and then kissing me desperately and I can't help but fall into him.

My clothes are on the floor and he pulls me to the bedroom in my bra and panties and we collapse onto the bed kissing. And then his head goes limp on my chest. He laughs softly again.

'Dan?'

'Sorry,' he says, bleary-drunk.

We can't stop laughing. My stomach muscles are starting to hurt from laughing.

'I can do this,' he says, but no matter how we try, he can't get hard.

'Oh God,' he groans, half-laughing, half-mortified. 'I'm sorry about this.'

'We had such big intentions to live out our fantasy of the grand one-night stand.'

We both laugh again and then he looks up at me. 'This is still pretty amazing,' he says. 'Just being here with you.'

'Let's not even bother about all that,' I say, and I realise I'm whispering.

He rests his head on my chest again. It's heavy and warm. I stroke his hair and the smooth milky skin of his back and he shudders. He is mine in this moment. I stop my hands from caressing his skin.

'Don't stop. Please don't stop.'

I keep stroking him and I can feel a searing pain that runs straight through the knots of muscles and nerves all the way through to his spirit. What has happened to this man? What has life done to him and what has he done to himself?

'You don't have anyone to do this for you, do you?'

'No,' he says, and turns his head to look into my eyes. 'No one touches me. No one looks me in the eye the way you do. No one talks to me the way you do. I don't have anyone in the world who can just be with me.'

We are transfixed by one another and the years peel off me slowly. I'm just a girl with a crazy, mad crush.

'Can I stay a little longer?' Dan mumbles, half asleep.

At four in the morning I wake him up and drive him back to his hotel.

'I want to see you again. Jacqui, you're incredible and I have to see you again. I want to start over.'

We exchange phone numbers and then he kisses me. Fuck, when did simple kissing get this good?

———◆———

I wake up to a message from Dan. He says he is out snowmobiling all day and asks if I will have dinner with him and his friends that night. I decline but agree to meet him for a drink afterwards, but I have a condition: he is to stay sober. He agrees, but has a condition of his own: that we fulfil our fantasy. We meet up after dinner and decide to go straight to his hotel. Like a seasoned lover, he gently takes my hand as we walk through the carpeted corridors to his room. He unlocks the door and I step inside.

'So, do you still want to have a one-night stand with a stranger whose name you don't know?'

'Absolutely.'

'I've gotta tell you, I'm living out my wildest fantasy here. You're a stranger from another country with an accent and you're driving me crazy.'

Dan leads me to the bed and starts undressing me, slowly and deliberately. I don't feel the cold even though I'm in nothing but my white underwear. He strokes the lace edging of my panties and then runs a finger over my stomach. I start to shake as he undresses. His eyes are wide and blazing as we start to kiss again and then he pulls away, strokes my hair and runs a fingertip down my cheek.

'Look,' he says holding up a hand. 'You're making me shake.'

Kissing, just kissing, in our underwear makes me feel like I'm having the teenager experience 30 years late. He doesn't get hard and this time he doesn't laugh about it.

'I'm so sorry. Jeez, this is so embarrassing: it might be from the altitude medication or something, I don't know.'

'What's there to be embarrassed about? This desire, this tenderness, is enough.'

We spend the night caressing each other and talking. We are catching one another up on everything we've missed in the long, long time that we've been separated, only to pass out mid-sentence sometime after 4am.

I wake up in his arms the next morning and blink sleep from my eyes. We whisper our hellos to one another, not wanting to break the softness.

I roll over, sit on top of him and stroke his hair from his face. My hair is falling loose around mine. It is as if we are in a secret hideaway.

'This is the most beautiful experience of my life,' I say – or does he say that?

It doesn't matter; we both feel it. We talk about how our lives have led us here and about our relationships. I tell him about Michael and how much I love him, but that I need to leave to save both of us. It is strange – to tell the man between your legs about how deeply you love your husband – but Dan understands. He loves his ex-wife, still.

'Sometimes, no matter how deeply you love someone, the relationship just isn't one that allows you to be yourself.'

I suddenly feel a stirring under me.

'What's this all about?'

'I honestly have no idea.'

He's pressing against me now. We are making love and it is staggering. He is touching me everywhere with his lips, his palms, his fingertips, his tongue and I can hardly see the room around me. He is quivering and I hold onto him, nails digging into his back, not wanting to lose him, this, everything. It is gentle and raw. My hands are in his soft hair and at last I feel myself shaking, hear us both. We are being torn apart and lovingly put back together. It is almost too much, but still not enough. It will never be enough and he knows this and does not stop, even though I'm shuddering. I lose control of my senses, back arched. Again. And again. And again, until we are spent and collapse into one another, trembling. I've never felt this free. We lie side by side in a haze, looking into one another's eyes. There is nothing asked and nothing expected.

'You've completely changed my world,' he says.

I do nothing, I think nothing. We exist in the moment, twin souls reuniting, melting into each other.

'I needed that too, Dan. I needed something so honest, naïve, simple.'

We lie there, stunned, until it's time to leave. It's his last day and I will never see him again. He insists I keep his T-shirt, because he doesn't want me to forget him. In the parking lot we stand and kiss beside my car.

'I don't even know what to say. Please don't forget me,' he says.

'There's nothing to say. I won't forget you. It was perfect the way it was.'

And we are kissing for the last time, hearts breaking, souls racing, kissing like it is the last time we will ever kiss anyone on this planet. In a way, it is.

CHAPTER TWENTY-TWO

You will not be punished for your anger, you will be
punished by your anger. – Buddha

DAN LEAVES TOWN AND A part of me is relieved. But then within hours he messages me and invites me to see him again for a weekend in Branson, Missouri. Just one weekend, he says. I don't want to go. I want to focus on my book. I pour myself a whiskey in the cabin and sip on it while I read from my manuscript. Amanda says it's okay to drink alone sometimes, but it tastes like ethanol. I force the tiny sips down. I'm reading the chapter where my father, who never even acknowledged that I was studying for an MBA, demands that he be invited to the graduation and I lose it with him, telling him he is not welcome. Boring! I toss the manuscript aside and wonder if anyone really wants to read a book called, *If Only I'd Had Bruises.*

After years of therapy, I now know that I was not to blame for the words my father chose to let fall out of his mouth. Nevertheless, a more powerful and violent inner voice tells me differently. You could have stopped it before it happened, it says; you could have saved everyone from his abuse, but you kept quiet. You were so obsessed by the fact that you were his number one, the bearer of his secret, that you didn't come clean. You let it fester until it got so unbearable you practically lost your mind.

I'm wracked with guilt for wanting a different father, a different life story. So I silenced my shame just like my mother. There's no winning in the fight between my ego, my inner critic and my true self. It's endless. I need to take control of what falls out of my mind and into my mouth.

I put my whiskey glass down in the sink and measure out dog food in a cup. I'm taking care of Blue, a collie dog who belongs to Stanley and Christine, a couple I'd become friends with in Columbine Lake. Blue stares at me anxiously. He is either sympathising or wants to go to the bathroom. I really can't tell with him, so I take him outside, ignoring the messages from Dan that are streaming into my phone. Blue and I weave through the snowy woods.

'Blue, it's time for me to focus on myself and stop feeling so guilty about everything,' I say.

Blue whines in answer. I'm speaking to a freaking dog.

We walk steadily down the paths. 'What went wrong?' I ask myself. 'I need to know, so that it doesn't happen again.'

First, it was my ego. When given a choice between working for a non-profit and taking on a court case, fighting for the truth and protecting my husband, I went for the second option. I wanted to prove that I was brave enough to take on Deloitte, strong enough to fight for Michael, right and wrong. I was just like Erin Brockovich, or so my friends and colleagues declared as they cheered me on. I was the woman who parachutes, bungy jumps, tackles down muggers, saves lives, jumps motorbikes. They saw me as a bad-ass, crime-busting, take-no-shit-from-nobody boss lady. I feared nothing, or so I told myself. As a result, Michael and I lost millions and we lost one another. And now I blamed Michael for it all, but it was my fault for not standing up for what I wanted. *It was my fault.* There it is again. Shame, guilt and blame in one neat package.

'Why am I so obsessed with all of these stories, Blue? My childhood stories and everything that happened in the last few years? What's the deal?'

It's a momentous question and he doesn't even know it. He's barking at a squirrel. I ignore him and follow the thread of thought. It's a bit insane, to be honest, but without my stories, what's left ... I'd just be me. No reasons. No justifications.

'They're just stories,' I say out loud. I say it again. 'They're just stories!'

My voice floats through the air like a feather and lands on the snow.

I look up at the sun glittering through the snow-heavy branches. Blue leaps around in the snow, tail wagging. It's exquisite. It's these small things that I want to carry with me and remember, not the pain of my stories. In holding on to these feelings, I'm suffering through them, again and again. How do I find love for my past pain stories? Do I break up with my past, but how in God's name do I do that?

'What if I tell a different story then, Blue? What if I act a different part? Blue?'

Blue has run off and I chase him through the woods and drag him back to the cabin by his collar. I stomp the snow off my boots and make myself a cup of tea. For a moment I consider pouring a shot of whiskey into my tea, but who does that? That's a slippery slope right there, Jacqui. Next thing I'll be a crazy old lady who talks to her dogs and drinks whiskey out of a tea pot.

I sit down in an armchair. Immediately my thoughts head straight for the part of my mind where I keep my suicide attempts. My mother still denies they ever happened. It's like it's not real: no mother could forget that, I tell myself, but my hands are shaking as if I've just swallowed a jumble of pills. It comes tumbling out at me and I cower in my armchair. It's not happening now: you no longer have to feel ashamed of that. You don't have to feel angry that your parents didn't care. Maybe I should just forget things like my mother does and pretend it never happened.

I'm standing in the living room and it's getting dark outside. I don't know what I've been doing. My hands are still shaking and I don't want to remember anything else. But I do. I remember the fear on my father's face when I first confronted him about the fire. His fear looked just like mine feels now. I'm with him in this moment and I've never felt so close to my father.

'You know I'll go to jail if I admit it,' he'd whispered.

Maybe it wasn't the jail time he feared. Maybe it was the humiliation and the rejection he feared. The shame. Just like I do. It was the gut-wrenching pain of looking at an awful person and admitting to the entire world that actually that awful person is you. My father and I are the same. The only difference is that life has bent him out of shape and he hasn't managed to love himself or others. That's what I need to do in order for me not to become like him. But I'm scared. I guess, just like he was – like he is. But I don't want to become depressed, obese and mean as hell like him. This makes me sad. I sit down on the couch, cross my legs under me and try to clear my mind. I'm so afraid of the past and the future that it's ruining the present moment. When did I become so scared?

My stories will never change, but I'm sick and tired of suffering because of them.

That day, nearly four years earlier, when I fell apart and cowered under my desk, was the turning point that started this journey. A journey to free myself from my pain. I want to live openly with my past and find love for it.

My phone buzzes again with another message from Dan, begging me to meet him in Branson. And why the hell not? Why shouldn't I go to a new place and have a little fun with a man who desires me and wants to spoil me? I text him back and tell him I'll think about it.

CHAPTER TWENTY-THREE

Out of suffering have emerged the strongest souls; the most massive characters are seared with scars. – Kahlil Gibran

BRANSON IS HALFWAY BETWEEN GRAND LAKE and Detroit and I've no idea what to expect from it or this weekend with Dan. I'm at Denver airport and suddenly I want to turn back. It's not right for me to see Dan again, even if it feels like Michael has been pushing me towards other men for nearly two years. Michael told me outright to have sex with another man if it would make me feel better. Our marriage was so corrupted by the end that we would both laugh about it openly and in front of Michael I would tell friends that I couldn't wait to find another man, as if it were all some big joke.

The truth was, Dan was not the first person I'd slept with outside of my marriage. The first one was Trevor, a colleague of mine and Michael's, who had recently become Michael's friend. It happened a few weeks before I left for America. I didn't do it because I wasn't getting any at home – quite the opposite. Our sex life was healthy in terms of frequency, but unhealthy as we'd lost that sweet intimacy we'd once had. It was just another habit. In the last six months before I left for America, I had asked if we could stop in order to try and find a more intimate emotional connection. I was falling apart and just wanted someone to hold me. After his breakdown, Michael had had the fight kicked out of him and, years later, it still hadn't come back. He no longer initiated sex or took the lead in anything in our marriage. I managed everything – the business, the court case, consulting work on the side, the groceries, the bills, the cooking and even when we had sex.

Trevor flirted so aggressively with me that even Michael, who lived in his own world, started to notice. In our last few months together, when Trevor would come to the office for a meeting, Michael would call out, 'Jacqui, your boyfriend has arrived.' It drove me mad and I begged Michael to stop, but he wouldn't. And neither would Trevor stop pursuing me. His desire was visceral and I was desperate for attention. I guess I enjoyed being desired more than I feared the shame that would follow if I slept with him. And so I did.

Back in Denver, I'm in the queue at the check-in counter and I wish Michael were waiting beside me. We travelled all over the world and travelling without him still feels strange. When we first married, we ate, breathed and slept love all day and every day – and then slowly it started running out. Now we're starved of love, but still I miss him. He has no idea about Trevor or Dan and I want to tell him. I find myself dialling his number.

'Mike?'

He's driving somewhere and the radio is on in the background.

'Jacqui? Hey! How are you?'

'I'm good. I just wanted to hear your voice. Where are you?'

'Trevor and I are going to a race. We've got the mountain bikes ready and we are going to kill it!'

'Kill it!' Trevor says in the background.

They sound like two high-school boys, giddy with arrogance and testosterone.

'What's up with you?'

'I'm heading to Missouri, but I wanted to talk to you.'

'Can't wait to destroy this race, hey! Man, I wish you were here to watch!'

'Tell Jacqui I send love,' Trevor shouts.

Michael explodes into too-loud laughter.

'Trevor sends his love and he's also sending you an open-mouth kiss.'

'Michael stop saying that shit to me! What the hell is wrong with you?'

'Ag come on, it's just a joke. You know Trevor's your boyfriend –'

'Michael stop it!'

'Come on, I know he wants you,' he sniggers.

'Fuck off, Michael!'

I hang up on him and notice people are staring. Fuck the whole lot of them. Thank God I'm doing what Michael has always wanted me to do and having this little fling, because my marriage is so fucking done.

—————◆—————

I expect my taxi to drop me off at a motel, but the driver stops outside the Hilton on Branson Landing, the waterfront hub on the lake in downtown Branson.

'Are you sure this is the right address?'

'Dead sure,' the driver tells me.

Dan must like me a lot, because he has booked us a premium suite. I pick up the phone and dial Amanda's number.

'Amanda, you won't believe this. You know I said Dan's a ditch digger or some kind of blue-collar worker? Anyway, I was expecting a cheap motel in Branson. Well, he booked us a suite at the Hilton.'

'I guess he must dig a hell of a lot of ditches.'

We laugh hysterically and then she reminds me to have fun and hangs up, leaving me to take a look around the suite.

What on earth does Dan do for a living? We've been speaking on the phone every day for the last week, but I somehow forgot to ask.

I'm a little nervous and so to calm my nerves, I walk around town before Dan arrives. I spot some dresses (yes, dresses for the tomboy) in a boutique window and try three on. Why the hell not? While I'm agonising over choosing one of the three dresses, Dan messages me saying he's about to arrive, so I head back to the Hilton, my heart pounding with fear. There's a moment of confused embarrassment when we see one another.

'What are we supposed to do now?' Dan asks and I can see that, like me, he's trying not to laugh.

'Um. Why not start with a drink and we can chat?'

'Sounds good.'

'But first, I want you to do me a favour. I've never bought a dress before unless I *really* had to. I tried on these dresses in a shop close by and I want to buy one but I need someone else's opinion. Think you could help me out?'

'You're so weird,' he laughs and grabs my hand so that I can lead him to the dresses.

When we get to the shop, I try on the dresses for Dan. The sales assistant passes me a pair of high heels that I can barely walk in, making me strangely aware of my legs for the first time. They're bare underneath the dress and I am aware of my thighs touching each other. I hesitate before stepping out of the changing cubicle, feeling completely out of my comfort zone. Still unaccustomed to looking at myself, I glance at myself in the mirror, quickly, just long enough to check that everything is in place and then force myself to look a second time, the way my therapist has been encouraging me to. I step outside to get Dan's opinion and I can almost feel his pulse quickening from across the shop as he sees me. Everything is honeysuckle and sunshine when he looks at me and I feel like the most beautiful woman in the world. His breath seems to have caught in his throat and he's just smiling at me. I do a silly twirl on the spot and he laughs.

'You look incredible.'

'I do?' I ask. Silently this dress is giving me a thrill of excitement that I can't explain.

'Go try on the others.'

The next dress is ultra-feminine: white, loose and swishy, with little uneven dots all over it. I could step out on the French Riviera in this dress.

'Jacqui, you look perfect. You are perfect.'

Did I just giggle? I did. I'm actually giggling like a schoolgirl. What is happening to me?

The final dress is one I still can't believe I've picked out. It's black, which immediately makes it seem a little risqué, and although it's a shift it somehow accentuates my figure in a way I've never experienced before.

'Exquisite, Jacqui. This is the one.'

'Do you think so?'

'I've no idea. You looked amazing in each one. Buy them all!'

I tell him he's being silly as I have no idea where I will even wear one, let alone three, and so I settle on buying myself the first one I tried on. Afterwards we stroll aimlessly around. With no preconceived ideas of each other, we walk hand in hand and talk about everything under the sun.

———◆———

Over drinks and dinner, I learn that Dan and I have many things in common. We love slow-cooked meals, loads of guacamole and the simple joy of eating bread with thick butter and a sprinkle of salt on top. We have the same sleep cycle and we both have a dog called Max. We're adrenaline junkies, but we both love golf. Our favourite brand of water is Fiji and we're mad about card games. We love dancing, but we don't dance enough. Does anyone dance enough? And then it's time to get serious and I ask him the question I've been putting off.

'So, how long have you been divorced?'

'Actually,' he says hesitating, 'I'm like you. Still in the process of it.'

'What! I said I'm not going home with a married man and you said you were divorced,' I say, speaking with a little heat.

'It's been a long time coming.'

I pause. He lied, but really, does it matter?

'I get it,' I say. 'I'm hoping to finalise my divorce within a couple of months.'

'I'm sorry I wasn't honest when we met. Jolene – my wife – and I have friends who got divorced but kept living under the same roof, so that they could gradually separate homes without disrupting their children's lives too much. We want that for our daughter, Kelly. We don't want her to feel lost or like she has to choose.'

'That makes sense.'

'Jolene and I are like brother and sister. She is a sister to my four brothers and very close to my mom. She's always going to be in my life and I have come to accept that any future partner needs to understand that she'll always be family.'

'I feel the same way about Michael. Michael is my family. I couldn't imagine my life without him.'

As we sit and drink, he tells me the story of Dan and Jolene. They married very young and although he loves her, he says it's never been romantic love.

'Actually, I've never been senselessly in love with anyone before,' he says, and there's something in his voice that makes the blood rise to my face.

I don't say anything and he keeps telling me about them. All he knows is life with Jolene. It's been an incredible journey, but behind closed doors their relationship is apparently toxic. Two people who aren't in love can't keep on acting the happy couple. He wanted to get divorced years ago, but then she finally fell pregnant after twelve years of trying and he thought maybe that would make them happy. But, he says, children aren't a cure for unhappiness, even though their daughter is the best thing on this planet. She's everything to them, but she's not a glue that's supposed to fix things. It's beyond fixing and Dan's tired of living with someone who can't escape the fighting and the negativity. He's says he has been living a lie for decades, from even before the wedding.

'I wanted to put it off, but everyone told me it was just pre-wedding jitters. I also believed no one else would ever love me, so I went through with it.'

I reach out and take his hand and squeeze it and it keeps pouring out of him. He tells me he was about to leave when his daughter got sick with cancer – and then he couldn't. But she's well now and it's time. He has stayed until now because there was always one more drama, one more time that he had to step up and be the man, but all that's over now.

'I do love her,' he says, sounding guilty.

'I understand. Jolene's your best friend: of course you love her. But sometimes it hurts too much to keep going.'

Dan notices the emotion in my voice and nods slowly.

'I guess you know all this already, though, don't you? You see right through me.'

We go back to our room and undress one another without needing to say a word. Everything is known between us. When we come together, touching slowly and kissing deeply, it's the most peaceful and intense thing in the world.

For three days we live slowly, lying amongst white hotel sheets and remembering everything we can about one another from all the lifetimes together. All of our plans to explore Branson drift away and hours pass lying in each other's arms. I tell him everything – *everything*. The fear that I suffered in Columbine Lake, that no one would be able to bear being with me after they knew it all, has evaporated completely. I even tell him about Trevor. He simply puts his hand under my chin and tells me, 'it happens: I did something similar with a work colleague. It's okay.'

Once again, he accepts me when I fear that I'm pushing it too far with all this sharing, that I'm on the brink of rejection. For the first time, I can speak of my childhood without losing myself in the pain of remembering.

'Those are my stories,' I say at last.

'Thank you for telling me.'

Dan holds no judgment. He's just here with me.

'I always thought that if Michael or his family knew everything, they'd abandon me.'

'Aren't we all afraid of abandonment?'

'But it wasn't about them. I never spoke about this stuff to anyone except a therapist and a few friends until now because *I* couldn't love that part of myself. Dan, I'm done with that. I'm done with thinking about wanting to kill off that part of myself. Damn it, I just want to love myself beyond my shame stories.'

'You deserve to love yourself. We both do.'

'And then there's people out there who are looking at me and saying, what a self-indulgent woman. Dammit, don't they understand that figuring out who I am isn't a vanity project, it's what's going to save my life? I'm not trying to be cool by travelling alone in America, I'm trying to survive.'

There's a bubble of anger in my chest. I leave it be and Dan's low voice makes it float away. He is talking about his childhood. His first memory is staring at his mother and she is wiping her eyes. He feels her pain and sorrow as she stares at him lying in her arms. He wants to cry because she's scaring him, but he doesn't want her to hurt. He gurgles. She laughs a little and strokes his chubby hand. I don't ask what the story means.

It's Sunday and our time together is almost over. We go out for a goodbye lunch and halfway through the meal, Dan puts down his knife and fork.

'I want to ask you something. Why would a woman like you be interested in me?'

'Dan, what are you talking about? You're amazing.'

'You've never said anything about my scars. Look at them, Jacqui. You look at *me* like no one else does. Can you not see my scars?'

I look and, true enough, he is scarred. His lip is twisted up and deep scars run underneath his nose on the left side of his face. His teeth are crooked. The same thing happened weeks ago in Grand Lake when I first met Sean. He, too, had a scar over his lip from a motorbike accident, one that I didn't notice until he called me out on it. I suddenly remember Dan had seen Sean in the bar the night we met. I feel the same awkwardness now as I did when Sean asked why I didn't mention his scar.

'I didn't notice.'

He stares at me.

'Dan, it's a long story. When I was 16, I stopped registering people's physical form. I disconnected from my body when I was going through all of that stuff, but I'm working on it.'

'You can't see the body?'

How on earth do I go about explaining this?

'I can see your scars now that you point them out. I just don't process that kind of information or see it as relevant when I am with someone. I relate to your spirit. Because I disconnected from my body, I also disconnected from other peoples' and it's taken me years to even look at myself again, let alone study other people's bodies. My therapist said that because I don't know what I look like, I don't pay any attention to other people's physical exterior. But I'm getting better at looking at myself and noticing small things. I recently painted my toenails for the first time, which was a huge deal, and hell, I've just bought a dress for no reason. Maybe I will start wearing pink soon or even learn how to put on make-up.'

He was silent and I could feel he was hurting.

'Dan, do your scars bother you?'

'Not anymore, I guess. When I was a kid I sensed it caused my mom a lot of pain. I guess it hurt her so much to see me like this because she – she knew what I'd go through before I did. I was just a little guy, I didn't know what that meant. It's like I carried the pain she felt. Her pain was the first thing I knew and I think my first impulse was to try and protect her.'

'You probably suppressed your emotions for your mother. I get that. I tried to do that for my mom too.'

'At times when other kids saw me for the first time, they would scream out of terror. I had so many operations and some of the time I was wrapped in bandages. Jacqui, when you look at me, you see right into me.'

He grips my hand across the table. His hand is warm and calloused.

'People always say to me, Dan you're so strong, you're so warm. Look at how you always take care of everyone. And I wanna say to them: Christ, can't you see I'm dying inside? I've built this fake-perfect life so carefully that no one can tell that I'm unhappy inside. I've put on a brave face for so many years that that's all anyone can see. I want to break out and do more with my life. Be more.'

His voice is tight with despair.

'You see past the brave face. You know my every thought and a part of me hates it, but I love it, too. I've always wanted to feel seen and known, but now that it's here – it's hard.'

'I know.'

'Of course you do.'

We laugh and then suddenly our precious few days have slipped through our fingers and we're saying goodbye to one another. I have to un-mesh my spirit from his. Meeting a twin soul like Dan at the wrong time is agony.

'We'll stay in touch,' he promises, wiping tears from my cheek with his lips. 'We're going to help each other, right, Jacqui?'

'Yes,' I say. 'We'll be there for each other, every step of the way.'

CHAPTER TWENTY-FOUR

If you are depressed, you are living in the past. If you are anxious, you are living in the future. If you are at peace, you are living in the present. – Lao Tzu

T HE SNOW IN THE MOUNTAINS around Grand Lake is starting to melt. Spring hiking is the worst. It's slushy and muddy and exhausting and after tripping for the hundredth time and falling splat onto the trail, I decide I need a break. My body is done with the gruelling hikes and my pride is done with the spring mud, so I decide to go on a road trip. I'll start in Denver. At some point I will find myself in Los Angeles with Michael's cousin Megan, whom I've been meaning to visit, and I'm leaving on my 46th birthday. That's as much of a plan as I've got.

I pack up the things in my cabin, say goodbye to Stanley and Christine and their dog Blue and drive down to Denver to spend the night with Amanda. On the morning of my departure, Amanda gives me a giant hug.

'You're going to have a great time, Jacqui,' she says, more seriously than I expected. 'You deserve this. You *need* this.'

I'm on my way to Santa Fe. By evening I'm driving through the rolling hills of New Mexico and I arrive in Santa Fe just as the sun starts to set, casting a purple-red glow across the adobe houses. They try to blend in with the surrounding desert, but fail due to bright green awnings and turquoise door frames.

The next morning, I rise early and ask the receptionist at the hotel for a breakfast recommendation.

'The Plaza Café. It's an institution,' he says without hesitating – and he's right about that.

It's crammed with locals and tourists all popping in for breakfast and being greeted by the owner. I study the menu and my eye is instantly drawn to the 'huevos divorciados'. Dan would kill himself laughing at the choice. We are now spending an hour a day on Skype or on the phone. I order the divorced eggs and receive the heaviest plate of food of my life. Everything is jumbled together in a spicy hot, hot, hot dish of New Mexican madness – corn tortillas, eggs, chipotle and tomatillo salsa, hash browns, guacamole and sour cream.

I spend my days in Santa Fe trying to take it all in, but there are too many different elements. Latin American meets Native American meets the Wild West meets the American South. Michael would love Santa Fe, I think, and then reprimand myself: everyone and anyone would love Santa Fe. That's why it's always so full of people. Don't think about Michael, don't think about anyone.

I look up and find that I've wandered to the government records building. A sign with gold lettering above a black cast iron gate reads: 'What is past is prologue'. I repeat the words to myself. *What is past is prologue.* Prologues establish setting or give background details that draw you into the real story. My past is not the heart of this story. Now, this, here is the heart of it.

I start walking fast back to the hotel where the manuscript lies in the boot of my car. I'm not going to write about my father and about what Deloitte did. I'm not going to try and convince the world of the damage of emotional abuse and explain why our relationship has fallen apart. My book is too conditional, expecting him to change. I don't like or respect a lot of what he has done, but I don't like or respect a lot of what I've done either. The fact is, I love him regardless: it is myself I'm struggling to love. I need to stop doubting myself and let him do as he chooses. And that means letting go of the book, the past, once and for all.

It was the book that led to our final parting of the ways. I told him that I would write about the fire and that was the end for him. What the future holds for my father and me, I don't know. He is enough, whether or not we ever have a relationship again. *The past is prologue.* I wanted a different father. I wanted to have a different experience with Michael. I wanted a different experience with Deloitte. It shouldn't have taken me so fucking long to actually *do* something about the fact that the whole book is about victimisation and revenge. I don't want my story to be about that.

When I get to the car I'm sweating, despite the unexpected cold weather. I get the manuscript from the boot of the car and slam it closed again, hard. I find the nearest trash bin, attached to one of Santa Fe's bottle-green lamp-posts, and drop the manuscript in. It lands half on top of a Frito Pie, the gooey melted cheese, beef and pinto beans sticking to the pages. And now? What now? I think about my plans to go fly-fishing, hiking and horse riding, but what about after that?

My thoughts don't stop racing even as I stand in a pair of waterproof dungarees, trying and failing to fly-fish for the first time. The guide's name is David, just like my little brother. Maybe it would be best if I returned to South Africa to be with family. I could sort things out properly with Michael and try yet again to establish a relationship with my father. I could finally look for a new job at a non-profit and maybe work part-time while writing – what? What would I write now? What did I have worth writing about apart from those stories?

'Concentrate now, I think you've got something! I really think you've got something at last,' says David.

But it's nothing. I've gotten my line stuck in a branch in the river and if I go back to South Africa, I'll just get myself stuck all over again.

I'll get stuck into all those relationships where I find myself unable to be anything else but what I was.

'It's almost five. I'm tired, please can we call it a day?'

'No way, José! You can't give up until you've achieved what you set out to do, my friend,' David jokes.

And what had I set out to do, all those years ago? I wanted to move to North America. Let me not fail. Let me not give up, I pray. I stare up at the sky and pray for a fish to tug on my rod. Let me achieve what I set out to do. At that moment, I feel a light tug and then another tug on the end of my line. David cries out in excitement and helps me reel in a brown trout. As soon as I see it, I feel sorry for it. Poor guy didn't ask to get caught.

'He probably has a family,' I say.

David laughs, insists on taking a photo of me with the fish, then takes the fish and releases it back into the water.

———◦———

I'm driving Route 66, Santa Fe to Los Angeles, and decide to stop for the night in Kingman, Arizona. It's late afternoon and the sun is harsh. Silver-bellied trucks speed through town. It's eerie, so I check into a hotel quickly. The carpet in my room is tacky and it makes the hair on the back of my neck stand on end. I wish Michael were here with me. I miss him and decide to call him. He picks up on the first ring and on hearing his voice, I'm home. The grief that I've been avoiding on my trip settles over me gently as we talk. God, I miss him.

'The road trip has been good so far. I'll be in LA tomorrow and I'm staying with Megan.'

'Jacqui – do you think you could not, uh –'

'I don't want to tell her about the divorce.'

'Right. Because it's not final, anyway, so if we change our minds…'

He tails off and I find that I'm gritting my teeth.

'Mike, we're going to have to start coming to terms with the divorce.'

'Well, it's better not to tell Megan.'

'Have you not told anyone about the divorce? What about Evelyn and Donald?'

Evelyn and Donald are Michael's sister and brother-in-law – and they don't like either of us.

'I haven't told them. It just seems so final.'

'But Michael, it is. You get that, right?'

He mumbles something indistinct. If only I could hug him.

'Mike, you don't have to tell anyone. It's got nothing to do with any of them.'

There's a silence on the line. I want to tell him I love him. I want to tell him about Dan.

'I miss you, Jacqui Burnett.'

'I miss you too, Mike.'

'Can you promise me one thing?'

His voice is heavy.

'I can try.'

'Promise me you'll keep your married name. Promise me that whatever happens you'll always be Jacqui Burnett.'

'I promise, Mike. I promise.'

———◆———

The morning sunlight does nothing to improve Kingman and I'm more than relieved to leave it in the dust as I drive on through the Mojave Desert to Los Angeles. At lunch I pull over on the side of the road at a rest stop and walk out into the desert. The sun brutalises red sand and I want the coolness of snow again. I turn slowly to look at distant rock-bodies and tall cactus-men. The desert is alive, with bugs screaming in the heat and colours exploding in the air.

Someone once told me that the City of Angels is just like Cape Town. As I drive into LA, I decide that person lied. Lane changes, off-ramps, highways twisting over and under and around each other like roller coasters – I've only ever seen this many cars, trucks and hissing buses in China. Google shouts at me in an American accent and I miss one turn-off, then another. Streets flash past me like slides on a projector screen and Hollywood is nowhere to be found. What I see outside my window reminds me of home. I am a white woman in an SUV, protected. On the streets, the homeless sleep in makeshift tents and trolleys filled with trash are pushed up against each other. People crawl into damp sleeping bags, ready for night to settle in, while others wander with unseeing eyes. I keep driving. The American Google lady at last tells me where to go and I find myself back in suburbia, where purple carpets of Jacaranda blossoms line the streets. I am taken back to Johannesburg, where I used to drive the streets on my way home to Michael, listening to Jacaranda FM.

Megan greets me in the driveway and practically pulls me out of the car into her arms.

'Jacqui, thank God you made it! I've been trying to call, but I couldn't get through to you!'

'Sorry, my phone died! So great to see you, Megs,' I say, squeezing her in a hug.

Megan and her husband Dylan ask me everything about my time in the cabin and my road trip. They've prepared a birthday celebration dinner for their friend Jayden. When Megan brings the cake to the dinner table, I see that it has Jayden's and my name on it.

'I've never had a cake with my name on it.'

'Wait till you're 50,' Dylan says. 'Then we're gonna party.'

'You'll have to come back to LA for that,' says Megan.

'Who knows, maybe I'll be living this side of the world by then.'

It slips out and all three of them look at me curiously.

'Pipe dream,' I say, trying to smooth it over, but I can tell that Megan won't forget.

The next morning, I go for a run on the promenade and we spend the day walking around a market in town. In the evening we go to a party in Malibu. Skyscrapers stretch into blue skies out of the same earth as palm trees and even the tar is alive with the spring heat.

CHAPTER TWENTY-FIVE

*Knowing your own darkness is the best method for
dealing with the darkness of other people. – Carl Jung*

MEGAN AND I HAVE DECIDED to road trip and check out the Big
Sur coast and Carmel. We'll stay over in Santa Barbara and
Pismo Beach and then go on to San Francisco. Our last trip together
a decade prior was to Victoria Falls in Zambia. Unlike me, Megan is
bright-eyed and bushy-tailed and has everything packed and ready by
the time I stumble out of my room.

'Breakfast on the road?'

'Sounds good!'

I say my goodbyes and then we're off, with me behind the wheel.
Megan lets us get out of the city before she reminds me of my slip-of-
the-tongue from the previous evening.

'So you still wanna move out here, after all these years?'

'I do.'

'What does Michael say?'

'Michael loves South Africa.'

'You two all right?'

Before I know it, I'm telling her things I wanted to leave alone, but
I manage to steer clear of the divorce.

'I don't know how we're going to forgive one another for everything,' I say, wiping my eyes. 'I just don't know.'

Megan looks stunned. From all of our 'happy couple' correspondence, she must have thought that everything was fine.

'Marriage isn't for sissies, that's for sure. It's damn hard work. You two will make it through all of this. You're tough as nails.'

I wish I could ask her to see a different side of me, but I don't have the courage. It appears the only three people who know and accept the soft and vulnerable side of me are Amanda, Jill and Dan.

'We'll figure something out,' is all I can manage to say about it.

'Look, I don't know what's gone wrong, but you'll just have to forgive him.'

'What if he doesn't want my forgiveness?'

'Oh, sure he does, honey. Everybody wants forgiveness.'

That's not true at all, I think, but I let it drop and we make happier small talk as the coast slides on by, changing in front of my eyes. We're winding through Big Sur now. It's foggy when I get out of the car and follow Megan down a sandy path to a deserted beach. The waves surge and suck at the rocks and gulls swoop through the wind.

There's something about this coastline that I find impossible to define. Words like pristine, craggy, glorious and wild mean nothing when held up against the sheer physicality of the area. Even simple signifiers like cliff or bay cannot capture the way the land, ocean and light meet here.

Each day of our trip is different to the next. One is glassy and still, with a golden breeze and air so clear I can taste it. Another day is the deep green of twisting cypresses and towering redwoods, ending on granite cliffs with a sunset glass of whiskey in hand.

One morning, I'm sitting alone at Pismo Beach, my toes massaging the cold sand. It's early morning and Megan is still asleep back at the hotel. We plan to spend the day in Carmel. It's a strange name, Carmel. Where did they find it? Was it named after the man who first decided to colonise this space or was it named after the Mount Carmel of the Bible, a symbol of beauty? Sometimes I get sick of the random Biblical knowledge I carry with me, product of that hard Christian upbringing where the Bible was twisted to mean whatever best served fear. It worked well for my father. I remember the tone of his many letters.

> I've learnt to take all of my mistakes and place them in front of the Lord Jesus Christ and ask for His forgiveness. Jesus has taught me to forgive unconditionally without naming requirements and making demands of others the way that you do, Jacqueline, when you say that you cannot spend time with me, your loving father, unless I, in your words, come clean and or change my behaviour towards you. I've come clean in front of the Lord and if it is good enough for Him it should be good enough for you. If you cannot find it in your heart to understand that I am not responsible for the words I speak when pushed beyond the limit, you are not the person or the child of God I thought you were. In Bible study years ago Reverend Connor told your mother and myself to put our sins committed knowingly and unknowingly into a container, seal it and throw it into the deep ocean and never go fishing there again. I may need a couple of containers, he said.

Hey, at least my father had a sense of humour about it. And without fail he would add something in to remind me to be ashamed of myself.

But it was always the same with my father. Whenever anything went wrong, the answer was to get forgiveness from Jesus – it worked every time. It boiled down to saying, 'No matter what I've done, I am right and you are wrong because I am a good Christian and Jesus loves me and that's the end of it. Oh, and also, if you don't move on, accept

Jesus as your only saviour and forget about what happened, I cannot love you.'

I get up and dust sand off my clothes. The light has changed from pale to golden as I stroll down the beach.

There is something sour about my forgiveness of my father and of Michael. It reminds me too much of my father's love of the moral high ground. I don't want to hand out forgiveness like a priest selling indulgences. I just want to accept how events have played out and the fact that every player has a different perspective – and not judge them if they see things differently from how I do. I might never be able to bring my father round to my point of view, nor will Michael ever understand precisely what went wrong between us in the same way that I do. Nevertheless, it won't help me move forward if I say *I forgive you*, but continue to judge and blame – and to suffer.

I find that I've walked all the way back to the hotel, where I wait for Megan to wake up so that we can go for a coastal walk before breakfast.

'I've thought of something, Megs,' I say. 'About how to forgive Michael.'

'Tell me?'

'For Michael and me, the only way forward is to be grateful for what we've had. If we say we forgive one another, but we're still holding on to who is right and who is wrong, then what's the point?'

'I get that. But how are you going to be grateful for the hard times?'

'I think that I have enough love for Michael and the path we've walked together to just accept what is and be grateful for it.'

Megan is quiet and stops walking. The morning sun is bright all around her silhouette.

'I suppose,' she says.

'The way I see it is that if you don't limit love, you won't have judgment going on in the background.'

'But it still hurts,' she says.

'Yep, it still really fucking hurts.'

CHAPTER TWENTY-SIX

We must be the change we wish to see in the world. – Gandhi

MEGAN LEAVES ME IN SAN FRANCISCO and although I've loved our time together, I'm grateful that I will no longer have to hide the truth of my divorce – or my connection with Dan. Although we haven't chatted in a while, we've gone past the boundaries of a one-night stand. The intensity of our connection makes me think that this isn't quite what Michael meant when he said 'What happens in America stays in America'. Our friendship – if you can call it that – couldn't even stay in Grand Lake. It follows me wherever I go and each time my phone buzzes in my pocket as I wander through San Francisco, my excitement is tinged with shame. I'm not ashamed of what's happened between Dan and I; I wish it were as simple as that. Every time my phone buzzes I'm reminded that I've lost out on what was supposed to be the perfect life with Michael and I'm still in love with him. I'm ashamed of wanting something different, for not having the strength to fight on and for giving up on my dreams to take care of his.

I'm riding the cable car alone while children screech and parents snap photographs of them. I'm silent as the city unfurls through the wood-framed cable car window. I get off the cable car at a sign that reads: 'Fisherman's Wharf of San Francisco'. It's shaped like the helm of a ship. The bustle of tourists who get out with me stampede onwards and I follow them to a stand on the wharf which is selling crab chowder in bread bowls. I leave them there and pass other cafés – Crab Station, Nick's Lighthouse and Fisherman's Grotto – before stopping at Alioto's, which offers me a Budweiser with my clam chowder for only a few dollars more. The chowder is thick, creamy, salty. Fisherman's Wharf is packed with people and not a single fisherman in sight, but it's a hot, sunny day and everyone seems happy to be here on this kitschiest of waterfronts. I wander down the pier to the Ferry Building Marketplace. I wind my way back into the city, between skyscrapers and Victorian row houses. I walk all day and find myself at last at Crissy Field in Presidio National Park. Dunes of fog roll in over the city. Golden Gate Bridge disappears and my hair stands out around my face in tendrils. I keep telling myself that it's good to be without Michael and that it's okay that I can't seem to shake my connection with Dan – Michael would understand this, even though he might never understand the many reasons why I hurt him. *I hurt him.* I need to accept that. I did what I did. I said what I said. We both did.

When I get back to my hotel, I call Michael.

'It's so good to hear from you,' he says. 'How was the trip with Megan? How are you?'

I tell him all the highlights and we laugh about the fact that Megan didn't want to drive on the road trip, not even once.

'I bet she wouldn't let you speed, either,' he says. 'That must have killed you! Remember our wedding cake? Remember that?'

A Formula One Ferrari. Of course I remember. That must've been the weirdest wedding cake the baker had ever made.

There's a strained pause.

'Mike, I just called to say that I'm sorry for blaming you for everything that went wrong. Do you think you can accept what happened without hating me for it?'

'I could never hate you.'

'But can you accept it for what it is and – can you forgive me?'

'Of course I forgive you. I love you more than anything and our marriage has always been my happy place. We can move past all that.'

I try to explain that we will move past it, but still go our separate ways, but he doesn't seem to take me seriously. At last I tell him that we'll talk again soon and that I have to go.

'I love you, Jacqui.'

'I love you too.'

My heart is aching. I try to calm myself by counting the city lights but after twenty I lose track. I thought I would feel relieved to hear him say he can accept the past and what I've done, but I don't. There is no relief for me, because I'm still clinging to the idea of a different life. My mind fills with the countless sensations of Michael. The way he sneezed and how he shuffled his pillows before going to sleep. The way he sipped his coffee and the sound of his footsteps in our home. The smell of him and how he would shout-laugh when we did motocross. I lie on his side of the bed and listen to myself breathing and I'm not sure if it is worth it, leaving him to be with me. I fall asleep dreaming of him and what I've lost and then wake with a start to the sound of my phone ringing. Half asleep, I answer.

'I needed to talk to you,' Dan says. 'I just needed to hear your voice.'

Instantly I can tell he's had a few too many drinks. I look at my watch; it is past midnight. I tell him it would be best if we speak tomorrow, but he insists. I can't help but listen to Dan. There's something about him that makes one want to hear more. He's charming and funny and open – and when he talks, everyone leans in to hear the special story he's telling, the story that must be meant just for them.

'I've fallen in love with you, Jacqui Burnett. I've fallen head-over-heels-upside-down in love with you and there's nothing I can do about it.'

'Dan –'

'You're the woman I've been waiting for my whole life.'

'Dan, please.'

'No, Jacqui. I love you. I'm in love with you.'

A warmth spreads through me and I want to tell him that I love him too, but I baulk because it isn't true and I don't want it to become true. I tell him we'll talk tomorrow when he's sober. Before I know it it's tomorrow and I've barely slept, but it's clear what I need to say to him.

'Dan, in Branson we agreed to stay in touch and to support one another on our journey, but a relationship is not an option for me. I'm in no position to even think about that right now.'

'But you feel it too. The connection we have is out of this world and we can't let that go. I've been waiting for you my whole life and now you're here and all I can do is love you.'

'Of course I feel it. I could fall in love with you and there's no question that I have a lot of love for you. But I promised myself to take care of myself, alone, and to see this journey through.'

'I know you want to be a writer and move to America and all that – '

'Dan, it's not "all that": it's my life. It's the most important decision I'll ever make. I don't want anyone to interfere with that.'

'I didn't mean to come across like that. I just meant that I want to help you make it happen and if we're together, imagine how easy it will be.'

I want to love him and feel supported, but I don't know enough about him yet. We've only known each other for a couple of weeks. It's crazy!

'I'm just not ready. Michael – it's too fresh, Dan.'

'I understand completely. But can we meet again? I'm desperate to see you.'

'I'm not sure. I love chatting to you, but I think it would be best if we didn't chat as much. Do you think you could do that? Make a little more space between us, I mean?'

'I would do anything for you. It'll be hard, but of course I'll do it. Do you think we could make time to see one another though, in real life?'

I can't say no to him and we make plans to meet up again in Park City near Salt Lake City in a week's time and before we end the conversation, he tells me he loves me again. Oh, Lord! What have I gotten myself into?

————◆————

Dan loves me.

I walk through the streets in a haze and life throbs all around me. I experience everything all at once because of those three words that encapsulate the purpose of life on earth. *I love you.*

The rush of traffic is a distant hum, a bee in the spring sun. Nothing in the world is single, everything is jammed together like the crush of people riding the San Francisco Muni.

Dan loves me.

Blood pulses from the tips of my ears to the ends of my fingers. The city under my feet is a miracle. Everything from the number of dogs bounding around, to people in fancy dress outfits for no apparent reason, to the ridiculously delicious burritos, puts a smile on my face.

Dan loves me.

I love myself.

I'm wearing a dress today and the wind keeps blowing it up around street corners and I have to Marilyn Monroe to keep it down. I wrap my new cerise scarf around myself and stop to take a selfie beside a pink Victorian house. I think of what Michael would say if he saw me in a dress, taking a photograph of my own face next to something pink. For decades I've avoided the camera and here I am, voluntarily taking happy snaps of myself. This must be love – or insanity. I don't know which. I start walking down a street, I don't know which – is it Bradford or Broadway? – and it's beckoning to me.

Suddenly I'm running downhill like a crazy person, arms outstretched, ecstatic. Nobody bats an eyelash: this is San Francisco and people here do weird shit all the time and, more importantly, Dan loves me.

CHAPTER TWENTY-SEVEN

You, yourself, as much as anybody in the entire universe, deserve your love and affection. – Buddha

I'M SPEEDING OUT OF SAN FRANCISCO towards Dan and Salt Lake City and nothing can stop me. Just as I'm leaving my hotel room, Michael calls and we chat.

'I miss you.'

'I miss you too, Mike.'

'This separation is only bringing us closer. You see, already we're talking again, talking like we used to –'

'Michael, this is no longer a separation. We're getting a divorce.'

'You feel that way now, but –'

'Mike, don't talk to me like I don't know my own feelings, like me wanting to get divorced is just a cry for attention. This is real, okay?'

'Listen, all I'm saying is that this break has given us both time to reassess things and I think if you're honest with yourself –'

'You're not listening to me! I am being honest with myself! I've never been this fucking honest with myself in my *entire life*! I hate that I'm hurting you. I hate that I'm hurting so much inside that I feel the need for this divorce. Can't you get it?'

'Jacqui, I'm sorry.'

'It's too late for sorry now, Michael: it's done, you broke my heart. I gave up everything for you again and again.'

'I've changed, I've taken time –'

'Come on Michael, how many times have you told me you have changed in the last ten years?' I start to shout, *I CAN'T LIVE THE REST OF MY LIFE WITH YOU ATTACHED TO ME LIKE A TWO-YEAR-OLD. I'M DEPLETED. I'M 46 AND THANKS TO YOU I'VE WASTED A DECADE OF MY LIFE, MY FUCKING LIFE, MICHAEL, AND NOW I HAVE TO START OVER BECAUSE YOU COULDN'T BE THERE FOR ME –'*

It goes on and on. I start to say the meanest things. At last one of us slams down the phone.

I stop for the night in Reno, but even its seediness and monthly hotel rates can't get me down. I drive under its explosive neon sign that reads 'Reno: The biggest little city in the world'. I'm out of Reno early the next morning and in the pale light it seems like a town where you come to lose things and never find them again. I turn my radio on loud, then louder, in an attempt to drown out my loneliness. I'm listening to *Angel* by Sarah McLachlan on repeat. 'In the arms of an angel, fly away from here, from this cold, dark motel room and the endlessness that you fear.' I use it to help myself cry as I hate myself for how I spoke to Michael the day before.

This morning before I left, Michael and I spoke on the phone, both of us sounding like we'd stayed up all night without much sleep.

'Michael, I love you and I hate what I do to you. I can't go on speaking to you like that and then hating myself afterwards. Can't you see that we're destroying one another? You say you don't want to get divorced, but we've tried everything else. We're stuck in this pattern. We've both been trying to change for years, but I can't within our marriage.'

I'm speeding down the highway. Is Nevada really so desolate or is it just me?

'Mike, I can't bear to keep hearing about your misery, how you hate how your family treats us, how much you hate your job, how I should take over the company, or how I'm better at it. I never wanted to run your company. I don't want to live your life and I don't want to keep having to build you up every day and then scream at you when I feel depleted –'

Tears are streaming down my face, remembering our words from the call just that morning, and I pull over. I hear how we pleaded with one another, still in love. I believe he deserves better than how I treat him now. I believe I have to leave him to save us both.

'Jacqui, I know you're still not over what I put you through. But maybe in time, you'll forgive me.'

I know I am finding it hard to forgive him after everything I have sacrificed for him, for our marriage. I don't want to judge it anymore. I don't know how to not surrender to his every wish when we are together. I always put what I believe is right for me aside. I have to find 'me' again.

'I love you so much.'

'Me too, I'll always love you.'

I wish I had told him that even though we will no longer be married, he'll never drift out of my life. Michael is my family and has stomped a footprint onto my heart. The mark will be there forever – a mark of love and of pain. Perhaps that's the only kind of mark we leave on another – love and pain, always together. I think of my sweet mother, how she suffered and how worried I was that I'd become her, unable to leave. I made the same marriage vows in a church as she did, but I've left him and there will be life after him. I won't become depressed, bloated, suicidal and angry – I won't become my father. Michael will never learn cruelty the way I learned cruelty in my home. This divorce will preserve him from learning those awful lessons and save me from sinking into them.

I tell myself these things as I speed along the highway past trucks and empty hills. It aches to forgive and to remember all the precious, secret moments we shared. It aches to let go of the future that we cannot have.

Angel has been playing on repeat the same way my thoughts have. I should probably turn that song off and concentrate on my next part of the journey, wherever that may lead me.

CHAPTER TWENTY-EIGHT

In the sweetness of friendship, let there be laughter and
sharing of pleasures. For in the dew of little things the heart
finds its morning and is refreshed. – Kahlil Gibran

I ARRIVE AT THE AIRPORT in Salt Lake City and look forward to a
few days of distraction with Dan, what with all that's been
happening between Michael and me. I've had a few too many hours
for self-reflection since I left Megan in San Francisco. When I see him
coming through the arrivals gate, it's like no time has passed since
Branson. He booms his greeting from across the hallway and sweeps
me into a crushing hug. We don't stop chatting from the moment we
see each other until we step through our hotel room door. Everything
is simple and happy – and then he stops talking and kisses me until
I'm dizzy.

'I missed you,' we say at the same time.

When he looks at me, I feel like a goddess.

'What are you thinking?' he asks.

'Oh, nothing,' I say, and start to laugh. 'I'm just happy to see you.'

'Me too, sweetheart.'

I pull away so that I can look into his eyes and he starts telling
me about his week. We don't need sex to connect and for now I just

want to hear his voice. We go and sit outside where the hotel has an open fireplace. No one else is around and Dan sits down beside me and puts his arm around my shoulder. I love the smell of him – it's light and summery at first and then ends with amber. He brushes a hair from my cheek and then stops speaking.

'What's up?'

'I had a fight with Michael and lost it with him in Reno. I hate that about myself.'

'I can't imagine you screaming at anyone.'

'You'd be surprised.'

His face clouds over for a moment.

'Jolene, now Jolene can be cruel. Once when we were going through another difficult year of trying to conceive, we got into a fight. She's screaming blue murder and then she jumps up – Jolene's tiny, you know – and takes down a painting. She throws it right at me and she screams, 'You're not even man enough to give me a child: you're pathetic!'

'I've done something similar to Michael. I threw a display board across his office. So don't think of me as the good party in my marriage, because we've all got ugly parts inside of us. If anyone is looking for the perfect partner, that person doesn't exist,' I say. 'I'm sure I'll like Jolene. Or be able to relate to her, at least.'

'I'm sure you'll like her a lot.'

It's a sticky moment, one of the only awkward moments we've had between us. I'm reminded of him telling me he loves me and I want to back-pedal as fast as possible. Dan raises an eyebrow and smiles at me and I relax again.

'Come on, let's get out of here. I wanna take you for dinner. What are you in the mood for?'

'I'm up for anything.'

'You always are,' he says, kissing me on the cheek and pulling me to my feet.

The night takes us to three different places for cocktails, dinner and then a third spot for dessert. The fact that we only have three days makes us act like a couple on honeymoon and we're soon back in our room, tearing our clothes off just to be together again. We make love on the floor in front of the fire.

'That was –'

'I know, right?'

'Are we great or what?'

We burst out laughing and Dan gets up and walks naked to the bathroom, where I hear him running a bath.

'Come get in,' he calls. 'I'm bringing out the champagne. We're celebrating!'

I go and get into the hot bath and rest my foot on the tap, a spot of delicious cold in the heat.

'What are we celebrating?'

Glasses clink in the kitchen and a pop and fizz means the champagne he ordered from room service has arrived.

'Each other. Life. Love,' he says, stepping back into the bathroom with two glasses in one hand, the bottle in the other.

He slides into the water opposite me and I can't help but admire his body.

'You checking me out, Missy Burnett?'

I snort with laughter, choking on my champagne.

'Oh shut up, don't get all vain on me. I already know you use hairspray, so I guess it shouldn't come as a surprise!'

'Hey! I thought we agreed that after you discovered the hairspray, we would never discuss it again. The hairspray is our one dark secret, okay? I can't let it get out that I'm thinning on top!'

The nights and days slide on too quickly for me, with us laughing and enjoying one another as much as possible before we separate again. We eat out and order in, eating meals in bed or having dinner and champagne in the bath tub. We play cards and tease one another and talk. We talk all night and all day until our throats hurt. He writes 'I love you' on the fogged-up shower doors, on my heart and in my soul.

The first flowers of May wink from between patches of snow that have forgotten to melt and cloud patches float through a piercing blue sky. Dan and I have gone for a walk and have stopped to sit side by side on a rock, looking out across Park Lake.

'When I'm with you, it's like I'm remembering the words to a song I heard a long time ago and starting to sing again. And then when I go back home – it's awful,' he says, rubbing his eyes hard with one hand. 'Half the time Jolene comes home from meeting with her clients and she's already had a few too many glasses of wine and she is as mean as anything. We have no real connection other than the experiences we have shared. I say she's like my sister, but no sister would ever treat a brother like that.'

'You don't know that,' I say, and I tell him about attacking David and how frigid things are between my brothers and me. 'They never call me, not even on birthdays. I think I've only seen them ten or fifteen times as adults. Even between brothers and sisters, it can be hard. Strange that we both have four brothers, hey? You're so lucky that you and your brothers are still close.'

'I am lucky.'

He smiles at the thought and we watch a butterfly land on a white flower.

'You know, I never felt butterflies with Jolene. The first time I ever felt butterflies was when I met you. Why did I leave it so late to leave her?'

'You've got to forgive yourself for wanting things to be different.'

'What do you mean? How do you know all this?'

That makes me laugh, hard, as honestly I don't know.

'I'm just going through the same thing as you,' I say. 'And I've had a lot of time to think since being away from home.'

'I've tried to leave so many times. I don't know why I always go back. Sometimes, in my darkest moments, I think it would be easier if she accidently died,' he says. 'And then I can't believe anyone could have such a dark thought.'

His voice is muffled because he has covered his face in his hands. I take one hand in mine and open his face again and he keeps speaking.

'That would be so much easier than dealing with the humiliation and the fall-out of a divorce. We're both going to be seen as such failures. Young marriage gone wrong, the typical story. Am I evil for thinking that?'

'No. I know what you mean. Being a widow attracts support, whereas divorcée, well that's a cuss word in my family. This time round, I'm just trying to accept it all. Forgive myself for it all, you know?'

'How can you forgive so easily?'

'I can't always and it's never easy. Forgiving myself is so slow sometimes it kills me. So I've been working on acceptance.'

'Accepting what your father did must've been harder even than forgiving yourself or Michael.'

'It was, especially because he's never had to face the consequences of his actions.'

'How did you manage to accept that your father is who he is and let it go?'

'I am still deep in the process, but I had my first big aha moment when I was 34. Michael and I were newly married and my father was having none of this second son-in-law business, never mind that I found out that he was having an affair with an ex-prostitute and drug addict that he then employed. My mother was working as an estate agent while my father *still* worked on his multi-million-rand deal. He was always talking about the business deal of a lifetime. He'd even taken a couple of thousand from me and, on top of that, he threatened to sue me for parental support.'

'He *what?*'

'It's not important, Dan.'

'You sure?'

'I didn't care about the money, I was just tired of the screaming between us, so I organised a meeting with him. I go in and I tell him I've been working hard with a therapist to change my way of being and to let go of my anger, but I'm going to need him to help me if we're going to improve our relationship. He acts like he doesn't know what I'm talking about. Then he tells me it's always been my fault and that, since I was a child, I just couldn't accept things for how they were. I always had to keep questioning and making him say and do things that he didn't like. I tell him I have finally realised I am not responsible for the things he does, or for what comes out of his mouth. I tell him I'm writing a book and in the book I'm going to come clean about the fire. I wanted to give him a chance to come clean. I said to him, "You always told me your father used to say that, should you ever be found guilty of murder, that while he won't condone your actions, he would hold your hand as you go to the gallows because that is what the Lord Jesus Christ would expect of him." I wanted him to know that while I did not condone what he had done, that I would stand by him and love him unconditionally. For me, it was all about him admitting what he had done and allowing me to break my silence without feeling like I'd thrown him to the dogs.'

'Wait, why in the hell would your grandfather ever make a statement like that? I don't get —'

'Also not important. So I tell my father this and say I will stand by him. He went nuts, telling me I've always been trying to ruin his life. It was — it was the most painful experience. All I wanted was for him to accept our past and to love me. But his love was conditional upon my keeping my silence and although I think I had always known that, it hit me hard that day. He said he wouldn't hesitate to bring the full force of the law crashing down on me if I so much as fucking dared to tell the story in the book, especially as I had no proof. He said I must stop judging and living in the past and accept the Lord Jesus Christ and learn to forgive. And then he said, "If you're not prepared to go that route, which is the only route for salvation, then I'm more than prepared to accept that I don't have a daughter." I told him I wasn't and, well, he said, "You can go to fucking hell, Jacqueline."'

Even in remembering that conversation, I miss him. Not that part of him, but the better parts, the loving father that could've been. Dan puts an arm around my shoulder.

'What happened after the conversation?'

'That was the end of it. I've only seen him at funerals and weddings since. I've slowly been realising that the way I've been holding on to all the things that went wrong between us hasn't been helping me. I developed an unhealthy attachment to the fire, to his redemption. I wanted to change him and I wanted a different past, but I now want to be done with that. I threw away the manuscript that obsesses over these stories.'

'So, do you forgive him?'

'I don't know as, in my heart, forgiveness feels unnecessary. I do know that I love him and accept him.'

'How can you still love him?'

'He's my dad. I've come to accept that he's not what I wanted in a father and I'm not what he wanted in a daughter, but that's okay. All that matters to me now is that I've forgiven myself for wanting something different.'

———◆———

Dan and I hike back down the path and I watch him as he strides out in front of me, the sun on his back. I can't believe my luck in meeting him. Everything is comfortable with him and even conversations about topics that we are taught to avoid – religion and politics – are unmarked by tension. Over a late breakfast in bed, we start musing about it.

'Only believing in one limited thing, say Christianity or Islam, for instance, doesn't make sense to me. It's got to be bigger than that. God has got to be bigger than that,' says Dan.

'For me, my problem is that in the Christian tradition, God is supposed to be Love. But in the Christianity I experienced growing up, there was overwhelming fear and love was conditional. Surely love transcends everything, so I don't see how a God that is Love can be captured in a single religion or dogma.'

Strolling through Park City hand in hand, we talk about how the world feels out of control. The year has seen a horrifying amount of violence. Hundreds have died in bombings in Syria, Iraq, Yemen, Somalia and Nigeria. The Syrian army is massacring civilians. The Israeli army has run air strikes on the Gaza Strip. Rockets were fired from Gaza into Israel. In Mexico, people are being decapitated, hung from bridges, dismembered and dumped on highways as part of the drug war. 10,000 Peruvian gold miners clashed with police in Puerto Maldonado. Hundreds have died in South Sudan over cattle raids and ethnic clashes. And it's only May.

Our few days go by gently, despite all the talk of religion and suffering. Dan shares how he struggles living in a small town with a conservative community, even though he loves the people. I share how hard it was when I felt held back by my family's narrative and the pain I've felt from their rejection. We're lying on the bed in the hotel dressing gowns and he says,

'But you're here now and I'll never judge or reject you.'

'I know.'

'One day you will write a book about us and it will be the greatest love story the world has ever seen.'

I can't help but laugh.

'Dan, what we've got is remarkable, but I'm not quite sure it's on the level of Romeo and Juliet.'

'I love you.' He sits up and twists to face me properly. 'I love you, Jacqui. I love the way your eyes crunch up when you laugh. I love your shoulders. I love that your favourite indulgence is chocolate coated strawberries but you still don't see yourself as a sensual kind of woman. I love how much you love fast cars and height and thrills.

I love that you're brave, but more importantly that you're courageous. I love how silly you can be, like when we're in a grocery store and you don't mind just acting the fool. I love that when you laugh, and I quote you, that you can be heard four New York blocks away.'

'Dan —'

My heart is brimming and if he goes on, I'll get lost in him.

'Jacqui, we're meant for each other. You said that you had no plans to come to the bar that night. It's a sign, like two meteors colliding. Love, the universe, God or whatever you want to call it, wants you and I to be together. We were meant to meet in that bar that night. Since I met you, you've become my world. You're all I think about and hell, you're all I want to think about. When you look at me, I feel more myself than I've ever felt in my life. To love you is the simplest instruction God has ever given me. I fell in love with you within the first five minutes of meeting you. Jacqui, I know I will never stop loving you. It's the only thing that keeps me going.'

'I love you too and I could fall head over heels in love with you in a moment, but I can't right now. You're incredible, but I can't be the only thing that keeps you going.'

'Are you scared?'

'No.'

'Silly question,' he says, and smiles and touches my cheek.

'I'm afraid of not focusing on what I need. With you, I see what I've been struggling to see for years. I want a gentle and fair divorce. I want to figure out what I have left after it and see if I can afford to move my life to Canada or America. I need to find a way to earn money that doesn't crush my spirit and I know at first I won't earn from writing. I can't do all that and also commit to you.'

It sounds so clinical. I want to say, screw my hopes and dreams, I love you, let's elope, goddamn it! Dan can see this and smiles at me again and shifts closer. He lies down and curls himself around me.

'I can't live without you,' he murmurs into my hair.

'But Dan, you have to. This is the most I can give you right now.'

He is silent, crying into my hair. I've never cried nor laughed as much with anyone. It was a shock at first, allowing myself to experience the pain of my shame in front of another person.

'My love,' I say, and I'm whispering. 'You need someone else, not me, to help you through your divorce and you need someone to tell you objectively what to do about your feelings for me.'

'You're right,' he says, and he is so close to me I can see the tears in his eyelashes. 'My big brother Adam went through a divorce and it was real tough for him. I've always looked up to him. I'll talk to Adam, I promise. But no matter what he says, you've got to know two things: I love you and I will fight with everything in my power to be with you forever.'

'I know, Dan,' I say, and kiss him, even though all I really know is that Michael is waiting for me at home and that my future, wherever it may take me, is just about to start.

CHAPTER TWENTY-NINE

I grasped the meaning of the greatest secret that human poetry and human thought and belief have to impart: the salvation of man is through love and in love. – Viktor Frankl

I'M NOT IN LOVE THE way Dan wants me to be, although sometimes I wish I were, because Dan deserves no less than that, but he doesn't seem to believe it. On our last night in Park City, he plays me *Creep* by Radiohead and we dance naked to it after too much champagne.

'The lyrics of this song – that's what goes through my mind when you tell me you love me,' he says. 'Jacqui, you're so fucking special and I'm a weirdo. You're educated, you've travelled the world, you're everything that I wish I was and when you say that you love me, I don't understand how you could love me: it's incomprehensible.'

Dan has a chip on his shoulder about not having gone to college, even though he's been very successful in developing his construction company. I wish I could tell him that I'm in love with him, because he's craving to hear that from me, but all I can tell him is that I adore him and I love what we've found. It doesn't seem to help him understand his own worth. I turn off the song and turn to him, and say, 'Dan, college and degrees don't matter. Travelling, nice clothes, having a fancy job or a nice car don't define me. We all buy into creating a fake image about ourselves, thinking it's the most important part of us. But the truth is we're all weirdos! Doesn't love go beyond that?'

'I guess,' he sighs, and I wonder if he feels annoyed.

Maybe it sounds like I am lecturing him, and what do I know, anyway? When I'm still struggling to love myself and live in peace with my own past. But I press on.

'Surely love is a connection that transcends human beliefs. My love for you has nothing to do with what you have done in your life or what you have accomplished or achieved: it has to do with who you are and all that makes you tick inside. You're perfect and I know that's hard to hear, but you are.'

As I drive away from Park City, leaving Dan behind, it gnaws at me that I may never make him understand how I could love him with no expectations and no agenda. Dan and I leave one another with no plans to meet again and I'm glad. I still feel like one giant bruise over Michael. I want clarity and stability and peace for myself, not romantic gestures or promises that no one can keep. Michael and my wedding vows seemed so simple at the time and look what we have done to one another. We've turned our love into a breeding ground of abuse, leaving me angry and resentful. Changing that is my only interest. Michael is my priority.

At last I arrive in Jackson Hole, Wyoming, and – wow! Grand Teton National Park is dripping with bright yellow blooms, spikey red flowers and pink-purple stems of lupine. I wake early every morning, shake off my heartache over Michael like a wet dog and then head outside to hike.

Today I'm going to hike around Jenny Lake and the dark, before sunrise, is heavy, sweet and still cold. It's so quiet I can hear my heart pounding. Then the birds start to sing and a moose – at least I'm guessing it's a moose – bellows in the distance. The peaks of the mountains are still striped with snow, but everything sings of summer coming. Being back in the Rockies without the snow is like meeting an old friend after many years – one who has dyed her hair and found a new lover. Kind of like me. I might still have the same hair, but I think – I hope – people will find me changed when I go back home.

On my last evening I head to the Mangy Moose bar. It's a bustling shrine to the Wild West and the decor alone is almost enough to keep me distracted from missing Michael. Michael would have loved to see the giant stuffed moose that looms over me with eyes that have been replaced with red lights, while murals of cowboys, historical flags, skulls, bison horns, collections of spurs and ancient advertisements cover every inch of wall. One day when we travel together again… but there will be no one day for us. I order another drink and as I take my first sip, my phone buzzes in my pocket. It's Dan. He misses me, he loves me, he wishes we were together. He wants to spend the rest of his life with me. It's crazy, but I can't help but smile. He's an incorrigible flirt with an inability to listen. Didn't I say: no commitment? What is it about the men in my life that they can't seem to hear what I'm saying?

I head back to my hotel and sleep comes easily to my tired body. I wake the next morning, perplexed. I feel the need to make Dan understand that he is enough and so I get out my camera and decide to video myself talking to him. The tension of seeing myself in the screen rises up, but it's just an old reflex, one that Dan is helping me unlearn. What will I say to him? I hit record and start speaking.

'Okay, so, you need to know that before I make a video for you I get some – uh – I feel a little shy. I don't mind making videos if I'm not making it for anybody in particular, because, um, because I have no idea if I'm going to show them to anyone else. But, um, oddly enough, I am making this video just for you. Um, I'm about to leave Jackson and drive up to Yellowstone. I wanted to make a video for you today because Dan, you – you have given me so much hope,' I say, and the awkwardness starts to fade. 'You have given me so much love and belief in myself. It's a reflection of who you are and what you are and how amazing you are and how kind you are and how loving you are. What this basically means is that you are so worthy of the love that you are looking for, of the love that I give you right now. And whilst I'd like in no uncertain terms to give that to you forever, at this stage in my life, I only met you seven weeks ago today and – and as I said, my heart is overflowing with love for you and I want so much more, but you have to put yourself first. You have to allow yourself all of that love that you are worth and whoever gives that to you is going to be a very lucky person. I'm not even going to pretend for a second that I don't really, *really* hope that that person is me, but as I sit here now I don't know that. But you're worth it my love and for what it's worth, I completely love you. I love every bit that you've shown me,' I say, and I've started to laugh for some stupid reason, but Dan always makes me laugh. 'And whilst I'm sure that there's a lot about you that I don't know and I might never get to know, just know that what you have shown me is beyond beautiful, beyond amazing, beyond intoxicating, beyond two meteors colliding somewhere in Grand Lake. It is just – you're beautiful. You're handsome, you're strong, you're everything that a woman could want. And – and I love you. I think I will love you forever. And don't forget that.'

The next stop on my trip is Yellowstone and Dan phones as I arrive at the lodge to ask if I've arrived safely. He worries about me and it feels unbelievably good to know how much he cares.

'I'm so glad you're safe, sweetheart,' he says. 'And as you know, I spoke to my brother Adam today.'

'What did he say?'

'He took one look at me and said, "You've met someone, haven't you?" He said I look different. He met someone while he was getting divorced, too. He said I should finish one relationship before embarking on another.'

'You know I agree with him. That's what we've been talking about.'

'And now I agree, too. To think of starting a relationship wouldn't be right by you or by Jolene. But – Jacqui, you're incredible. The moment your divorce papers are signed some guy is going to come around and snap you up if I take too long –'

'Daniel! Please. I'm not just going to be sitting around like a helpless princess, waiting for anyone to snap me up. You need to have faith that what will be will be. I can't promise you that I'll wait for you and you can't promise me that once your divorce is finalised, you'll want to be with me.'

'I will, though. I'm going to make sure that our divorce is finalised as quickly as possible to be with you.'

'You shouldn't,' I say, and I realise that I'm pacing through my room. 'Endings are just as important as beginnings and you need to respect Jolene and your marriage. I want a good ending with Michael and you need to respect that, even if you don't want to do the same.'

'You've changed everything for me. How many times do I have to tell you I fell in love with you within the first five minutes?'

'You've changed my life too Dan, but telling me that won't change my mind. You don't care about all the things that I've done in the past or things that have happened to me. Apart from my therapist, you are one of only a few people that I've ever told this stuff and I love you for that. I love you for making me feel accepted for the first time in my life. But that's all I can say.'

'I can try to make peace with that. But you need to know I'll wait for you.'

'I'm going back to South Africa in less than three weeks and Dan, when I do, we have to go our separate ways.'

'Jacqui, please, no. Don't talk to me about you leaving. Don't even bring it up. I can't bear it.'

'When I get back home –'

'It's not your home, your home is in the mountains. Jacqui, your home is with me.'

'Dan, please! It is my home. I want to go back to my family and figure things out. No matter what, Michael is family and we need to do this last thing together.'

He sighs over the telephone and there's a moment of silence.

'Jacqui, I'm sorry. I'll respect your wishes. Just know that wherever you are, you can always call me,' he says, and he sounds cut up.

'It's worth the world to me, Dan,' I say, and then wish him goodnight.

———

In Yellowstone, Dan is good about giving me space. He leaves me be so that I can hear Old Faithful speak. As the first geyser in the national park to receive a name, she blows jets of water out of turquoise depths into rust-coloured pools as if only for me. I see the Grand Canyon of Yellowstone and remember my experience at the Grand Canyon in Nevada – and marvel at how different I feel now. I wouldn't go so far as to say I'm upbeat and sunny, but I've definitely cut down on the weeping and cursing myself. Yoga helps – and hiking too. I hike every day. On one hike I see a coyote; on another, a brown bear. I do easy loops that show me otters, osprey and a lake full of trout; lakeside trails that lead me to secret beaches where lily pads cover the water; steep and dirty routes that reveal the Grand Tetons far in the distance and leave my legs burning.

Although I've spent the balance of my trip in Jackson and Yellowstone, it feels like I'm rushing towards the end of things. Every day goes faster than a minute did at the start of my journey. If I could pick a dream from a menu and order it, I would order my time in Yellowstone again and again. After Yellowstone, I drive to Denver and then fly to Florida to spend time with my cousin, who is also going through a divorce. Over lunch we get to talking about future relationships and I tell him about Dan.

'Just have fun. It'll be good for you.'

I want to say that being with Dan doesn't feel like a fun spring fling, even though we've got no future. Being with him is intense and profound because it's a love that, as twin souls, has a dark side, a past life known to both of us. It scares me, but that's hardly something you say to your cousin over seafood pasta.

That night in my room I lie in bed and want to message Dan, but I shouldn't. And then my phone starts ringing and it's him. I shouldn't answer. I want to answer. I must not answer. I answer. He's teasing and sweet and somehow – God knows how – he persuades me to meet him in Branson for a weekend at the end of May. He says he has something special to share with me.

'Branson, 20 May. Meet me at the airport. I love you and I'm hanging up before you can say no!'

CHAPTER THIRTY

*If you talk to a man in a language he understands, that
goes to his head. If you talk to him in his language, that
goes to his heart. – Nelson Mandela*

WE MEET IN BRANSON LATE on a Sunday afternoon and there's
a weight hanging over both of us. We really won't see one
another again after this. I'm heading home and I'm clear I won't be
back for two years or more. We chat quietly while the sun shines
through the hotel window and then we communicate in silence, a
language we both understand. I love that face, the hair on his throat
that his razor has missed, the scars on his mouth, the lopsided nose.
Most of all I love staring into his eyes. Words are useless to describe
what is happening between us. I see all of him in his eyes and try to
memorise it before I let him go forever.

'Not forever,' he says, reading my thoughts. 'You need space, I
know that. You owe Michael your attention. You need to look after
yourself now. And I need to have faith in myself that I will be okay
and find this kind of happiness, with or without you.'

He is wretched, but I'm glad: I feel heard. And then I'm sobbing
in his arms.

'I'm just a phone call away. I will always be here for you, okay?'

We spend our days walking the streets of Branson, stopping to sip Mojitos while eating heaps of guacamole, followed by apple pie doused in cinnamon ice cream. We sit by the lakeside, playing cards until the sun sets and we finally return to our room. Dan gives me one look and he is tearing my clothes off, running his hands over my shoulders and back, pulling me down onto the bed. His touch shoots through me, his tongue at my ear, my neck, everywhere, there.

'Relax,' he says, but it is impossible to relax.

We find our way into one another. When we're spent, we lie on our sides facing one another and fall into one another's eyes. This love will haunt me. Years later, or so it feels, we are curled up, warm and damp from the shower and as innocent as vanilla in each other's arms.

'I said I've got something I want to share with you,' he says. 'A few years ago, I looked at my future and I said to myself I cannot die without having true, romantic love. So, I did something kind of silly. I drew a picture.'

'What did you draw?'

'A woman, surrounded by symbols. When I was finished I looked at her and prayed to God to bring her into my life. Imagine a white piece of paper,' he says and pretends to hold one in front of me. 'Look, here is her blonde hair and blue eyes and a smile that lights up my world. Behind her are mountains, because she loves to hike. There is a dog at her feet. Like me, she loves animals. In her hand is a book, because she's educated, and in the sky is a plane, because she's seen the world. My drawing wasn't very good,' he says teasingly.

He points to another corner of the imaginary picture. I sense he is now making things up.

'Down in this corner are toys, because she allows herself to be childlike and goofy when she wants. She doesn't take herself too seriously, see. And in the sky, where there should be a sun, there's a heart, because she loves more and deserves more love than anyone else.'

He looks down at me and tucks my hair behind my ear, the way he always does.

'Sweetheart, she's you. I asked God, the universe to send you into my life and he did.'

'Dan, come on.'

'Jacqui we're meant for one another. We're twin souls. Maybe I embellished a little, but I promise you that years ago I asked God to bring true love into my life. I drew a picture and the moment I saw you, I knew you were her.'

'This can't be real.'

'Jacqui, I've been waiting for you for years. You're a gift from God and neither of us can or should deny that. We have to be together.'

'You're the gift, Dan. I – really, I'm completely overwhelmed. You make me so indescribably happy. It's more than happiness. I can be myself. I don't know how to put it into words because I've never felt this safe before. Being with you is extraordinary because we can hold this space of no judgment and of nothing but love, but – but you're asking too much.'

'I'm not asking you to not go back to South Africa: I just want something that tells me you will come back. You said you would eventually come back.'

'I can't. I can't give you anything except this moment where I'm here with you now. Yes, I want to come back but I sense it will take a few years. You know that I think you are the most amazing person and that I love you and believe that you're worthy of the romantic love that you seek. But – Dan, I can't promise you anything.'

We're going in circles with this and it's torture. He covers his face in his hands and lets himself fall back onto the bed. I curl myself up against him and hold him. Where will he be, in a year's time? What will his life be like? I hope he'll be happy. God, I hope you take care of him.

Three short days later and it is our last day. We pack up our things in silence, returning the hotel room to its original state. It's the same suite we stayed in the first time in Branson and it seems strange that a hotel room should come to know this much love.

'Before we leave, I have something for you. Just some little things.'

He pauses and pulls an envelope out of his jacket pocket.

'I prayed for you for years. Many of my previous prayers weren't answered, but if only one prayer could be answered in my whole life, I'm glad that this was the one. It's the will of the universe that we stay together. Ask yourself, what is the chance of you walking into that bar at that exact moment? It's a sign. Even though we're going to be apart, nothing will allow me to let you go.'

'I –'

'Don't speak. I don't care how long I have to wait for you. I brought you these little things as a sign of my commitment to you. This first one is a fun one,' he says, holding up a tiny model of a classic sports car. 'It's a promise that one day we'll race cars on the track together.'

He presses the little car into my hand and one of its minuscule wheels bites into my palm as I grip it. He then turns and picks a golf tee out from his bag.

'I got you this because when we're eighty and living near the mountains, we're going to play golf and I fear I'm going to get beaten by you every time, the way you beat me at cards – and I'm going to love every minute. Know that every time I tee up a golf ball in the future, I'll think of you until we are together. I'll be thinking of you and missing you every minute of every day.'

He sits down on the bed and buries his head on my shoulder. It's warm and heavy and I hate that I have to go back home.

'Next,' he says, and wipes his eyes, smiling.

It's a piece of Perspex with a car engraved on it.

'It may just look like the outline of a Porsche 911, but it also has the year of my birth engraved on it. As you know, I love symbols, maybe a bit too much.'

'I do know,' I laugh.

'I held on to this Perspex picture for years as a symbol that I would rise above my simple upbringing. We never had spare money with five boys in the house to feed and I promised myself that one day I would rise above it and buy a Porsche 911 – and I did.'

'Wow, that is so sweet –'

'Jacqui, you're the woman I always dreamed of. For decades I saw the number 911 everywhere around me, in the strangest places. I knew it was a sign. This Perspex is meant as a reminder to you that I will work hard every day to rise above this confusing start that we've had and be the man for you, the one you can rely on to support and love you for the rest of your life. From now on, whenever you see the number 911, you will know that I am there with you.'

'Dan, I don't know what to say except that I adore you,' I say, but it's painful for him and he presses on.

'I'm not done. This is a money band.'

'What?'

'This simple paper money band is a reminder that I will always look after you. You can focus on your writing and I'll take care of you financially. Look I've written 'I LOVE YOU!' on the band so that you don't forget who gave this to you. It might not seem very romantic, but it's important that you know you have this support.'

'Dan, this is too much.'

'No, it is not too much. Jacqui, I am going to love you, like nobody loves you. Listen to that Keith Urban song, *Making Memories of Us,* every day that you touch these small gifts. I will be a man of my word. You deserve this kind of love and support. Now for the last thing. This is the most important. It's not a ring, but it suits us better. It's a friendship bracelet that my daughter made for me when she found out she had cancer. She told me to wear it and never take it off, because it was a sign of faith that she would heal. It is the thing that is closest to my heart and I'm giving it to you now as a sign of my trust and my intention to stay true to you. I've always told you that my daughter, my whole family, will just love you when they meet you. This bracelet is a sign that I want you to be a part of my family.'

'Oh God, Dan, I don't know what to say.'

'You need to find yourself first and I will support you through this.'

'I'm scared to step out of this room and it will all be over.'

'It will never be over, my love. I'm committed to you. Everything I have is yours, forever. You need to trust me. God brought you to me Jacqui.'

'I'm scared to see Michael again and yet I miss him. I'm scared of the divorce as most of my money is tied up in the businesses and they are not doing well at the moment.'

'From what I've heard about Michael, he sounds like a good man. If you just ask him to look inside himself and honour everything that the two of you have agreed on throughout your marriage, he will. But if he doesn't, remember that you have me and that I will never, never let you down. I don't care how long I have to wait, be it two years or more. I can think of nothing more that I'd like than to find you at the end of my rainbow. In the meantime, take as much care of yourself as you can. You hold onto those gifts I gave you and remember everything that we've done and felt – and know that someday I'm going to come looking for you.'

'Do you promise?'

I feel like a lost child and the question seeps out of me before I know what I'm saying.

'I promise. You go do your work and I'll do mine and then I'll come and find you. I love you with all my heart and I know now that you love me too. I'm finally able to believe that. I need you in my life, I want you in my life and when it's time, I'll be ready to fight for you.'

We kiss and it hurts. I get up to go to the bathroom and when I get back to the room, Dan is crumpled over the kitchen counter sobbing. I go to him and hold his face in my hands. Saying something like it will be okay is pointless.

'I guess it's my turn to cry now,' he says.

His plane leaves before mine and he must go or he'll miss it. We cling on to one another for as long as we can, neither of us speaking, and then he is gone.

Chapter Thirty-One

Nothing you confess could make me love you less. – Jesus

I'M ALWAYS AT MY MOST patriotic when arriving at Cape Town International Airport. It's not the greatest airport, but it'll always be my home airport. The queue for locals at passport control is short and sweet and the woman behind the counter beams at me.

'Welcome back,' she says.

'Thank you. It's good to be home.'

But that irrational happiness evaporates as soon as I see Michael standing in the arrivals hall, looking at anything except the incoming people. We see one another and he gives me a two-handed wave. God, it's awkward. He bumps his jaw against mine in an attempt at a kiss on the cheek and takes my bags. I hold out my arms to hug him and he hugs me back, stiffly first and then relaxes. Tears again. I let them flow.

'Hey, don't cry. Don't cry.'

And with those words, I'm back. I want to snap that it's normal to cry, but I say nothing. I'm back to that, too. I hurt, I force it down, I smile bravely and I say nothing. When we arrive back at the house, Michael makes me a cup of tea and we sit in the living room like two strangers.

'I've been doing a lot of reading while you were in America and I think I finally understand what you mean when you say that I never supported you, that I don't make you feel safe.'

'Really?'

He seems genuine. He has even made us an appointment with our old therapist, as agreed.

The next day we're seated side by side on a leather couch facing the therapist. He is leaning back in his chair with his hands crossed in his lap, in the exact same position as five years ago when Michael and I started therapy with him.

'I won't do this anymore,' I had said that day, years ago. 'It's not about the marriage anymore. Michael is unhappy and I have to deal with his unhappiness every day and it's killing me. But it's not just him, his whole family is like that. God, I miss your father Michael. His mom and sister, they drain the shit out of me and I can't deal with their constant judgments, negativity and unkindness. When we sit down at the dinner table with them, they both immediately start bitching. It's either guess what so-and-so did or it's moaning about the price of potatoes – and I'm up to my fucking neck with it. It's horrible, the things they say, even about each other behind each other's backs. Now Michael wakes up in a foul mood every morning and says he doesn't want to go to work, moaning that he should have studied medicine and become a doctor, or that he shouldn't have bought the business, and I have to spend an hour before we leave the house trying to pick his mood up so that we can work together. In front of everyone else he puts on this jovial, bouncy, fun-guy act and I cannot take it for one more day. He doesn't understand I didn't buy this business and I don't want to run it any longer.'

I walked out of that therapy session then and didn't go back. Michael glances at me and I wonder if he's remembering it, too. It's kind of funny, to think that Michael's family and their constant rejection of me was one of the issues that came up then. Little did I know then how much more fucked up things would become because now they don't even like him. I am not sure they like anyone.

But as I sit in the chair listening to Michael speak, I realise that I don't want to sit here and complain about his family's ways or why I sacrificed my dreams for him. And I definitely don't want to talk about our sex life. This conversation would be just like the one from years before. I stare at my wedding ring as he talks on and on about how we're going to fix our marriage.

'I'm leaving you Michael,' I cut in. 'And there's nothing that's going to stop me.'

I turn to our therapist.

'I have no clue what this means for me. We sat here with these same issues five years ago and nothing has changed except for the fact that now I don't trust a word he says. He has never honoured any of his commitments to me, both emotionally and financially. In fact I don't even trust myself. He has even destroyed the very successful business I handed back to him and I've turned into a really mean bitch every time he runs to me for advice,' I say, and I hear my voice breaking, 'I don't like me anymore and I'm leaving. I'm leaving this session and can you please explain to Michael that I'm leaving our marriage and I'm not coming back because I have to fix myself.'

I walk out of couples therapy again, but this time I allow myself to cry.

Later that day we are sitting at the dining room table staring at one another, our food only picked at.

'Jacqui, I know you feel like there's no winning here and that our marriage can't be saved. But —'

'Michael, please stop. I hate who I've become and I just want this to end. So I'm going to say this to you ten times and I don't want you to interrupt me or say a single word. Ten times. I love you but I can't be in this marriage and nothing you do or say is going to stop me. One. I love you but I can't be in this marriage and nothing you do or say is going to stop me. Two.'

With every count his body convulses. It's like he is taking bullets.

'I love you but I can't be in this marriage and nothing you do or say is going to stop me. Three.'

Four. He shudders. Five. Tears start rolling down his face. Six. His lips are pressed tight. Seven. He's gone grey and he drops his head in his hands. Eight. I'm broken inside. Nine. My hands, veiled in gun powder.

Ten. In finally acknowledging our pain, face-to-face, we are closer than we have been in years. We lie in bed, night after night, both of us in the foetal position with our backs touching. Even this pain I will miss once it passes. If it ever passes.

I have moved out of the house and am staying with my close friend, Jill, because Michael and I can't stay living together. It's too painful. I feel Michael needs to know about Dan and, although I shudder to think of it, Trevor. I arrange to meet with him and we sit around a dying fire in our living room – or whose living room is it, now?

'Mike, I need to tell you some stuff.'

'I think I know what you're talking about.'

'What do you mean?'

'Last week, when you asked me to fix something on your computer, I took a copy of your hard drive and I read all of the stuff on there. I don't know why I did it. I broke your trust again. I'm really sorry.'

'Michael, it's okay. I have recently broken trust with you as well. What's done is done, but I do need to tell you about it, okay?'

He looks at me blankly, as if unable to believe that I haven't flown into a screaming rage.

'Talk to me,' he says, and I do.

I open up to Michael and speak to him with more honesty than ever before about the way I feel about myself – and then I tell him about Dan. It flows out of me.

'It's a powerful connection, Michael. I know it hurts to hear it, but it's one of the most powerful things I've found in my life. But it is in America and it's staying in America. I've been completely clear with Dan about my need to spend time working on me and on the end of our marriage.'

'Working on the end of our marriage?'

'Hear me out. People spend so much time and energy on the beginning of a relationship, but at the end, they just up and leave. They cut it off and it hurts so much more that way. We need to end this together, the way we started it. If we don't do this lovingly, I don't know how we will ever recover from separating from one another. But there's something else I need to tell you about,' I say, and take a deep breath. 'It's about Trevor.'

'Trevor?' He looks puzzled. 'In an email I read, you mentioned him but I couldn't figure out the context. What did that mean?'

He looks innocently curious. My courage deserts me for a moment. What I'm going to tell him is going to hurt like hell.

'You and Trevor started out as work acquaintances, but I know that a few months before I left, you started to bond as friends, and that you've gotten closer since I went away. Our marriage got so fucked up that you were telling me I could have sex with other men. I know what I did was wrong and I am not trying to justify it but. But. Every time Trevor rocked up, you would say that I'm his girlfriend. Michael I was so angry at you for so much. One day I just gave up and had sex with him.'

He has gone white, his fists in balls, his face stricken.

'Oh God – no! How could you? How could you, Jacqui! *HOW COULD YOU DO THIS TO ME?*'

I thought his reaction would be different – sad, distressed, but this was rage.

Michael has always been the stingiest man I know, even though he has a large inheritance coming his way. He used to joke that he was T-Rex, with arms so short they couldn't reach into his pockets. I made the money and I paid the bills to the extent that Michael didn't even know *how* to pay bills. When I left for America in February, I paid all of our rates and utilities six months in advance because I knew he would never do it. His favourite complaint was, 'Why is everything so damn expensive?' I heard this old refrain again in the months leading up to my departure for America while Michael was on the phone to Trevor, planning for a mountain bike race and new tyres for Michael's bike.

'Come on Trevor,' Michael had wheedled. 'Tyres are so expensive. You're sponsored, so it won't cost you a cent. Give me those tyres after the race. I know you fancy my wife. How about if you give me those tyres, I'll give you access to her G spot?'

I went berserk on Michael that day. I was angrier with him than I'd ever been and now, somehow, he has managed to turn the whole thing back around on me.

'ARE YOU FUCKING SERIOUS? YOU HAD SEX WITH TREVOR? ARE YOU SERIOUS WITH ME RIGHT NOW OR IS THIS A SICK JOKE?'

He's flipped my bitch switch and I want to hurt him because it's all about him again. I don't want to take responsibility for what I did – all I want is for him to acknowledge the pain that drove me to Trevor.

'Yes, Michael, Trevor and I went to a hotel and had sex,' I say bitterly, 'But don't worry. After we had sex, I told him to send you his second-hand tyres, because I only did it for you. Fuck, I do everything for you. Did you ever get the tyres from him?'

Michael groans.

'Why Trevor? Jacqui, why Trevor?'

'Goddammit, Michael! You kept on and on telling me that I should have – not that I could but that I *should* have sex outside of our marriage. For years you told me that. *Years.* The day I left for America you told me again that it was okay. What happens in America stays in America – or have you forgotten that sweet goodbye? Who the fuck says this to their wife? Do you even love me?'

'But this wasn't America, Jacqui: this was Trevor!'

'So now you're trying to tell me that you wanted to have a choice in who I should have sex with? You're saying you wanted to choose the man? Do you now realise how fucked up our marriage is?'

I'm crying and when Michael looks up, I see he is crying too. He takes my hand in his and whispers something. I don't know what it is. Maybe it's 'I'm sorry'. That night we lie huddled together in pain. Within a few days, we decide to move into separate places permanently. I stay in our house and Michael moves in with a friend.

CHAPTER THIRTY-TWO

Let yourself be silently drawn by the strange pull of what
you really love. It will not lead you astray. – Rumi

WE HAVE NOBLE INTENTIONS OF nurturing the end of our marriage, but it's easier said than done, so Michael and I agree to see a mediator. We don't want to get two separate lawyers and use them like fighting dogs.

I just want something that's fair. The shareholders and directors know that I've got a lot of money owing to me from the company in loans and unpaid salary, but while I'm in no hurry to get my money, it's a little more complicated than that. Michael's late father had loaned Michael money to buy and develop the business. That loan was now in his mother's name and tied to Michael's inheritance. Poor trading conditions and high-risk business strategies in recent years had also seen Michael's mother and I stand surety for extra funding for the business. My father-in-law and I were close. He was a fair man who believed we were to respect our unpaid salaries as much as we were to respect his loan. However, everyone knew that the money owed to his father's late estate would be repaid before mine.

To discuss how we're going to sort it all out, Michael and I arrange to go to a coffee shop for one of many chats, but when

Michael starts talking, it's not what I expected.

'You always said how important writing was, but I never appreciated that. I've heard you on Skype to Amanda the last couple of weeks. When you talk about your writing, you have this sense of peace. I don't know exactly what you're working on, but you mustn't stop. You're free and childlike, like when we first met. I see how happy writing and being in America has made you. I want you to go back to America and I want you to continue to write. We wasted a decade on a stupid law suit and I don't want you to waste another second because you've sacrificed everything for us.'

'That's not all. Your savings, the money you made while consulting, the salaries that the business owes you – all of that is tied up in the business and I'm going to make sure that you get every cent. You know I can't pay you now and I'll never be able to give you back the time that you sacrificed for me, but I want you to trust me.' Michael promises to honour all of our agreements.

'Jacqui, *please* trust me and promise me that you'll write and get your health back. Please take care of yourself and no one else.'

I am overwhelmed with emotion, 'Michael I feel so loved and supported right now. I will trust you, I promise. I don't know how to thank you.'

Michael offers me a fair settlement with interest. He agrees to start paying it out in small monthly portions to start with and, when he either sells the business or inherits, he will settle the balance owed to me. I cash in all my last savings and put the money into the business to help him reduce the debt. Even though the business is struggling, I know Michael and his team will turn it back into the successful business it was when I left it three years ago. I had recently asked Alison, my childhood friend, to step in and help Michael as she had the right skills, plus she needed a job. It'll be years before Michael can settle the balance with me and until then the monthly portions won't be enough to support me without a job. But that's okay. I'll find something that will allow me to work part-time so that I can write.

The thought paralyses me with fear, but I tell Michael that I accept his offer. Getting the business back to good health and protecting the jobs we have created needs to be put ahead of my fears now. Despite all of this rationality, and all of my yoga, I'm consumed with fear over what will happen when I abandon everything I've grown to love – my husband, my pets, my home, my friends and my country. My life stretches empty before me, strewn with doubts.

———

Michael says this is finally his time to support me so he pays for my ticket to return to America, supported by his encouragement to get back there as soon as possible. Before I leave, I go to see my brother Steve and his wife, Olivia. They manage a Christian campsite and conference centre near Hermanus, where we went caravanning as children. Driving that road brings back waves of memories of all of us squeezed into the car with enough *padkos* (food for the road) to last for days, even though it was only an hour's drive from our home.

Steve hugs me hard when I arrive and I immediately cry. I never did like crying in front of any of my brothers, so I try to suck it up, but I can't. 'Come on Jacqui, get your shit together'. That voice in my head nags at me, but I ignore it. They take me to their cottage and we talk for hours. I tell them about the divorce and how I need to change. I tell them as much as I can, but only as much as I think they can handle.

My family does not believe in emotional abuse, so there are always limits to our conversations. Steve barely knows Michael. He barely knows me anymore and I cannot say out loud, to my brother, that I've become like Dad. My family does not talk about the past; shame is locked in a cupboard and these stories are cloaked by surrendering ourselves to Jesus Christ – and that is that. But at the same time, they believe they know me and rumour has it that they seem to believe that the divorce, shocking as it is, can only be my fault, and if I only looked to Jesus…

'I just don't believe in Jesus Christ the way that you do, but I know how important Jesus is to you,' I find myself saying. How on earth did we land up speaking about religion?

They keep pressing me and I get it. They believe that Jesus and the Christian faith are the *only* way to God. I just don't make sense to them. To be fair, they don't make sense to me. I don't seem to be able to articulate that I have only experienced God as undivided, all embracing, all loving. I share that I don't think God's word is as narrow-minded as a single religion, but they just don't see things the way I do and that's okay. I don't want to get into a religious debate and I sense they don't either.

When I leave, Olivia presses a letter into my hand that she must have disappeared to write and holds me for a moment. I wonder if they struggle as I have in my marriage. My brother and I can hold different truths about our explosive upbringing and neither one of us needs to be wrong. We each have our own truth. But I cannot help but feel that no matter the different stories each of us hold, it must hurt him too, because I've seen our father come out in him, too – in his bitter and harsh judgments of others. I drive away from them with a heavy heart.

Before I've gone far, I pull into a petrol station and while the attendant fills up my car, I open Olivia's letter and begin to read.

> Dear Jacqui,
>
> Thank you for coming out here to us and sharing a bit of where you're at. I feel there is so much beneath all of this that is unspoken and I would love to be able to get right through all the layers, lay my hands on the real issues and hurts and heal that pain.
>
> I know you have been through a lot over the years and you have also taken steps during your journey to deal with your issues and heartache. I have no idea why you have chosen to have different beliefs than us about Jesus, but as you said – you have faith in God.
>
> I believe in Father, Son and Spirit and I will pray

for you and your situation – especially that His Spirit will go with you as you make your decisions and that you will make the time and have the inclination to be aware and listen to His prompting.

You have beauty, brains and a big heart.

Let His light shine on the broken places.

With lots of love always,
Olivia

When I reach the end of the letter, I'm crying. I want to turn around and go to Olivia and tell her that at this point I feel like I'm nothing *but* broken places. The petrol attendant asks for my card, but my hands are shaking so much I can't slide it out of my wallet. At last I get the card out, pay and drive away. I drive up over Sir Lowry's Pass, a haunting place that has always had a hold over me. When we returned from Hermanus to the ashes of our home, this is the pass we drove. We were all silent in the car that day and today I am silent too.

I let the view sink into my eyes. When we moved to Ladysmith, it was this view of the Cape that I longed for. I pull my car over to the side of the road and turn into the parking lot at the top of the pass, cross my arms over the wheel and pray.

'I'm sorry I don't believe Jesus Christ is the only way. But I need you to give me a sign. I need you to give me a sign that we're all angels. That each and every one of us are your children and that none of your love is conditional or confined to one religion. Please just give me a sign. I'm tired of the pain and the conflict and the feeling that I need to justify something I know to be true. You've shown me this love in all my near-death experiences. But I need a sign that you are more powerful than just the Christian faith I was brought up in. I need to know that you exist everywhere and in everything when we can simply *be love*. I need a sign that you are beyond my human fears, that you are the truth. I just need a fucking sign.'

I look up from the wheel and see four conservation workers in green uniforms staring down the side of the mountain pass. They're probably watching a baboon. I dry my eyes, get out of the car and walk over to them.

They look forlorn and I ask them what they are looking at.

'Lady, we have to catch feral dogs who come up from the township below and fight with the baboons. There are two dogs here and they're both wild and dangerous. We caught the one early this morning and took him to the SPCA, but his brother, he won't come. The ones we can't catch, we're supposed to shoot. We've spent hours trying to catch him, but today we don't want to kill this one. We can't. We've been standing here for hours and we don't know what to do.'

Without thinking, I climb over the wall and down the side of the mountain. I lie down on my side between the bushes and let our fear – mine and the dog's – pass through me. I hear whimpering, but it's just my own voice. The white dog has scars on his muzzle and a tear in his ear and is hiding a little way down the hill. I don't look at him. I send him love and he slowly comes to sniff me. I look up and into his eyes and he blinks, but doesn't move away. I slowly raise my hand to stroke his head. One stroke, two strokes and he runs away. The whimpering continues. *Please help me,* it says. The dog comes again. Silently I tell him it's okay and we stare at one another over the distance. I smile at him, letting him know that beyond his fear, through love, as Spirits, we are one. Slowly, as if smiling back at me, he comes again. He lies down next to me and nudges me with his muzzle. I stroke his back, tell him he is safe and then heave him into my arms and carry him up the mountain side. He does not struggle. I gently place him into the back of the conservation workers' truck, close the flap and start to walk away. One of the workers runs to stop me. Standing in front of me, he stares in amazement into my eyes.

'How did you do that? These dogs are wild. Are you an angel?'

I place my hands on his shoulders and just as I had with the dog, I look deep into his Spirit and answer, 'No more than you are.'

Without thinking, we embrace. He smells like sweat and soil. I hold on to him until the hug comes to its sweet end. We look into each other's eyes and smile as a sense of knowing contains us. He leaves with the rest of the group, while I sit on the rock wall and look out over the bay.

'Thank you God. I know now without doubt that beyond our fears we are all connected with you through love. I see now that you are love and when we can *be love*, all fear is gone. That's the miracle. As Spirits we are all your children, brothers and sisters alike. Why can't the whole world see it?'

I thank Olivia on that rock for having the courage to ask the light to shine through my broken places, although I don't know exactly what this means. I know only that it means as I continue this journey, that I must explore *being love* to experience true purpose in life. I know that this is where I'm going to go. Somewhere towards love, whatever that may mean.

CHAPTER THIRTY-THREE

*Lovers don't finally meet somewhere. They're in each
other all along. – Rumi*

'Hello? Dan? Listen, I can't talk right now –'
'Well I'm telling you, you have to talk to me!'

'Dan, I'm standing in a line at security with my passport in my hand and I can't talk to you right now.'

I've packed my bags and am ready to board the plane, on my way to Amanda in Denver. I have told Dan that I am coming back. But I'm not planning on picking up where we left off.

'Jacqui, you're coming back to America and you can't even tell me when I'm going to see you again?'

'You're still married, Dan. You need to focus on that now. We've been through this. I have to go.'

'You will talk to me right now! You have to tell me when I can see you again, Jacqui. You can't be so selfish: you can't make this decision alone. It's not just about you. I want to see you!'

He is shouting and I'm sure that the people queuing with me can hear. I'm kind of delighted that Dan can express his anger. It's good to see Dan standing up for what he wants, but now is not the time.

'I'm about to go through security and I'm not going to answer my phone again.'

I end the call, allow my hand luggage to be scanned and then go and sit at my gate. As I watch the planes land and take off, my phone keeps vibrating. I ignore it in my hand bag, but after ten minutes I can't take it anymore. Dan has been sending a barrage of text messages and I know what they will say. Ever since I've told him I'm returning to America, he's been begging me to meet him in Snowmass, Colorado, a little town near Aspen. I don't know if I want to see him again. I have told him I think it is too soon for me.

I read the first text. 'I was a real jerk on the phone and I'm sorry. Sweetheart, I just can't take not knowing when I'll see you again.'

I turn my phone off, irritated, and then at last it's time for me to board. I fall asleep before the plane has even taken off. A weariness has settled into my bones, even though Michael tells me that I look more alive than I have done in years. Apparently it used not to bother him that I looked half-dead. Michael has signed the divorce papers, but has asked me not to sign them for 90 days. He thinks there is a possibility that we can still repair things and I don't have the strength to even think about it.

'You look exhausted,' Amanda says, when I arrive at her house in Denver.

'You look pissed,' I say. 'What's up?'

'These arrived for you,' she says, and points to a weird arrangement of exotic flowers on the hall table. 'From *him*.'

I pick up the card, open it and read it.

'Beautiful Exotics for a Beautiful Exotic. Love you lots, Dan'.

I burst out laughing at Dan. He's so deliberately ridiculous. Amanda raises her eyebrows at me.

'Come on, it's just a joke. We can talk about Dan another day. Let me just unpack first, okay?'

A few days later, and a few thousand phone calls with Dan later (for all my talk, I can't reject his calls), Amanda brings him up over a game of gin rummy one evening. She never can hold back for long and I love that about her. She puts her cards down and starts on me.

'Honestly, Jacqui, I don't know what you're doing with this guy. I'm grateful that he brought the game gin rummy into our lives but that's his only redeeming feature. He's married, for God's sake. Married. Michael has signed the divorce papers already, whereas Dan's wife doesn't even know about you. I just think the whole thing is dodgy.'

'You don't know Dan,' I say, with all the assurance of a lover.

'Listen, you need to cut yourself loose from that man entirely, because you're hurting over Michael. I heard you crying while you were unpacking. Crying. You feel me?'

'I'm not in the best of places, you're right.'

'You're in the worst shape I've ever seen you. And it makes sense – you've left behind your whole life and you haven't got anything to hang on to except your writing, which you love, but it's not exactly stable ground to stand on. You need to just focus on you.'

'That's what I've been telling Dan.'

'Then why does he send flowers to my house? And he phones you at all hours. I can hear you giggling on the phone. It's all so fucked up, Jacqui. Why can't you just let him go?'

'I'm sorry it's upset you, but he's persistent and I don't know how to let him go. We're helping each other deal with the difficulty of our respective divorces.'

'You have me,' she says fiercely.

'I know. There's one more thing I need to admit,' I say, scared that she'll take it back and say that I'll lose her if I don't listen to her.

'Don't tell me you're going to see him. You told me a hundred times that you refused to go to Snowmass.'

'I did, but I gave in today. Amanda my heart is broken over Michael and I need some laughs. When I am with Dan, it's incredibly fun. Plus, soon I will have a job and then when will I get a week off to go hiking in the mountains? I also know what he's going through.

He says all he wants is to hike and talk and spend time with me.'

'Oh my God, Jacqui, are you kidding me? I don't trust him.'

'You've never met him. He's the most genuine –'

'Bullshit. Bull. Shit. I don't support this for one second. I said go out and have fun, not go out and get tangled up with a depressing married man.'

'He's a good man, Amanda. He says it's completely over between him and Jolene. When his daughter is done with school, Jolene is going to move down to Florida. If you got to know him –'

'Got to know him? I don't want to know him. I don't want to know about this fucked-up relationship. If you and I are going to make it work living together here in Denver, it'll have to be as if he doesn't even exist. Okay?'

'Your house, your rules,' I say.

The words have been drilled into me and pop out without my noticing, because I'm already dreaming of the tranquillity of the Snowmass mountains and laughing again, with Dan.

———◆———

Dan and I are strolling around Aspen, after having spent our lunch at a fancy restaurant playing card games and laughing too loudly, obnoxiously happy to be together again.

'Let's get ice cream,' I suggest.

'Now?'

'Yes! Now! I haven't had a cone since I was a kid.'

'Ice cream it is then,' Dan says, turning to ask a stranger where we can find the best ice cream in Aspen.

It's a blue summer's day and then, as if the heavens heard us talking of ice cream, rain starts lashing down.

'Come on, let's get under that shelter,' Dan says.

'No, let's walk in the rain.'

It's splashing in my eyes and as I start to laugh, a drop lands in my mouth. We start to run as the heavens unleash a mighty downpour and the people under the shelter cheer us on to claps of thunder. I feel like a child again – simple, carefree, loving. The rain wets the tar and flattens, adapts itself to new circumstances, evaporates, rises again. I'm in love with this moment, with myself, with Dan. My hair is wet like in the movies when we finally get to the ice-cream shop. This has to be the start of forever. Every now and then a flash of warning – don't go too far, Jacqui, it's just a fun week – runs through my mind, but I block it out.

'Two mint choc-chip cones, please,' I say to the woman behind the counter.

I lick the ice cream, bite into it and get brain freeze.

'This is the best brain freeze I've ever had,' I say.

'It's worth it for the pain,' says Dan, licking his cone.

The next day we eat lunch at a champagne bar. Over another game of cards Dan leans back in his chair, his hands behind his head.

'You know, I'd kill for another one of those ice creams, but I'm way too lazy to go and get one. I want one here, in this chair, now.'

'Pity it's not on the menu,' I say. 'Just quickly going to the ladies. Back in a sec.'

I privately approach our waitress with fifty dollars in my hand.

'Could you do me a favour? Could you go down to Paradise Bakery and get me a cone of mint choc-chip ice cream and give it to the man sitting with me – yes, that one – and tell him that it comes with love? And you can keep the change.'

'But that'll cost less than three dollars and this is fifty, so –'

'Trust me he needs something this sweet and I have just won that fifty from him, as he lost the game again. Please, keep the change.'

There are hardly words to describe Dan's face when he gets his cone. He is beaming at me while tears stream down his face.

'No one has ever done anything this sweet for me in my life.'

He reaches out to grip my hand as tears begin to well up in his eyes. Dan says he doesn't know this kind of simple romantic sweetness. He does not know this kind of spontaneous love.

Dan kisses me then and he tastes like mint choc-chip.

Throughout our week in Snowmass, moments like this come up and I realise that Dan is in more pain than I know. Late one afternoon I walk up behind him on the patio of our hotel room, brush his shoulder and kiss him on the neck before sitting down on a deckchair beside him.

'Promise me that when we are together, when you walk into a room, you'll just touch me on the shoulder, just like that. If my brothers or people are there, just reach out and touch me. Just do that for me.'

I knew from that first night at the cabin in Columbine Lake when I stroked his back how much Dan craved touch.

'Jolene doesn't give me this kind of tenderness. I need this. I was just a kid when I met her and, well, I hadn't really had a girlfriend before her. I haven't been touched by anyone in what feels like decades. She doesn't look me in the eyes and we don't have any kind of sexual contact unless she's had too much to drink. I'm not even allowed to hold my own daughter's hand anymore because Jolene says it's inappropriate.'

'Of course I will Dan.'

'Do you mind that I always talk about Jolene?'

'I don't mind at all. Like me, you're still mourning the loss of that relationship and it's important. The fact that you're still working through things with her doesn't take anything away from me or make me feel like you care any less.'

His phone rings and he says he has to take it. I pick up a book and start reading.

'No, Dad, I'm fine. I said I'm fine. Yes, I'm alone. I told you guys already, I'm out here hiking for a few days. I just needed some time to – yes, I understand. Dad, I told you already! Fine. Fine. Okay, bye.'

'There's drama coming your way,' I say, flipping through the pages of the book. 'Does he suspect you're here with another woman?'

'It's not that. My father's just worried about work and stuff.'

The next morning, while we eat breakfast on the patio, his phone rings again.

'This time it's my mom,' he says irritably. 'I'm just taking this inside.'

He comes back to the patio again.

'You okay?'

'I don't know. My mother, who never worries about me, is suddenly all worried about me…'

He trails off but I feel he is seething underneath. It's like sitting next to an open fire. Five minutes later the phone rings again.

'Fuck. Jolene.'

'Take the call.'

'I don't want to take the call.'

'Dan, you should take the call. You need to speak to Jolene. I'll go inside.'

A little while later Dan comes inside, slamming the screen door behind him.

'Now she's also worried. She says my mom called her and told her that she should be.'

'That's nice. I guess.'

I have a one-second sense of warning before he loses it.

'Now they are fucking worried about me, when I'm out, when it's done, when it's finally all over, now suddenly people act like they care! Christ knows I love my mother, and I know she loves me but I was putting aside my tears for her every single day because I wanted to be strong for her and to protect her!'

He is breathing heavily.

'Jolene's whole fucking life, her whole fucking life has been about what Jolene wants. Non-fucking-stop! Where was anyone for me when our daughter had cancer? Nowhere. I was the one who had to be strong. I was the one who had to give and give and give until I broke – and even then no one saw. No one cared about me! I had to tell everyone she would be okay, they would be okay. Who held my tears?'

It goes on and on and I start to get worried. He's like a wild animal in pain.

'Dan, come here. Lie down.'

He can't stop shouting. He's been waiting years to say all this and now I'm the only one listening. I want to cry for him. He still has so far to go with Jolene and his parents and with himself before he will be able to be in a normal relationship with me or anyone.

'Dan, come to the bed and just lie here and let me rub your back.'

I take him by the hand and lead him to the bed, where he lies like a child and cries.

'You need to calm down. It's going to be okay.'

His phone is in his hand. He looks me in the eye and then hurls it with all his strength up into the air. It hits the corner of the wall and smashes.

'*FUUUUCK! FUCK THEM, I AM DONE!*'

Time goes by and I feel his breathing slow under my hands. I keep stroking his back and remember my mother smearing sunscreen onto my father's back. Each of our stories is unique, but we all bind ourselves to our stories of suffering in the same way, through our emotions. Did my mother hold my father like this in their bed and tell him that it would be okay, and that if he just let it all go and accepted that he was angry and forgave himself for that anger, that it would be okay? I don't know.

I think Dan has fallen asleep under my hands, but then he speaks.

'I love you.'

It is a test to see if I will stay, now that I've seen how far he still needs to go before he can be in a relationship with himself. I shift down in the bed next to him and curl him into me. I wish I could give him something better.

On our last day I bring up what I've been wanting to say.

'When you first suggested we meet here in Snowmass, I said no.'

'And then no again. And again. And again,' he says, and he starts to laugh.

'But you convinced me in the end. You said that we're meant to be together and that I can't see what you see. I want you to know that I do see that now. Dan, I'm in love with you. I've been fighting falling in love with you since the day we met, but I can't fight it anymore.'

'Thank God,' he says, and he pulls me to him.

'No, wait.'

'No?'

'Yes. I mean, no. Just – hold on a second. What I'm trying to say is that even though what we have is out of this world, I stand by what I've been saying all this time. I need to focus on my writing, finding a job and my relationship with myself.'

'What? I don't understand. You're back now –'

'I didn't come back for you!'

'Don't do this.'

'Dan, I have to. There's clearly a lot you need to deal with in your family and in your divorce. You need to take care of those relationships, especially with Jolene. It's July now and it will only be a few more months probably. Then you'll be free and then we might be able to start a relationship on a clean slate.'

'I can't do this Jacqui. I want to be with you.'

'It's not your decision. Out of the four of us, me and you and Michael and Jolene, only Michael has signed the divorce papers. That's twenty-five per cent,' I say, trying to make a joke out of it. 'That's a fail.'

'I'll do all I can to get it finalised sooner, but I can't go on not knowing when I'll see you again. It's not fair. Do you not believe that I'm getting divorced or something? Is that it?'

'I trust you. I don't doubt you're getting divorced, Dan. I have to ask this but have you ever bothered to tell Jolene or your mother that you need their support? Have you asked your family for help?'

He is silent.

'Look how Michael is finally being fair and even supporting me, the way that I supported him. Because we communicated. While you go through this divorce, I think you two should go to counselling.

Have you and Jolene considered therapy? Because I don't think you've processed the pain you've experienced in your life.'

'No, we haven't, because ours isn't a relationship, it's hell, Jacqui. There's – there's a part of me that's scared of her,' he says, and in that instant he looks it. 'I can't stand her like that, but I don't want to hurt her and I don't want to be with her.'

I can't help him. To get past whatever's been happening with Jolene, he has to do it alone. The way I did with my father, although I hope that their relationship isn't nearly as destructive.

I drop Dan back at Denver airport. He asks me to trust him, saying we will be together in time and then he reminds me to read a poem he scrawled on the back of hotel stationery the day before. Before he can walk away, I take the piece of paper out of my pocket and read.

> If I could dream a dream today –
> For my sweet Jacqui who came my way –
> Oh Heaven please put her here to stay –
> Eternal and loving for all of my days.

'It won't be long now, and then I'm coming to get you Jacqui and we will grow old together,' he says, and then he turns and leaves.

CHAPTER THIRTY-FOUR

Your pain is the breaking of the shell that encloses
your understanding. – Kahlil Gibran

IT'S A HOT AUGUST IN Denver, almost too hot to write. Almost, but not quite. Amanda and I are taking a break from work and sitting outside on the patio, looking onto the garden.

'Amanda, I want to thank you properly for letting me live here. It means more to me than I can express, because I've never had a safe place to go to. Usually when bad things happen, people move back home, but that's never been an option for me. My parents have never held that kind of a safe space open for me and neither could Michael's family. You're the only one. We disagree and have our fights but you never make me feel that if I don't do or act the way you want, that you'll stop loving me, even when we're too angry to talk to one another. Even though we've had times when we weren't talking, I always knew that if I really needed you, you'd be there. I always felt like my family and in-laws drew invisible lines and if I crossed one, they would cut me out forever. When they'd lay into me or make comments that hurt me, I used to think I was overly sensitive or reacting badly. But you, even when you're really speaking your mind, you never try to shame me or make me feel bad. I've been here for a month and a half and it feels more like home than any place has in years. I want to thank you for letting me become your family.'

'You are family, Jacqui. You're my son's godmother.'

'I feel like one of you. I feel so safe here and no one has ever made me feel that way, no one. I know they loved me, but it was different. Their love felt so conditional. A part of me still wishes that I could have gone home to my mother and just cried in her arms, but I couldn't and I've been mad about that. I've been so angry with her, but I think with time I'm slowly accepting her for everything.'

'For everything?'

'For all the little things that add up. For forgetting that I tried to kill myself twice and God knows what else she has cut out of her memory. For saying that my father was a wonderful father to me and always supported me. For blaming me for my divorce. For not standing up for herself and leaving him. I wanted her to be different for so long, but she was the mother I got and she was the mother I needed. She's so sweet and naïve in many ways and I love her for that. And today I'm happy. I think it's going to be okay. You've been like a mother to me, in ways that she couldn't be, and I thank you for that.'

Amanda smiles, gets up from where she's sitting and wraps me in a hug. When she lets go, I blink back tears but I'm smiling.

'What was it like growing up with her?'

'It's hard to put into words because each one of us in my family has a totally different story on what it was like. When we talk about old times, it's like we're trying to build a jigsaw with pieces from totally different puzzles. I sent her a text message not too long ago and said, "Mom, when we were growing up, did you have any idea of what we were going to be one day?" She said that she and my father had definite ideas of what my brothers would become. But then she said, "Well, actually, when it came to you, your father and I never thought about that. It felt like it just wasn't relevant."'

Amanda doesn't say anything for a moment.

'That is the saddest thing I've ever heard.'

'I've never felt seen by anyone except by my closest friends, you and Jill, and – and by Dan. While Michael loved me – no, loves me – it isn't the same. I feel so unseen by Michael. It is as if my needs weren't relevant. I always felt like I needed to protect him, give him a safe space. I love him, but somehow I, the real me, got lost in our marriage. And my parents just saw a female. I was meant to become a wife and mother by nineteen and the fact that I have failed and failed again at that appears to be an embarrassment for them.'

'Nineteen? Are you fucking kidding me?'

'Nope. That was their dream,' I say.

'If I'm honest, my parents had the same dream for me. It was, after all, the mid-'80s in South Africa. I guess it was like the '50s or '60s in America.'

Amanda and I look at one another and then at the same time we start to laugh. We laugh deep from inside our souls and there is something vulnerable about how we are both happy and sad, all at the same time, in this moment.

———◆———

Amanda comes into my room with a cloud over her head. I know why she's angry. She's just heard me on the phone to Dan.

'I thought you weren't seeing one another anymore. I just heard you on the phone with him, laughing like crazy. What's going on?'

'Dan has started therapy with Jolene. He's doing so much better. There's this lightness in his voice and I really think that it's helping him.'

'So what does that mean for you?'

'I don't actually know. Being in Snowmass with him was incredible. He knows I don't want a relationship now. We're keeping in touch, though.'

'Keeping in touch? Don't be so naïve. First he fell for you, but then couldn't believe that you could love him back. Then he realises that you *do* both love one another, even though you're not properly in love, but you're going back to South Africa. Then you come back to America and you both fall back into one another again, but you resist seeing him because you want to heal yourself. Then you go to Snowmass and fall seriously in love, but nonetheless decide not to see one another again because he needs to work through his shit. Now you've decided to *keep in touch*. Jacqui, what does he want? What do you want? You better figure this shit out, because all the while you're dealing with getting over your life with Michael. It's too much for any one person to handle without losing their mind. God, I feel like *I'm* losing my mind just watching it. You need to ask him for some *hard facts* before you see him again, Jacqui!'

Amanda is right, of course. Dan and I have been going back and forth for five months now, but it feels like a lifetime. We either need to accept responsibility for what we're doing or we need to separate completely. I sit down and write him an email that ends up looking like a cross between a business proposal and a personality quiz in a fashion magazine, in an attempt to find out what he wants. Dan and Jolene are unravelling their marriage gently in therapy, I know, but I want to know what that actually means.

In Dan's reply, he tells me in unequivocal terms that he and Jolene are getting divorced. The only change here is that it could be sooner. He says that if I have any doubts, I can call his father or his brother Adam, who will reassure me, and he sends me their phone numbers. It's touching that he's told them about me and that he's happy for me to reach out to them.

It's high summer now and he tells me that they will have finalised everything at latest by early spring and his daughter will be told long before then. He and Jolene have agreed on how to split everything and they will have received a mock asset separation from their attorney by the end of next month.

He writes that by the end of this month, August, he will be looking for a new place to move into by January. He says he will buy a lot and start to build a house for himself and, he says, for me too.

'As far as Jolene goes,' he writes, 'it's just like living with another human being: effective, helpful, but totally void of mutual affection. Trust me, there is no reason for you to be jealous.'

It's not that I'm jealous, it's that I abhor dishonesty. Jolene does not know about me, while Michael knows about Dan. Our contact, without Jolene knowing, is starting to feel sordid. So I decide that I'm going to tell Dan that we can speak when he has moved out in January.

Before I can phone Dan and tell him for the last time that I want space, he sends me an email.

> Jacqui my love,
>
> I get a feeling around you that I haven't felt in my life. I recall every single second of taking you to the restaurants on our dates and remember vividly as I stood in the shower getting ready for our first date that I actually got butterflies. You will never appreciate how much of an honor it is to walk with you into a room. I am simply in awe of you Jacqui. Our timing is bad as far as my situation goes but I believe true love doesn't discriminate that way. It happens, no matter what. My head and my heart tell me I have found someone who makes me who I want to be. I so desperately desire to be in a home where I can smile naturally, stare affectionately, kiss deeply, hold genuinely, sit near, cuddle with, cook for, laugh with, commiserate with, grow old with and just adore the person I love. I have been so sad for so long. Jacqui, I am just tired. And you wake me up in so many amazing ways. I'm awake now and I've been asleep for years. All I can ask from you is to try to give as much as you can to allow us to make this work. Many things logically tell you that we shouldn't do this. I am asking that you listen to your heart. Being and becoming us involves

risk, but please find a way to trust me in this process. I don't want you to be in another situation where you are fixing someone. I was looking for you for a long time, looking for someone who made me feel the things I had been wanting to feel, things I thought were not even remotely possible to feel until you came into a small bar in Grand Lake and turned my world upside down.

Love always,
Dan

It's hot in my room, but reading his email makes it swelter. I put my laptop aside, get up from the bed and go and stand at the window and stare into the garden.

I don't know what to say to him.

It's hard to read his words after I've decided to put silence between us until he has moved out. I can't just leave him in the dark, can I? I can't ignore him. And so I call him and tell him what I've been telling him over and over again: I adore him, but it's for the best. I tell him that I 'woke up' from the unhappy life I was living and realised I needed to change long before I met him and I don't want to be his catalyst. I don't know if he's far along enough in his process to start dating, even if true love doesn't discriminate. Of course, he tells me he is ready, but I don't think he is. I don't even think I am. I don't want to affect his and Jolene's process and I don't want him affecting mine and Michael's.

'I'm letting go of you, Dan.'

'Sweetheart, we may have to be separate for a while, but you will be on my mind constantly until I come searching for you to bring you to a place we can share. A home where you will be wanted.'

'Keep writing, Jacqui. Remember, our love story is the greatest ever told and it needs to be told.'

Dan loves telling me this, although I'm not sure where he got the idea that my book is about us. I don't correct him, because not even I know how the book will turn out. Maybe it is our love story. We say goodbye and I don't know how long it'll be before I hear his voice again.

—◆—

As it turns out, these were not our goodbyes. Dan messages and emails me as frequently as ever and it breaks my heart to ignore him.

'Jacqui,' he writes, 'I love you and you have returned that love tenfold in such a way that I never even dreamed possible. Baby doll, I feel blessed every second I get with you and I want to pursue that until we are together. Grand Lake will always be special to me, as it was where I met my soulmate, or twin soul in your words, the woman I will grow old with. I will be moving out on the 7th of January and I will love you more each day until I can call you. You are true love and I can't give up on us. Even if we go through pain, you are worth it. I am used to pain in the process of getting what I want and what I want is you.'

True love, a home, a twin soul is everything I wanted, but there is a limit. There is a limit as to how much pain one should go through to be together. Yes, Romeo and Juliet went through hell and back. But they also died in a double suicide. But God knows, I want a home, a room of my own. But I want to be the one who builds it. I want to be my own hero and as the days wear on, Dan becomes more or less a crazy man. The text messages continue to flow in.

'For God's sake, Jacqui, I can't just get cut out of your life. Please say something.'

'I didn't realise that you were going to excommunicate me when you said we should wait. I still love you to pieces even though you're ignoring me.'

'Please, baby, quit being mad at me.'

'You're crushing my heart with this silence.'

'I am praying for January, when things will be sorted out and we can be together.'

Why is he acting like we had a stormy break-up? We agreed on this.

'Why can't we start planning our future? I promise nothing bad will happen. All our communication will be completely safe, just talk to me.'

I ignore him for over a week, but this text message triggers me and so I respond.

'Dan,' I reply, 'I don't want safe communications. I want honesty'.

'I've spoken to Jolene and the way it's going now, we will be living separately before January, long before. Please quit being mad at me.'

'Dan, I'm not a child and I am not mad at you. I love you, but you have to grow up, back off and leave me out of decisions between you and your wife. I want no part of it.'

But even this does not stop him.

'You hate me. Is the mechanics of a relationship really that important to you? Would you rather be with an average guy who is emotionally available all day or a guy that you're actually in love with, who happens to still be married, meaning that you have to temporarily work hard to create the most amazing thing ever?'

I can scream.

'Stop badgering me to engage and respect my choice. In both cases, I would rather be single.'

'I just can't take not knowing about you. I'm stubborn, remember sweetie?'

'Dan, get used to it. You chose to live with Jolene while getting divorced and I respect that. But your choice affects people and I've made my own decisions about how best to cope with the fact that you are still living with your wife and that your daughter doesn't know about the divorce yet. Now goddamn it, show me some respect!'

'Yes, Ma'am!'

'Really? Sarcasm?'

I'm dealing with a spoilt child who cannot handle not having my attention. But still it hurts, as I do adore him.

'I'm sorry, Jacqui. There's just no life for me without you in it. I will work my fingers to the bone to be with you. I love you immensely and

I'm not giving up on seeing you again. Soon.'

I wish I could disconnect, separate and just move on. It hurts too much to hear him say he loves me.

'Dan, we can't be together under these circumstances. Who knows what the future may bring? This is the hardest thing I've ever done and I feel I must do it alone. You have my heart, but please let me go. I am literally begging you to stop contacting me.'

This seems to work because a couple of days go by before he replies.

'Jacqui, I understand the hardship I am causing you. I know I've been a jerk. It makes my heart bleed to even consider you moving away from me or taking time off. But I need to respect that peace that you deserve. You have seen the man I used to be and you have made me see who I want to become again. I love you so much and I can't wait to grow old with you. But I need you to know that Jolene and I've confirmed that we will be under separate roofs very soon. I want to see you again. This separation is pointless. We know we'll never be able to stay away from each other. Please, I am begging you to meet me in Detroit.'

I was cavalier telling Amanda that we would separate, but being without him and facing my divorce alone is hell. I'm miserable. Surely I've nothing to lose from exploring this relationship further. My only worry is that he will lose himself in me, but my resolve to stop that is breaking.

Two weeks later I'm sitting at the kitchen table, ideas for my book spread out around me, and Amanda is making coffee. She fills the kettle up and then slams it back down onto its stand harder than necessary. I've just told her that I'm going to see Dan.

'Mands, I will practically be driving through Detroit on my way back from New York. It would just be a quick stop over in Detroit. We would see one another and talk, face to face this time. It's not a commitment and it's not going to detract from the fact that my focus is me and Michael.'

'You keep saying that Michael's the focus, but you're here, he's in Cape Town. Fuck, Michael sent you here and now you've decided to visit Dan in Detroit?'

'Michael is my focus, Amanda. I'm going to speak to him and see how he feels about me seeing Dan again.'

'Where do you want things to go with Dan? What's your plan?'

'I honestly don't know. According to Dan, in a couple of months he and his wife will be in separate houses. He say he wants me to move to Detroit so that we can date, build a relationship, marry and have a holiday house in the mountains. He's a hopeless romantic!'

Amanda starts to laugh.

'Hey, what's funny?'

'Detroit? Honey, you're gonna fuckin' *die* in Detroit. Have you seen it? You came here to hike. It's flat as a pancake and *way* too conservative for you!'

She can't stop laughing, but soon, as always happens between us, I'm laughing too.

'Jacqui, you don't have to justify yourself to me. I want you to be happy. So go and test the waters, okay? Plus, if Detroit is even a vague option on the far distant horizon, you better look closely at it first.'

CHAPTER THIRTY-FIVE

Being deeply loved by someone gives you strength, while loving someone deeply gives you courage. – Lao Tzu

I'D TOLD AMANDA I'D TELL Michael about visiting Dan in Detroit and see how he feels, but I haven't yet. Missing Michael feels like a constant toothache and I wish I could hear his distracted, bubbly, all-over-the-place voice.

The next day I'm sitting in the kitchen with Amanda, her son Joshua and a friend of his, listening to Joshua tell us why he will never drink when he is older. The heat is on and it's fogging up the windows against the autumn chill. We're just getting to the heart of Joshua's story when my phone rings.

'Michael! Mike! I was wanting to call you last night. How are you? What have you been doing? Hang on, I'm in the kitchen with Amanda –'

'Jacqui.'

'Let me just get to the study, I've got better reception there. Hi, hi! Hi. Talk to me, what's been going on?'

'Jacqui, I need to tell you something important.'

'What. What is it?'

'You haven't signed the divorce papers, have you?'

'No, you told me to wait. What's up?'

'My family is putting pressure on me and there's nothing I can do.'

'What are you talking about?'

'Donald, Evelyn, Mom, they all agree that I can't go through with the divorce the way that it is.'

'Michael, it's not their decision. This is not their marriage or their divorce.'

'I can't do it Jacqui. I'm going to have to renege on the agreement as it is.'

'You what?'

He draws a rattling breath. I hear him struggling to speak.

'I'm so sorry. I know it's wrong, but I'll figure out a way to make sure you get all your money. My family won't let me go ahead. It's not my fault. You've got to believe me: they just won't let me.'

'You *bastard.* I'm sick and tired of you buckling to your family. I'm so glad that I'm getting a divorce from you because you've never been able to honour an agreement in your life and nothing is ever, ever your fault,' I say, and I'm losing it. Then I start screaming. '*I AM SO GLAD THAT I AM LEAVING YOU AND YOUR FAMILY, AS THEY ARE SO FUCKED UP OVER MONEY. YOU CAN HAVE IT ALL, YOU CAN FUCKING WELL HAVE EVERYTHING. JUST SEND ME A FUCKING PAPER WITH ZERO WRITTEN ON IT AND TAKE IT ALL. I AM DONE!*'

I hurl my phone onto the desk and storm out of the office, only to see Joshua and his friend standing in the kitchen with wide eyes. All the fight goes out of me.

'Boys, I'm so sorry you had to hear that.'

'It's okay,' Joshua says in a half-whisper.

Amanda is standing behind them holding a cup of tea in one hand, looking as if she might drop it at any second.

'Boys, could you give us a minute?' she says, and they leave.

'Amanda, that's it. That is the last time I will ever scream at Michael again. I'm telling you right now that I promise myself that I will never do that to Michael or to myself again.'

'What happened? Jacqui, what happened?'

'You heard. He's reneging on the divorce. He's fucking – I can't even talk about it.'

'You need to go back to South Africa and fix this.'

'I don't want to go back to South Africa again. How many times do I have to leave before it sticks?'

'Just one more time. You've got to go and fight for your money.'

'I don't care. I don't care about the money,' I say, breaking down, and Amanda wraps her arms around me. 'Amanda, I am done with Michael now. I just want out.'

◆

I agree to meet Dan in Detroit before returning to South Africa. The moment we see one another we can't stop laughing.

'I'm so sorry for being such a crazy person,' he says, hugging me.

'It's okay,' I say. 'You were a real asshole, though.'

'I know. But it's only because I love you.'

Dan guides me on a tour of Detroit, his home town, and the different areas we could live in, as well as discussing a business opportunity with me. In his mind, he will start the business and I'll run it part time while I write – and this will lead to me getting my Green Card. He's decided that this is the best route to me staying in America. Over lunch we hear one of his favourite songs, *God Gave Me You* by Blake Shelton. He always says it's our song.

'I want to marry you, Jacqui,' he says, over lunch. 'That much is clear. But even though I think I'm a pretty great catch, I know there's no ways in hell I'll manage to persuade you to fly to Vegas with me and tie the knot the moment I'm divorced.'

'You are damn right about that. Dan, you know I think it best if we first live separately, in the same town, and date properly first.'

'Yes, that is why this business is the best way for you to stay in America so I can date you. I'll get my lawyer to sort it all out.'

I'm sinking my teeth into my favourite, a Reuben sandwich.

'Dan, I'm not saying yes to anything. I'm just here to see you and to hear your plans.'

'I know, but since we're here, I might as well show you all my cards. I'm a positive guy, remember? If I believe one day you'll be here with me, it'll happen.'

On our final day, we're shamelessly happy. As I leave Detroit, he starts messaging me and I can't help but shed a tear – or two or three. This man has turned me into a complete waterworks.

'I can't wait to see you. In the meantime, here are a 104 reasons why I love you'.

My phone goes crazy as each message comes through one at a time.

'Eyes
Brains
Humour
Smile
Wisdom
Soul
Caring
Kindness
Loving
Taste
Cooking
Baths
Dancing
Voice
Gentle
Massages
Passion
Race car driver
Talent
Heart
Feelings

Little black dress
Candles
Strawberries
Moonlight
Charity
Sexiness
Laughter
Character
Nervousness
Cheeky
Naughty
Strategy
Card player
Mornings with you
You love the way I look
Your gaze
Your anger
Your confusion
Your love
Your reluctance to take anything away from me
The way you looked at me when you tried on the dress in
    Branson
Hiking
Outdoors
When you call me a ditch digger
When you call me handsome
When you call me Daniel - only my mother is allowed to do
    that
Our constant reminiscing
Drinking champagne in Aspen
Your hair up
Hair down
And messy after ...

And your strength
And your pain
And your breakthroughs
And your persistence
I love your hopes
And your desires
What you believe you deserve
I feel like I am home with you
Love the thought of being in front of a fireplace with you
Beating you at backgammon
Watching you wash yourself
Seeing you get ready for our dates
Walking into a room with you
The way you step out of a cab
The way you reach for me
The way you love my smell
How you look at me when I'm driving
Love, love, love the fact that we can lie in a pile in bed and
   just talk…'
The texts continue until he finally signs off saying,
'…That you make me whole
And love me back completely
In the end Jacqui
I simply love you.'

Dan has taken root in my heart so deeply that I fear I will never be able to pull him out of it. I'm not sure I want to. He knows that I'm not ready for a commitment and that anything might happen. But we both know that what we want is for January to bloody well hurry up and get here so that we can explore dating one another. I've never had anyone offer me so much in my life. I have always done all the giving. It's refreshing that he now accepts that all I can give him is the thought that I love him and will miss him, wherever my life takes me.

It's September now and autumn is settling over Denver as I

arrive back. Soon the snow will come back and in January, in the thick of winter, Dan will be in Detroit in his own house. I don't know if any of this will come to pass, but Dan is adamant that I will be with him and that once a month, on a Sunday, we will stay in bed all day, doing nothing but lie in a pile watching the snow fall. That's all he knows for sure.

———◆———

One night, shortly after returning from Detroit, I am just about to fall asleep after texting Dan goodnight, when my phone rings. Of course it does: I'm living my life over the telephone these days. It's Dan! I thought he was out at a dinner function.

'Hi Dan!'

'Who is this?'

It's a woman's voice. I go cold.

'This is Jacqui Burnett. Is this Jolene?'

'Who is this? Who are you? Who are you in Dan's life?'

My heart is in my throat. The last time Dan and I discussed telling Jolene was a while ago.

'Jolene, this is something Dan should tell you,' I hear myself saying from a distance.

She hangs up. I sit up in bed. Frozen. My mind blank.

The phone rings again. I answer it without thinking and Jolene's cold voice speaks again.

'I'm calling you on speakerphone with Dan. I just want you to confirm that you are from South Africa.'

'Yes.'

'You are a writer.'

'Yes.'

'And you and Dan have been spending time together.'

'Yes.'

The next twelve hours pass in a haze, cut through only by Amanda's looks, all of which say I told you so: you can't trust him.

The next day, my phone rings again. I don't even know where in the house I am or what I am doing. My entire being is in suspense as I pick up the phone.

'Jacqui, I'm so sorry about that.'

'Dan, it's so good to hear your voice. What happened? Why did Jolene call me?'

'She went through my phone and saw some of our messages. After she called you, I explained everything to her. You know I've been wanting to tell her about you and now it is done. It was a hard conversation, but now she wants to fly to Denver to meet you.'

'What?'

'Jolene wants to meet you because you will be part of our daughter's life.'

'But Dan, I'm not ready to meet her. I know that there's a chance that one day we could end up together, but I'm not ready to meet your wife or talk about being a part of your daughter's life.'

'I don't understand,' he says. 'It has to happen sometime. I told you Jolene will always be a part of my life.'

'I get that, but this is way too soon for me. We are not even in a relationship, so it's pointless. It's just way too much too soon.'

He sighs and I can picture him running one hand through his hair.

'I'm so sorry about that, sweetheart. You won't meet her for a while then, not until we've figured out where she's living and where we're living – and not until Kelly knows everything gently. Okay?'

'Okay. Okay,' I say, slowing my breathing.

I don't know why Jolene's phone call is upsetting me so. Everything just seems to hurt. I am in my bedroom, curled up on my bed and sobbing. I feel disorientated and, confusingly, I wish I could speak to Michael about it all, but we haven't spoken since I slammed the phone down on him.

Why can't anything be easy? I just lost Michael, I miss him and now I've hurt him by screaming at him again because I can't trust him. I think I want to be with Dan, but I can't get stuck between him and his wife. God, Jolene must also be hurting right now. She must feel this. We all feel it. Divorce is just one massive mess of pain.

There's a soft tap on the door and I look up to see Joshua standing in the doorway.

'Jacqui, I want you to know something.'

'What, Joshua?'

'If Dan hurts you like Michael has, I'll kill him,' he says bluntly.

I can't help but smile. Joshua is 14 and wants to protect me in a way I want my life partner to. I silently hope he'll never lose this ability to love.

'Don't worry Joshua, he won't. I promise you.'

———◆———

I find myself back at Denver International, with my bags and my crushing exhaustion. I have to go back and face Michael. Even Dan thinks I should go, but I don't want to. I wish I could fast-forward through the divorce to a place where Michael and I are friends and don't have to deal with any of this shit anymore. I check my new watch, a gift from Dan, and groan. I've still got two whole hours before I board. Dan had the watch delivered to Amanda's house. Attached to the package was a poem that Dan had written saying that he wants me to have this *instrument of time* as a moment-to-moment reminder of the *us* that will be together for the rest of time.

I get up from my seat and buy water from the nearest shop. I've lost a lot of weight since my world fell apart last year and I've only received compliments about it. I should advertise divorce as a miracle diet. So long as no one pays attention to the side effects, it'll sell like wildfire. A video file from Dan buzzes onto my phone's screen and I open it. The moment I see his face, everything in me softens. I put my earphones in and listen.

'Hey baby, it's me. I've just hung up with you and I miss you already. You've got a big day today and a lot of travelling to do and I just want to make sure you have me with you. I want you to know how important you've been to my life these past few months and how amazing I think you are – and how amazing I think we are together. I want you to go do your work and I will do mine – and my hope is that we will be together real soon. I promise I won't make you wait very long. I know that we are going to do great things together. I look forward to a time very soon when I can spend all of my time with you. Go there, do your work and be safe. Don't be lonely. Think of me often and we'll talk as much as we can and we'll be together and we will be fantastic. I will miss you but I will see you and I will talk to you. I just want you to know that I love you. Have a great trip.'

I watch him again and again and I wish that I could be with him. I watch him as I board the plane and as I land in Cape Town, knowing that it will give me strength to face what is to come. I finally have someone who will be there for me, no matter what.

CHAPTER THIRTY-SIX

Greed is not a financial issue. It's a heart issue. – Andy Stanley

To START FROM SCRATCH IS an evocative expression. *Scratch.* It is the skin ripping slowly under something sharp – a cat's claw, a rusty nail. It's a trapped animal trying to escape. It is picking at a sore you're not supposed to touch. It is striking out a name with a pen, over and over again. It is groping in a dark place for something that you can't quite find. I'm starting from scratch again. Over my few months in Cape Town I've been whittled down to nothing by the people I loved most.

First it was the Burnett family. After I arrived back in Cape Town in October, Michael came to see me. I remember how he first told me he would not honour our agreement. 'My mom just can't let me go through with the divorce the way that it is.' It was always about his mother and while I was sick and tired of dealing with her constant unkindness, I suspected something else was amiss. Michael told me his mother would drag me through court for five years if I signed the old agreement. Michael says her intention is apparently to break me emotionally and ensure that by the time she is finished I won't have a cent to my name – and the Lord Jesus Christ knows, she's got the money for it. I had called her in June to chat, because even though

275

she'd publicly noted her hate for me, we had shared a few wonderful moments over the years. I fondly remembered sitting with her at the bedside of my father-in-law the day he died. He lay in a coma and I was hugging her as she cried. In this tender moment she asked me why I continued to love her even though she had been a real bitch to me over the years. I told her love was a choice. I wanted to tell her again that despite the fact that I'm getting divorced from her son, I'd always love her. Ruth cut across me before I could form a coherent sentence.

'You know what Jacqui, I never liked you. I knew you'd never fit in, so I decided at the beginning not to let you in and I'm glad I never did – and I didn't care that my husband disagreed with me. He may have liked you, but I didn't.'

I should be used to humiliation and rejection by now, but somehow I'm not. As I listened to her criticism I remembered the first time she and I went out in public. She used to complain to her husband that she wanted a daughter-in-law she could take to tea parties and the like, someone pretty and gentle, maybe a school teacher, but definitely not a businesswoman and a divorcee who was four years older than her son. Michael's father and I were very close. He told me that he'd snapped and told her to make an effort with me – and so she invited me to a ladies' charity dinner. I took extra care with my appearance that night and tried to dress in a feminine way for her. On our way to the bar to get a drink, she introduced me to a friend, who was clearly drunk. The woman looked me up and down and said, 'Oh, is this the little bitch you're always telling me about, Ruth?' Her friend laughed in my face while Ruth forced an uncomfortable laugh and asked me to fetch our drinks.

I tried to block out her words over the telephone but it was impossible. It spiralled on and on.

'I don't know what Michael ever saw in you, but he does have a tendency to mess up. I told you to not leave the business because he'd ruin it and now my money is at risk and it's all your fault.'

I had tried standing up for myself with her over the years, even asking her to leave our home twice after she'd attacked me during a wine-fuelled rage. Afterwards, she sent me flowers and apologised, but it would only take a few months before she was back to her usual ways. She'd even threatened to disinherit Michael over petty things related to me. She used to mock him about how she had paid him to do well in school, but I wondered if now she wished she'd saved her pennies to pay him not to marry me. Am I really as bad as she thinks I am?

That phone call was a nightmare. She wouldn't stop.

'And I suspect you took money from the business to go on your trip to America and while I have no idea what's true and what's not with you, I do know that you left my son to go to America with no one to take care of him.'

On it went. After she hung up, I sat on the kitchen floor and let myself cry. After that, Michael tried to defend me, but his family refused to see any good in me. So began the process by which I had to prove to the family that I had not disrespected the business and that I had not yet drawn my outstanding salaries for most of the years I had worked for the business. Michael and I, Ruth's financial advisor and Donald, her son-in-law, sat in an endless meeting to hash it out. Donald was there representing the family and, despite the tension, he was respectful enough to say that I'd done a good job ensuring the business was managed with squeaky clean bookkeeping. He also thanked me for respecting Michael's father's loan for all those years. I was always obsessed with being honest in business to a fault, probably in reaction to my father's shadiness. But despite the clarity of everything, our meetings went around in circles.

I felt everything should be split down the middle.

'The business can't afford to pay out that outstanding money to you, Jacqui.'

'Michael, don't give me that. Your dad agreed when I entered the business that your and my unearned salaries must be treated with the same respect as his loan. You know I recorded it all. These outstanding debts were addressed at every single board meeting. Despite my chronic fatigue, I was working over a hundred hours a week between the business, my consulting and the court case, to protect your father's money and ours. Your dad was proud of me and he told me that he was grateful that I was there making the business a success and protecting his loan. But now suddenly that means nothing. You can honour your mother's loan, but my money now means nothing to any of you?'

'I'm happy to write off *my* unpaid salaries,' he says.

'Yours? Michael, please. Your unpaid salary amount is small because I made sure you earned your salary way before me. You can afford to write yours off as you will inherit a huge sum one day. I don't have that luxury. This is all I have. You get half of mine in the divorce anyway. Why do you want it all?'

'Listen, all we're trying to do here is protect the trust and protect Ruth's money,' says Donald.

'Oh, for god's sake Donald, there is more money in that trust than either of you will ever know what to do with and frankly this has nothing to do with either of you! All I want is my fair share, the share I worked for. The same as every other employee in the business. It's not fair for me to have to write off what's owing to me just to protect the trust fund, which doesn't even need protection! I'm not asking for my money now. I'm happy to wait in line behind the bank and Ruth as a creditor. I don't care if I have to wait ten years. If the business fails, it won't affect your and Evelyn's portion of the trust – it falls completely on Michael's shoulders and will be set off against his inheritance. I'm the most at risk to lose everything.'

'That's assuming that Michael is going to inherit,' Donald snapped.

I had heard this kind of threat before and so I reminded Donald of how Michael's father had trusted me by sharing how he set up the trusts to ensure Michael's mother could never do this. Michael's father had even asked me to take care of Ruth and Michael on his death bed, saying he didn't trust Donald and Evelyn.

'We're just trying to look out for our family.'

'Our *family?* Where were you for our family when Michael was struggling to take care of the business due to his breakdown, or when I collapsed from fatigue? Nowhere. I personally came to you and Evelyn and asked for your help and you said it's not your problem. Evelyn practically threw me out of your house, saying she doesn't care and wants nothing to do with it, and to top it off you called Michael a spineless fuck within a week of that. He was sick! So don't sit there and tell me that this is about family. Just be honest about the fact that this is about money, like it always is with you two.'

But despite my tough words, I can't fight them. I am broken and they don't care. I don't have the strength to fight anything. I don't know how to say no to Michael and so I give him what he asks for.

And then there was my family, who by their silence wore me down. Not a word from one of them, except a mention through Jill that they had decided that the real reason I was getting divorced was because I was a lesbian. I'd finally come out of the closet and damned myself to hell: this explained every single moment of strife in which I was involved throughout my life, from my father's abuse to my divorce from Michael. I guessed it all made sense to them now and there was no point in any of them reaching out to me, because I was beyond saving. I soothed my pain with my inner knowing that it was a sure sign that they didn't know me. Had I been lesbian, I would have been the chairperson of an LGBT organisation and the whole world would have known my sexual orientation.

———◆———

Dan has either Skyped or phoned me every day since we last saw one another. He is the one bright spot in my life, but I could really do without his wife. Twice since I've been in Cape Town, Jolene has called me. The first time, she tells me that she thinks she might want to save her marriage or at least have Dan and her live together until their daughter goes to college. She asks if I could respect that. I tell her that I do respect that and I understand more than she can know. But soon afterwards she calls me back and says that they are done and all she wants is time to end things properly with Dan and that I should give them space to do that. Again, I tell her I do, and remind her that it is Dan who has been reaching out to me every day, not vice versa. If he calls, I answer, it's as simple as that. Dan continues to call and support me every day.

Dan says: 'I told you before and I'll tell you again. None of it is worth it. You can't let people treat you this way. You've been to hell and back: just get it over with.'

'I don't know what to do. I want out, but I don't want to lose all my money. I worked hard for it, you know? There's got to be a better way than me giving everything up, but I don't see one.'

'I know at this point it looks like you're not going to get what you're owed, but how many times do I have to tell you that you don't have to worry about anything? That I'll look after you?'

'Dan, we don't know that.'

'We do. You've spoken to Jolene. She said to you, in her own words, that we're ending things. I have even told my father and my brothers about you. And if you move to Detroit at the end of January as I have asked you to, things will be great. It'll be a fresh start. You'll be running the new business part-time, sweetheart. All I want is for you to know that I'm here and I'll support you. I want you to clear your mind, forget about everything you've been through and write.'

'I don't know. Everything is just confusing at the moment. On the one hand it seems like I should fight for my money and stay here, get a job and just work hard at getting what I'm due. But on the other hand, I want to say screw it, I'm outta here as I don't want to fight against this greed. Dan, I am tired of fighting.'

I start to cry.

'Remember that giving up and letting go is different. You can't get into another court case: it'll kill you. We will work on recovering the money and for now all you need to do is turn your back on all that ugliness and focus on what's important to you. Jacqui, I will never let you down. I promised you that. And as soon as my divorce is processed, we're going to be together forever.'

'I know,' I say.

'You know? Are you saying that you agree with me, baby doll? Is this the yes that I've been praying for?'

It'd slipped out of my mouth before I knew what I was saying.

I start to laugh. I always do when he calls me baby doll as he knows I can't believe that I allow anyone to call me baby doll. He knows that a laugh is what I need right now.

'Once I've sorted everything out with Michael, let's just be together. I'm broken and for the first time I have to admit that I'm scared, but when I think about you, I feel strong and I should listen to that feeling.'

'I've never been happier to hear anyone say anything in my entire life. I don't think I've ever been as happy as I am at this moment.'

'I'm happy too,' I say. 'It feels weird to be this happy and this sad at the same time. Your constant support means the world to me.'

'It's going to be great. I hope you know that means you'll need to buy a white dress someday soon, baby doll.'

I laugh and it feels unfamiliar in my throat.

'Dan, you're ridiculous. Take it easy.'

Dan and I say goodbye, not knowing that I'm about to find out about another person who will whittle me down to nothing: Alison. When Alison destroyed her career, she came to me looking for work. I had just managed to extricate myself from the business two years before, but in the short time that I'd been gone, it had started making massive losses. Alison was smart and tough and had a good education. I offered her a place in the business as Michael and I were fighting all the time. I couldn't go to another board meeting where he hadn't prepared a single thing.

When I got back to Cape Town from Denver, Michael and I met with her and we all agreed that she should be rewarded to continue doing her good work. Alison asked for 26 per cent of the business. We agreed to each give her 13 per cent of our shares and I would give her full voting rights on my shares, so that they could continue to run the business without my input. All I now have left is my remaining shares. Michael and I meet with our lawyer. I believe we are here to sign the final agreement.

'We've got to change up the situation with Alison,' Michael says.

'Why? Why is that another hassle to deal with? We all agreed, so let's just leave it like that. I keep my shares, you keep yours, Alison keeps hers, but can vote on mine and continues doing a good job. What the hell is wrong with that, now?'

Michael says Alison wants all my shares, otherwise she won't stay. I'm dumbstruck. Rage starts rising up in me.

Michael continues saying he cannot run the business on his own and that she needs to stay to protect him and the employees.

'Are you seriously asking me to give up my shares to you in this divorce? On top of all the money owing to me and the fact that behind my back you two drew down on the house bond that is in my name while I was away, while she drew a salary and she expensed your drawings against my loan account? Are you fucking kidding me?'

The lawyer still hasn't spoken. Now would be a good time to mediate, but she says nothing.

'Jacqui, unless she gets her 45 per cent, she'll leave and I can't give her more of my shares without getting your shares –'

'*Michael!* Can't you see what's going to happen? She's fucking taking over my life again - my old job, my friends, she even fucked my ex-boyfriends in the past – now my shares! She doesn't even have the courage to have this conversation with me herself!'

'I promise I'll make it up to you! I'll draw up a separate agreement. Jacqui, my mother says she's going to break you. She wants to drag this out and Alison is now needed in the business. God, Jacqui, I'm so sor–'

'Don't even say it. Just don't.'

But of the people who reduced me to nothing, most of all, it was Michael. Oh, God knows that I love him in equal measure to my hatred and pity right now.

Michael and I had decided that we wanted to keep the family out of it and only have one lawyer between the two of us to mediate if necessary, but his look was telling me a different story.

'When did you get a lawyer?'

'I don't know what you're talking about.'

'Michael, when did you get a lawyer?'

'I don't know what you're talking about.'

'Michael, you know you can't lie to me. When did you get another lawyer?'

'Jacqui I am so sorry, my family made me do it. You know my mom will drag this out in court for five years.'

Michael continues to blame his actions on his mother, Donald and Evelyn. Once again, never taking responsibility.

'Give me the papers,' I say to the lawyer.

'What are you doing?'

'Give the papers to me.'

She passes them across the table. I take my pink pen and start drawing hard lines through the pages.

'Here,' I say, tossing them back across the desk. 'You can remove all of those pages. He can have it all.'

'Jacqui, you're emotional. Don't be silly,' she warns.

'No, I don't have the emotional or financial resources to fight these people. I guess I will just have to *trust* that he draws up that side agreement.'

'Jacqui, this isn't right. I know you are prepared to wait: please trust me, I will draw up a side agreement,' Michael says. 'I only need it this way for the family. They don't understand what you have sacrificed for me, for the business. I promise I'll pay you –'

'I can't believe you think it is okay to throw me under the bus for your family. You, your mother, Alison, your family. It's always about money. The greed makes me sick to my stomach.'

'No, don't say that. This agreement is for them: it's not how it should be between us. I'll make it good, Jacqui, I'll make it right: please, please trust me.'

He's desperate and I don't give a fuck.

'If me having next to nothing is what you need to appease them, you've got it. Now stop talking about it, honour your word for once and draw up that side agreement. But until then, you all disgust me.'

I am broken and incapable of looking after myself.

Three weeks later, on the day of our divorce, I'm sitting alone in the house, wondering where to from here. I will have to start from scratch. The market is in a slump and it might be months, years, before we find a buyer for the house. I've got a small amount of cash in my bank account that should get me through a few months and that's all. It's mid-December and it's sweltering in our house. Oh God, help me. What have I done? I sink to my knees on the kitchen floor and press my head onto the cool tiles. How many times have I not sunken to the floor in the last decade? The front door slams and I jump to my feet. Michael is striding through the house and then he sees me.

'HOW MUCH DO YOU HATE ME THAT YOU WILL GIVE ME EVERYTHING? TELL ME HOW MUCH DO YOU HATE ME?'

He has never raised his voice at me in this way, never really lost his temper at me.

'Well done for finally shouting at me. I'm proud of you,' I say.

'HOW MUCH DO YOU ACTUALLY HATE ME, JACQUI?'

'What you don't understand is that I've always loved you so much that I've given you everything,' I say, and my voice breaks. 'But Michael, I don't think I can ever reconcile how you have kicked me now, when I am already down and broken. Now give me that side agreement and get out of my life. I never want to see you again.'

CHAPTER THIRTY-SEVEN

The cure for pain is in the pain. – Rumi

I AM DEVASTATED AND THE only comfort I have is Dan. He distracts me from the pain by telling me what our future together will be and it helps.

'Jacqui, have you had a chance to send me pictures of faucets you like for our dream house?'

'I haven't had a chance. You haven't bought a lot yet, so this is all premature.'

'Can you at least send me photos of homes you like? My current home is just too much. Jolene says I should keep it as she wants to move to Florida, but I want something simple. In my head, I've designed the writing room that I'm gonna build for you. It's gonna have a beautiful view of the garden and the woods.'

Usually I love talking about our dream life, but today I'm exhausted.

'Dan, I'm pretty cut up right now. I can't think about taps and tiles. I'm only moving to Detroit once your divorce has *also* been finalised, so can we just take a step back?'

'I know, but that's going to be really soon, so I want to figure the new house out.'

'Dan,' I say, and then pause.

I've been wracking my brains as to where to go next, but moving to Detroit seems too soon for me right now.

'I'm going to base myself in Canada. In Toronto.'

'Toronto?'

'Yes, it will be easier for me to find a job in Canada and Dan, it's only a short flight away.'

'But I'm moving out of this house on the seventh of January, straight after New Year's. Can't you just come to Detroit at the end of January as we discussed?'

'God knows I want to. But I'm just so tired from these last few months in Cape Town and I don't want to have to rely on you or put any kind of pressure on our relationship. The idea that soon we will be an *us* is something I treasure and it's something we need to be careful with. I just want to date you like a normal person. I want to allow for us to just be silly and in love and not have to worry about things like visa permits and a legal commitment. I'll get to Toronto at the end of January and then we can just enjoy ourselves.'

'What about Detroit?' he says in a small voice.

'In time. You'll have time to choose where you want to live and to introduce the idea of me to Kelly. You can't just say, "Hey, yesterday Mom and I filed for a divorce and this is Jacqui, isn't she nice? I sure hope you think so because we live together now." That's just wacko.'

'You're right about that.'

'And it'll give you a chance to support Jolene as she adjusts in her own space. And then, after six months or so, if we feel it is right, I'll come to Detroit.'

'This is why I love you. You care about everyone. You even care about Jolene. Oh, sweetheart, I have to run — shit, I'm late for an appointment. I lose track of time when I talk to you. But send me those photos for our house anyway, okay? I love you, bye!'

<hr />

I wander around the empty house, lonely. I go to the study where I've printed out various job opportunities. If I could get a swanky job and build up a business that puts Michael and Alison to shame, would I be happy? Nope, that is not me. I don't want to just take some random job, but the pessimistic bitch inside me keeps telling me to settle and to soak up the misery of it all, because 'honey, this is all you gonna get'.

But even though all my possessions are half in suitcases, half in boxes for storage, half strewn all over the house (that's too many halves, I know) and I'm in limbo, I don't want to curse this uncertainty and then settle for the easy options. I want to arrive at a point where I can look at the wreckage and think positively about it, but right now the only positive thing in my life is Dan. I thank God, the universe and everything that is out there for Dan.

I sleep badly and the closer it gets to Christmas, the worse it seems to be getting. I wake up, thinking someone is calling my name and I get up and wander around dark rooms. It hurts to be without Michael. It hurts that I'll never have my own normal family. But still each morning the pain comes as a surprise and the day before Christmas Day is no different. Michael and I used to love the December holidays, as it meant trips to the beach and long lazy lunches. Michael and I wanted to build that happy, cheerful Coke-advert family and now it's gone.

It's okay, I tell myself. It's okay that you're missing that dream again. After all, it's Christmas time. Everyone gets lonely at Christmas time.

I don't get out of bed, because there are no presents to start stacking under the tree. There isn't even a Christmas tree, just some kind of pseudo-minimalist branch that I've tried to hang bits of paper on. I want to call Dan and tell him that if I can get through this day with a genuine smile on my face, then I know that everything else will fall into place, but Dan will be fast asleep by now. It must be around two in the morning for him. He and I haven't been speaking much over the weekend as we had a fight. I told him I wanted some space to consider what we are doing. He tried to console me by saying, 'Baby Doll, be patient. Jolene and I will be living under separate roofs in just three weeks – and five weeks from now I will see you in Toronto'. He has been spending the festive season with his entire family, but in true Dan style he has not given me the space I asked for and so I get a few classic Dan messages:

'I have to tell the world, shout it from the centre of the market place: I am totally, completely, unequivocally in love with this woman and her name is Jacqueline Burnett.'

'Please don't stop loving me.'

'I so totally love you. It's pathetic. Can't think of the rest of my life without you.'

Dan is always epically, ridiculously romantic and I love it. He doesn't mind being silly or over the top and he holds nothing back. Thinking of him cheers me up. I hop out of bed and go and make myself breakfast in the kitchen. I hear my phone ringing in the bedroom and bound back to it. Maybe Dan stayed up late singing carols or drinking egg-nog, or whatever Americans do at Christmas time, and is calling to wish me an early Merry Christmas. It is his number! It is!

'Dan! Merry Christmas for tomorrow, my love.'

'You *dare* to call him your love, *you home-wrecker!*'

'Jolene?'

'Yes Jolene, Dan's wife, remember me? Remember me, the one whose life you're trying to ruin?

'Jolene, what's going on? I don't understand –'

'Don't you play innocent with me, you fucking bitch! Don't act like you don't know what I'm talking about!'

She's drunk. Very drunk! I hear slamming in the background and Dan's voice pleading with her. She tells him to fuck off and her words are slurred.

'Jolene, I think you should just take a breath and remember that we've spoken before and you know that Dan and I are exploring our relationship and what that means –'

'Exploring your relationship? Fuck you! Don't you tell me to take a breath: all I want is for you to get the fuck out of our lives, you hear!'

'Jolene, please. I don't understand where this anger is coming from.'

'I've been with Dan forever and now he comes home and tells me he's never loved me and that he only loves you – and you say you don't understand where this anger is coming from! Please!!'

'Jolene, if what you need is more time to process this, then –'

'You think you've got some bright future with him? He's not an intelligent person like you: he didn't even go to college. Bet he never told you that; bet he never told you a lotta things! You think you know him? Well *you don't know nothing!*'

'Jolene, I do know all of this. I would like to speak to Dan. Put Dan on.'

'He is too fucking pathetic to speak to you right now. Tell me, Jacqui, what is a woman like you going to do in a dump like Detroit?'

'I can write from anywhere in the world. Now please can I talk to Dan.'

'That's a fucking joke. You in Detroit, ha! He's never gonna be able to keep up with a woman with your *intellect* who's travelled around the world, ha, no ways. He probably tells you some big shot story about how he's a big fish and wants more from his life. Dan ain't never gonna leave this town or this house or this marriage because *he is fucking weak,* ain't that right, Dan?'

I hear Dan's voice in the background again. Just grab the phone from her, grab the phone and end this now, Dan.

'I've made it clear to him tonight that I will destroy his life. He's not leaving me. I will tell everyone in town that you were a pathetic fling and the shame of it is going to drive that man into the ground. And if he ever tries to leave, I swear to God I will even destroy his reputation with his daughter. Think he'll be able to show his face around here again if he leaves me? No ways. Think my daughter will ever be able to even look at you? I will lie and tell her you tried to destroy our marriage if I have to and who do you think she will believe, her mother or you?'

Jolene starts laughing – a mad, hysterical laugh. She laughs the way I laughed when my father punched me.

'I don't know what's going on right now, Jolene. I think there's been a huge misunderstanding.'

'There is no misunderstanding. You think you and Dan are gonna live in a big ol' house, with a nice porch and a nice family? Think again because he's a piece of trash. You really wanna hang around with a man whose father takes his sons to strip clubs and gets them drunk. I bet he's telling you his Daddy is a nice man, but he's nothing but a liar, a liar!'

'Jolene you're drunk,' I hear myself saying. 'This is where I draw the line. I'm putting the phone down now. We can talk when you've sobered up. Goodbye.'

———◆———

I feel drugged, my senses dulled from pain. Dan hasn't contacted me and I don't know what to do. At first, I think it will be okay, that Jolene can't possibly mean what she's said about ruining Dan's relationship with his daughter and destroying his reputation. I think to myself: even if she did, it wouldn't make a difference. Dan is adamant that he will do anything so that we will grow old together. But as the hours pass, I doubt him.

I don't know where to turn, so I ask Michael to come and see me. Even though it's Christmas Eve, he comes straight over. I said I never wanted to see him again and yet here he is in the kitchen. Dan is breaking my heart as much as Michael did and yet Michael is still here. Still willing to talk. The conversation turns to Dan, but I'm too embarrassed, now that he is here, to tell him about Jolene's call.

'You changed when you started your relationship with Dan. You're different, somehow softer, more feminine,' he says, taking a seat at the table. 'Don't let that part of yourself go. I think you should pursue this thing with Dan and let him help you get into America.'

'Michael, I'm not sure I will hear from Dan again.'

'Why?'

'Things are complicated with his family. I'm going to Toronto soon and I have nothing. No one.'

'You've got me. Jacqui, I promise I'll give you what's fair and draw up that side agreement.'

There's dirt under my nails from all the packing. I should get my clothes out of the tumble dryer before they shrink. Toronto is going to be freezing and I can't be walking around in too-small clothes.

'Jacqui, are you listening? I said I promise you'll get your money.'

'I don't want to talk about it. I don't want to talk about the money, the divorce or Dan.'

'It's important, though. I want you to know that you'll get every cent.'

'Michael, please please stop talking about it and just put it in writing. I can't live on promises anymore.'

'You've got to trust me.'

'I honestly don't know who I can trust anymore. I'm broken in two and I'm leaving for Toronto in a month and I've no idea what's going to happen to me there and I'm scared.'

'I've never heard you say that before.'

'I've never been this scared before.'

'You always rise out of the ashes, Jacqui. I know you'll do it again.'

Michael leaves and I wait, hoping that Dan will contact me and explain things. But I have no faith in him.

Have faith and trust in me.

Those were the words I heard God speak or told myself I heard. I am just as much of a mess now as I was then at 16. What have I been doing with Dan? Are they all laughing at me in their Christmas jumpers? I cannot imagine that. Every hour that goes by, the chance for him to save things and for me to believe whatever he says grows smaller. Was I wrong about every single thing? I'm not going to be a fool for one second longer, so I email him.

Dan, I am in shock. Of late I've tried many times to end things between us as your 'stories' were just not consistent and I had no clue as to what was true, hence our fight again on Friday. I don't get your relationship with Jolene. I am completely shattered after that phone call, as clearly I was played. I feel used, taken advantage of and violated. I have never been this intimate with a man. I'm broken. Since I've been in South Africa, it has been pure hell as I haven't been able to trust anyone, but I decided to trust you as you asked me to. You said you were not like my dad or Michael and you begged me to believe that we would grow old together. I eventually chose to trust you as my love for you is so honest, so real. It's not what Jolene said, I can filter that, it's what you didn't say. In the new year I will organise with a friend of mine to collect the things you have of mine that I want. I guess the rest of the stuff you can toss out.

Hours go by and at last he replies. For a sick moment, I hope he'll deny all of my suspicions.

Jacqui,

I can fully understand why you would feel a sense of shock.

I have been thinking on what we have gotten ourselves into and this has been unbearably difficult. We just weren't very good at keeping our promises to let each other back into each other's lives. On some level I am almost relieved at how things now stand. Our ongoing contact has been making it difficult for me to get my life in focus. We have a special connection that is very powerful. I can assure you that you were not being played as you concluded from Jolene's phone call. I told Jolene that if I was guilty of something, maybe a lot of things, it was the stupidity of trying to figure out what I wanted for the rest of my life and trying to keep any love that I had alive. The funny thing is that you called me out on this on many occasions and maybe I just didn't want to accept it. It was selfish to think of only myself, even though it made me feel alive for the first time. The really painful part of this is that I am still trying to find answers. I didn't play you, even though you do have the right to understandably draw that conclusion. I have never been in any situation even close to this and I made horrible choices along the way, hurting people in the process, and for that I am truly sorry. That phone call was a nightmare, one that I couldn't even begin to explain, much less remember. Having to have that conversation, or any conversation for that matter, while I was on my way to being out-cold, was pathetic, but my ignorance caused it so I must deal with it. You can filter some of what was said and it would be wise to do so, but I didn't stand up for what I believed in and I am broken for it as well. You deserve better and I am so sorry that I put you in this position. All I can say is that love is a powerful thing that carries powerful consequences. I expect no one to feel sorry for me – but I am shattered. I wish you the happiness that you deserve. I know that God will help direct you in that pursuit.

Love always,
Dan

Night terrors. Cold sweats. Dry sobs that shake through me. Don't forsake me now, please God. Show me love, when all I feel is dread and fury. I'm stunned with sadness. All of the promises, his daughter's friendship bracelet, all of it was just words to him. I can hear my

Granny's voice in the back of my head.

'Remember, Jacqueline, a woman's worth is never defined by a man. What do I always say? She just needs two things in life: her dignity and a pair of fur-lined gloves'.

I miss my grandmother now more than ever. I need someone to hold me and tell me that it will be okay. Dan kept telling me to trust him and that he wasn't Michael or my father. *He* would never go back on his word; that I could always trust him.

Were there signs, like a sickness slowly spreading, whose symptoms I ignored? Yes. No. I don't know. Jolene called me. Jolene knew who I was: she wanted to meet me in Denver. Am I going crazy? I shrivel slowly into myself.

I'm broken. I have little but my pain, but even that is better than nothing. I can accept that. I refused to allow myself to write my story in a victim's voice many months ago and I won't tell this story as a victim. There must be some hard kernel of truth or value in my time with Dan, although I don't see it now. I decided to leave Michael and give him everything and now Dan has decided to leave me. My heart breaks for him, for Jolene, for all of us – how many more times can it break? How many more times, God? But this pain is surely a sign that I can love. I use this love as I write to Jolene asking her to love Dan with all his imperfections, signing off by saying that I will keep them both in my prayers.

Maybe she will read my letter as fake rubbish. I don't care, but Jolene is no different to me or my father in her moment of unkindness. I believe she deserves the love I feel I am not getting from my family, Michael's family or Alison. I just hope that she'll come back to it in a little while and read it with the intention of love with which it was sent.

———◆———

A fortnight later, I wake up from a nightmare and find that there's a bizarre two-voiced voicemail on my phone.

'Jacqui it's Dan here and I'm phoning to say – what must I say again?'

'*Tell her Dan! Tell her you don't love her!*' I hear Jolene say angrily.

'– that what?'

'Tell her you don't love her!'

Jacqui, I don't love you –'

'*Tell her you never did! Tell her, tell her!'*

'Jacqui, I never loved you, and – and –'

'*That you NEVER want to speak to her again. Say it. SAY IT!'*

'And I never want to talk to you again.'

My hands are still shaking when Dan phones me eight hours later.

'Jacqui, it's me.'

'Okay,' I say.

'I'm calling to say I'm sorry about that voicemail from earlier.'

Hearing his voice has made me numb.

'Are you okay, Dan?'

'No. I'm just so, so broken. I hate that I've hurt Jolene. I told her I never loved her the way I love you. But I can't carry on like this: it has gone on for too long. I deserve better. I want more.'

'Where are you, Dan?'

'I'm sitting on the floor of the garage.'

'Why did you say those things to me on the phone?'

'Fuck, Jacqui, she beat me and it's not the first time she's gone that crazy. God, you must think I'm spineless. But I was asleep and she came out of nowhere. She had something hard in her hand and she just started beating me and punching me with it. Then I realised that it was my phone. She was smashing my phone into me. She went insane. I've got bruises all over me. She attacked me.'

'Oh, God. Dan, she must be in so much pain to do that.'

'Jacqui, I love you. You know none of what I said on that voice message is true. I asked God to bring you into my life and no matter what went wrong afterwards, just... just know that I love you.'

I'm silent. What's the use of empty words?

'I just need some time. I can't live with her. I don't want to. I can't live with her telling me what to do or who to love. Let's just figure things out when you get to Toronto. I need to try. We both need to try. I know my letter said it's over, but it isn't.'

I don't know exactly what I replied, but I didn't say what I should've said. We say our goodbyes.

Now what?

All I can do is stick to my plan, move to Toronto and try my damn hardest to improve my writing so that maybe, someday, someone will get some good out of all of this. I need to let go of my fears, settle into this pain and let it be, the way I do with yoga.

'This is just yoga, Jacqui. This is an uncomfortable pose. Find comfort in the discomfort,' I tell myself.

'Life is not fucking yoga! I've lost Michael. I've lost Dan. I've just lost everything.'

'Find comfort in the discomfort. Try to stay present in this moment of pain and accept it.'

'Oh, fuck off trying to be so zen. It'll never get you anywhere.'

But it does – it gets me all the way to Toronto, even though, as I pack my entire life into a small suitcase and board the plane, I feel like I'm stepping off a skyscraper into thin air, my heart riddled with holes.

PART THREE

RISING PHOENIX

For My Self

i wanted God to be external
as i wanted someone to name

i wanted God to be external
as i wanted someone to explain

i wanted God to be external
as i wanted someone to blame

CHAPTER THIRTY-EIGHT

*No one saves us but ourselves. No one can and no one
may. We ourselves must walk the path. – Buddha*

I'VE BOOKED TO SPEND THREE months in a tiny room in Deer Park,
Toronto, while I figure things out. The place is small and cosy, if
not exactly what I've been used to, and I see that someone has put an
exquisite bouquet of 24 red roses on the dresser. It's got a card
attached and I open it. Instead of being a welcome note from the
owners of the B&B as I thought, it is from Dan.

'Welcome to your new world. Always and forever, Dan.'

I haven't heard from him, I don't know where he is. He told me
we would sort it all out in Toronto – whatever that even means –
and yet I haven't heard from him in over a week. I am too hurt and
too exhausted to give it much thought. I need to focus on finding
work.

Then Dan starts emailing. He says I hate him, I'm killing him and
I want to say, 'For God's sake, stop being a child!' He says he knows
that he is being impossible but that he won't stop pursuing me. He
says we need to see one another in Branson or Detroit or Grand Lake,
anywhere. I refuse. He says I must trust him and that he cannot
comprehend living without me. He will have to learn to imagine it.

If only I had listened to Amanda and to all the signs. I will never ignore another sign, I tell myself, as I throw out the roses he sent. It is as if he knows and so he sends me 24 pink roses. I throw them out as well.

Some days, while it is still freezing outside and the street is powdered with snow, I walk through the city, watching it wake up slowly. When it is too cold to walk, I take a streetcar or a bus and sometimes ride the same loop again and again. I've been hunting for jobs in Toronto and researching how to get settled as a legal resident – and as the days go by, I drift further from my writing. It's money, bloody money holding me back. In a matter of months my funds will get used up and I will slide into debt. I try to cheer myself up by remembering the good bits in my life – the friends; the snow and the sunshine; new places; jokes that still make me laugh years later; being born into a big family; summer holidays with cousins – but still, I can't help wondering about the point of it all. What's my purpose as a human being, if no matter the good I've done, I still hurt myself and others? Why does it have to be like that?

Most days I shrivel up alone in my room, unable to get up off the floor and feed myself or wash my hair. When I was little, my father would wrap me in a towel after my bath and comb my hair. I miss that feeling of being loved and protected.

Every now and then, Brandon and Owen, the owners of the bed and breakfast, open my door and check on me. These two men do not even know me, or why I'm so annihilated by grief, but they support me in a way I didn't know was possible from two strangers. I lie in my room and it is as if there is a blowtorch being held to my skin. They are the ones who dust away the dead skin and let me grieve over all the people and things I love that I've left behind.

I can't handle Dan's messages. He's pleading to see me and I tell him that if he's so desperate, he can meet me to talk in Toronto. He doesn't come, but keeps on at me, so one day I call him. Hearing the voice that has made me laugh, cry and feel more acceptance than I have ever felt in my life is torture.

'Jacqui, I know things have been hell, but I need to see you. There's so much I still want to say to you.'

'Dan. You know how I feel about you. But I can't do this. I can't be with you. I can't be a part of lying to Jolene. I just can't.'

'You need to listen to me. Last week I looked at myself in the mirror in Chicago. I looked into my soul and asked God to give me the strength to follow my heart. Please, just come and spend time with me in Branson so that I can tell you about it.'

'I don't think that's a good idea.'

'We're gonna grow old together and you might not believe that right now. But you need to trust me.'

I hesitate. I don't trust him, but there *are* things I'd like to say to him face to face.

'Please, I'm begging you.'

'On one condition. I'll come to Branson if Jolene knows about it.'

'Jolene will be fine.'

I don't trust this. When it comes to Jolene, Dan is blind.

'Perfect, then I'll call her and check.'

I immediately try to call Jolene, but she doesn't answer. I do want to see Dan. I want to know what was true and what wasn't. I want to sit face to face and get answers. But Jolene refuses my calls. The only solution I can think of is to call his father. He said I could call his father or his brother Adam if I ever doubted him. I was touched at the time. 'My dad will look out for you: he understands how I feel about you', he had said.

'Hello?'

'Is that Mr Biscotti?'

'Yes, who is this?'

'Hi, this is Jacqui Burnett.'

'Who?'

'This is Jacqui Burnett. I am – a friend of your son Dan's.'

'I'm sorry. I don't know who you are.'

I'm sorry. I don't know who you are. I am reeling.

'Fine. Will you do me a favour?'

'What?'

'Tell your son Dan to leave me the hell alone.'

It is done. The final lie. I can't handle anymore. He can tell me I wasn't played all he wants, tell me it's a misunderstanding and that he loves me all he wants. 'Love is a powerful thing that carries powerful consequences'. That's what he wrote to me. And now, as I lie here on the floor with tears running down my temples into my unwashed hair, I am dealing with the consequences of that love while he – what? He wants me to meet with him again in Branson? He'd said in messages again and again that he would get on a plane right then and fly to me if he could, but he couldn't because 'things are a bit tricky with Jolene.'

'I fucking know things are tricky, you lying halfwit!'

Did I shout that out loud? Shit, I think I did.

'Are you okay?'

It's Owen at the door, holding a mug and looking concerned.

'Sorry about that. I didn't realise I was speaking out loud.'

'Don't you worry about a thing. Here, have some coffee. Brandon and I are going out for dinner: why don't you join us?'

I look up at him from the floor. He seems tremendously tall and friendly from down here. A true Canadian.

'I think I will. I'll join you in a moment.'

'I don't know what hell you've been going through, but I know that you'll get through this. You are perfect just as you are.'

He helps me to my feet and hugs me and it sends love right through me. I start to cry, but he does not pull away.

'There's nothing to be afraid of,' he says, and even though he is right, in this moment I don't believe him.

CHAPTER THIRTY-NINE

---

*If you bring forth what is within you, what you bring forth will
save you. If you do not bring forth what is within you, what
you do not bring forth will destroy you. – Jesus*

SLOWLY, DAY BY DAY, I put myself back together again. I keep
looking for signs that will allow me to accept all of me, even the
humiliated parts. Even the parts that are still in love with Michael
and Dan.

One day, on a walk around Toronto, I find myself staring at a
Presbyterian church across the street. Snow is packed unevenly on its
roof and despite the below-freezing cold, the door is open and a light
shines from inside. People are entering in twos and threes for the
morning service. I haven't set foot in a church outside of weddings
and funerals since I was 16, but something pulls me towards the door.
I cross the street, step inside, someone hands me a programme and I
take a seat in a pew. I look around and notice the woman who greeted
me and gave me a programme at the front door walking towards me.
Her smile embraces me. She must be an angel at the very least – and
as I look at her again, regal and silver-haired, I swear I can see her
wings.

'Hello,' she says, walking over to where I'm seated. 'I'm Teresa. I haven't seen you at our church before?'

'I'm new to Toronto. I'm Jacqui. I was out walking and something told me to come inside the church.'

'I'm glad you did. Would you like to join me for tea afterwards? I'd love to find out how you landed in Toronto.'

I gladly accept her invitation and stare down at the programme. Printed on the front is the poem called *Meditation*, by Ruth Burgess.

> The desert always waits, ready to let us know who
>   we are –
> the place of self-discovery
> And whilst we fear, and rightly,
> The loneliness and emptiness and harshness,
> We forget the angels,
> Whom we cannot see for our blindness,
> But who come when God decides that we need
>   their help;
> When we are ready for what they can give us.

After the service, Teresa comes to find me.

Over tea I tell her I'm trying to settle in Toronto and that I'm struggling to find work. I share with her that I want to work in the non-profit sector and she promises to help me. I can't quite believe it.

Soon I am attending charity dinners and gala events, mixing with entrepreneurs and philanthropists this angel has introduced me to. Teresa has taken me under her wing, trying to introduce me to people and help me find a job – and I've never been more grateful. She knows about Michael and Dan and everything I've been going through. She telephones often and asks how I'm getting along or how the interviews she has set up for me have gone. All this time my mother has not picked up the phone to call me or taken the time to write a single email.

I come back to the B&B one day after another interview and flop down onto my bed. The interview was okay; nothing special. I keep hoping I'll find an opportunity in a non-profit that will capture my imagination, but so far everything has felt wrong and no offers are forthcoming. But I keep at it because somehow I believe I must. I am conditioned that way. The job hunting keeps me tied to the business world in the hope that I can help people through my work. If I can be seen as a good person, maybe I will become a good person. I'm afraid if I join a for-profit business in Toronto, I'll become aggressive and lost again. Maybe. But I need to take that risk, because money. Oh, money! How we all want it, need it. I have no back-up now, no savings, no job. Debt is terrifying and taking a job I don't love is even more terrifying. But it's what we all have to do, isn't it?

In the interim I spend my Sundays at Church. One Sunday I find an old programme lying inside a hymn book. I recognise the verse printed on it immediately: 'God grant me the serenity to accept the things I cannot change; courage to change the things I can; and the wisdom to know the difference.' Dan had quoted this verse many times in relation to his past with Jolene and his dreams for his future. I needed a reminder that I can't change what I did, the lies Dan told me or what Michael did to me. Terrible things have happened to me and I've done some terrible things. I suddenly remember that Viktor Frankl said we alone can choose our attitude to any set of circumstances. I silently pray for the courage to change my attitude – to love what was and what is. When I open my eyes, I feel a little lighter. The next minute I feel a rush of energy come at me: my hand grabs a pen from my handbag and without control I begin to write all over the programme.

> It matters not that you lied to me.
> It matters that I not lie to myself.
>
> It matters not that you asked for trust.
> It matters that I trust myself.
>
> It matters not that I forgive you.
> It matters that I forgive myself.
>
> It matters not that you broke my heart.
> It matters that my heart still breaks.

It matters not that I love you.
It matters that I still love.

On another Sunday, over tea, the minister and a congregation member, both about my parents' age, question my faith and I am encouraged when they share that while they choose the Christian faith, they are of the belief that it is not the only way to God. I am astounded and relieved all at once. I openly share my thoughts and they lovingly accept me despite these beliefs.

———

The next day, I'm sitting in Starbucks drinking a latte, watching a father and his son, and the poem I wrote is still in my mind. The boy is eating a croissant and messing crumbs all over. The father laughs and leans over to clean him up. They could've been my father and me. We've been through so much, but I still love him. I'm lucky that I still have that capacity. It's the same with my mother, Alison and Michael. With Dan, and even though I don't know her, with Jolene. It's time to stop hurting for what couldn't be. They probably wanted me to be different, but the best I can do is say that I'm trying to become a more loving and accepting person. This is my story, not theirs.

I get up and leave Starbucks, throwing one last look back at the father and his son.

———

Slowly, as time passes, I find that I no longer wake up with the heavy dread that keeps me tied to my bed. I cry – hell, I cry all the time. I'm hardly ever not crying, but I've made peace with the fact that, contrary to the belief I've held for most of my life, I am a softie. One day, while riding in a streetcar over the Queen Street Bridge, I read the words inscribed on the bridge's arch: 'This river I step in is not the river I stand in.' The icy river flows rapidly and every millisecond it changes. No matter what happens, my life will continue to change without my consent and I want it to keep changing for the better. I cannot abandon myself to my fear after all these years. As the sign disappears from view and the streetcar carries me along with it, I still feel scared and lost and overwhelmed by this vast city, but I now know those feelings can change in an instant.

I get off the streetcar and arrive home to an email with what feels like a terrible offer on our house. I decide to take it.

'Are you sure, Jacqui?' I hear myself saying. 'You could wait and get a better offer.'

I insist on selling. I need the money, now, as I am running into debt. When the sale comes through in a few months, I'll take my share and pay off my debts. Then I'll get a job in Toronto and get settled. Months ago, such a bad deal would have nearly killed me. But I don't have the fight left in me for negotiations over a house.

The next morning I finish a draft poem and then sit at my desk, staring at the wall, and dread starts seeping through me. I've gone and sold the house for peanuts and now I'm screwed. My only safety net is my credit card. But what was the first thing I did this morning when I got up? I sat down and wrote. I didn't arrange another interview or update my LinkedIn. Surely that means something.

Day after day, this keeps happening until I have to face the facts. No one is hiring me as my heart is not in it. I decide to take action. I don't want to waste another second of Teresa's time, so I call her and arrange to meet her for lunch. On my walk to the restaurant, I get increasingly nervous. At the table, my stomach is in a knot. I imagine the worst that could happen. She'll recoil, stiffen and shake her head. She'll be disappointed in me and think I've wasted her time. I remind myself that she is not my father.

When Teresa sits down opposite me, she is her usual warm and engaging self.

'So, what do you want to tell me Jacqui? Have you decided on a job?'

Oh, she's going to hate me.

'I'm really sorry Teresa, but I've decided to stop looking for a job in Toronto. At this point I want to focus on my writing. I am so sorry about letting you down. I know you've been through all of this trouble to help me network with people and setting up interviews, but I just can't do it.'

'Jacqui, Jacqui, honey,' she says, and she reaches across to take my hand. 'This is so right for you. I am so proud because I know how hard this is for you. I know how much you've been struggling, but if you stick to what matters to you, you'll be fine. The only time your eyes really light up is when you talk about your writing.'

The relief at her words is indescribable. She doesn't think I'm worthless or a time-waster or any of those things. And she doesn't disappear, either. She still checks up on me and invites me around for tea. I don't know why she cares about me. Perhaps she doesn't need a reason to love. Perhaps none of us do.

I rush home to call Amanda to tell her my decision.

'Jacqui, financially things are difficult now because of Michael. He still hasn't given you the promised side agreement. And on top of that, after what Dan did – I wish I could lay my hands on that bastard – anyway. I'm worried sick about you, so is Jill, so is everyone. If you don't take a job, how are you going to cope? I don't want you to get chewed up and spat out while you're still –'

'I've already been chewed up and spat out a few times,' I say laughing. 'It's a terrible thing to say, but honestly, how much worse could it get? I may have no home, country or income and I may still see Michael and Dan everywhere, but Amanda I am strong enough to live purposefully. I might have lost everything but I can't live in fear – not mine, not yours, no one's fear can hold me back now. My life is moving. This river I step in is not the river I stand in.'

'What?'

'Life is constant changes, but I'm going to make them positive changes now. I'd rather die than give up on the things I want.'

'What do you want?'

'I want to write. I want to share why love matters. It's the exact same dream I had as a teenager, before I started doubting myself. I feel like I've come full circle.'

Spring in Toronto is magnificent and while the cityscape reflected in Lake Ontario is not quite the Grand Tetons reflected in Jenny Lake, it's still magnificent. Cherry blossoms hover in pink-white clouds on the trees like great breaths of meditation that float around the branches. The blossoms whisper to one another and it wouldn't surprise me if in a moment, with a gust of wind, they all fluttered away, a crowd of butterflies off to beautify some other place.

The blossoms fill everyone with delight, even the locals who see them every year. The parks are packed with people coming to gape at the trees and I am one of them, sitting with my notepad and pen, watching. I am training myself to write more, write longer and write better – the way I used to train at running when I was a kid: every day, no matter the rain or having a cold or lost shoes or anything. Nothing would stop that Jacqueline from running and nothing is going to stop me from writing now, especially not that voice inside me who still sometimes whispers that I am worthless and unlovable. I turn a deaf ear to it, because like the winter cherry tree without its blossoms, I am perfect, I am enough.

I have a moment of discomfort as I consider this, but then brush the discomfort away. If this story isn't all about me, what is it? Dan always said I was writing the greatest love story on earth. It just wasn't the love story he thought it would be.

CHAPTER FORTY

Only love, with no thought of return, can soften the
point of suffering. – Mark Nepo

SUMMER IS LOOMING AND I don't know what to do with myself. I am writing and doing yoga every day and trying to make as many new friends as possible. But staying in Toronto is starting to feel like a constant effort. I'm being drawn forwards again, as if a string is attached to my navel. I want to keep living in a way that allows changes in my life to feel effortless, fun and not a hurdle. I've had enough hurdles as a result of not following this inexplicably delightful forwards-feeling that I now call true will. But before I can see what that means for me, I want to tie up one loose end: Dan.

We agree to meet for a day in Windsor, Ontario. It's close to Detroit, which means it's convenient for Dan, if not for me. But he has never worried about inconveniencing me and I'm just happy that I don't have to cross the border back into America.

'This is a mistake,' says Amanda over the phone before I leave.

'I'm meeting him on my terms. I need him to look me in the eye and tell me what is going on.'

'No matter what you tell yourself, Jacqui, I know that one word from him saying that he chooses you over her will make you want to give it all up and go back to him.'

'Regardless of his plans or whatever he says to me, I will not abandon myself again, Amanda.'

'God, I hate that man. I'm still so mad about what he did to you.'

'He didn't *do* anything to me: it's just the way things played out. Holding onto that anger is like drinking poison and —'

'Expecting the other person to die: yeah, yeah, I get it.'

'Amanda, I don't hate Dan or anyone who has done things that I don't like. What he did, he did because he believed it was right from his perspective. Sure, it hurt like hell and I have cried buckets of tears. But I can still love him.'

'All I'm saying is be careful and don't let your guard down with him.'

I don't even have a guard, let alone one that I can let down and put up at will. When I walk into the hotel lobby in Windsor, I expect to see Dan immediately. He's texted me to say that he has arrived and usually the whole room is drawn to him. I used to walk into rooms and find him bantering with a group of strangers that he had just met, bubbly and overjoyed to see me. At last I spot him. His shoulders are slumped, his eyes cast down and his hands hidden in his pockets.

We greet one another with a clumsy hug, head to the hotel restaurant and sit down. He can't look me in the eyes, but instead fidgets with the salt shaker.

'Dan, are you okay?' I ask, and he looks up.

A smile flickers on his face for a moment and then dies. Slowly, he starts to talk. It's strained at first and then the truth starts to pour out.

'Actually, I'm not okay. I hate to admit it, but I'm literally living from one drink to the next. I'm defeated. I want to be with you, but I don't know how to do it. I'm stuck. Everything I do makes Jolene mad. Everything about me is a trigger.'

'I've said those words myself about people I love. But Dan, it's not things you do. We can't control how other people behave — ' I pause, and then decide to stop speaking.

There's a long silence. He looks so defeated. When his food arrives, he fiddles with it.

'You know how I feel about you, Jacqui,' he says, changing the subject. 'You know that my feelings are true, but I hate how I have hurt Jolene. Can't we go back?'

'We can't go back to the way things were. Dan, you need to remember that Jolene was first okay with all of it. She only broke after you told her how you love me. This clearly triggered her deeply and since then she hasn't been kind to either of us. Either you need to cut yourself loose and together we can support Jolene or you need to move on from me. The middle road where you stay with Jolene, trying to help her and promising me that we'll grow old together, isn't an option.'

'But I can't imagine my life without you. I know I've hurt Jolene, but I love her like a sister. It may seem fucked up that I want to divorce her and that I just can't abandon her.'

'It's not fucked up. I get it. I love Michael more than anything and it almost killed me leaving him. Hell, I gave up everything to make sure he felt safe when I left. Dan, you can't carry on like this.'

'I don't know what to do.'

He doesn't meet my eyes and he is still slumped over, as if crouching away from something. He looks so tiny.

'Dan, if you stay, you can't keep denying who you are, who you need to be in the marriage. I know you're scared. But don't judge yourself. Make a choice and follow through with it.'

'I wish –' his voice breaks. 'I wish I could have a love like yours. Where no one judges me. Where I can just be me, tell the truth and know that at the end of the day, I'd be loved. But I don't know if that'll ever happen for me. You probably think I'm such a loser right now.'

I don't recognise the fear in his voice.

I'm trying to stay calm but I want to cry, because Amanda was right. All I wanted was to see him again and for it to be like it was. But that isn't what's happening. He's shattered and there's nothing I can do but watch him in pain.

'I'm not sure I can do this without you.'

'You can.'

I think about all the ways I used to drown myself in trying to save other people as a distraction from my own pain. Before I left, the last thing Michael asked of me was to promise I wouldn't try to fix Dan.

'I love you, Jacqui. I need a week or two to digest all of this and come back to you.'

His eyes are cast down and his voice is drowned in pain.

'I love you too.'

We go up to my hotel room without a word. We stare at one another.

It's urgent. Desperate. And over too soon. He shudders and I hold him.

'I'm sorry,' he says.

Moments pass and then he rolls to lie beside me and rests his head on my breasts. His tears trickle down between them while mine slide down the side of my face. I stroke his back one last time.

Later he says, 'Aren't you going to ask me what was real and what was a lie?'

'I know you love me, Dan. None of the rest matters anymore.'

'My dad did know about you, that day when you called. He couldn't speak freely because he was out with my mother.'

I remain, stroking his back as he cries. I'll always love him. The only thing that will let me walk out of this hotel room and let him go is my unconditional love for him. The same love that my mother always held for my father and me. The same love I accessed to set myself free from my father's conditions to earn his love. The same love that lets me love my father today.

'Dan, I'll love you forever and missing you won't stop me from letting you go. Don't forget that.'

As I hold Dan's fears for those last moments, I know that I also hold Jolene's, my father's, my mother's, Michael's, Alison's and in that moment, I do not forget to hold my own fears safely in the spirit of unconditional love.

He leaves. I shatter.

After dinner alone in the hotel restaurant, I come back to my room to find a frantic voice message from Dan, begging me not to answer my phone if Jolene calls, begging me to lie to her if she asks if he saw me today. I turn off my phone. I know that he has lied about it being okay for us to meet and about a hundred other things – and I know why. It is the same reason I didn't tell my family how I started shouting at Michael and why my father could never admit to what he did.

I suspect Dan also lied for the same reasons that my mother always protected my father. By telling me that Jolene was okay with things, that Jolene was ready to let go, he was protecting himself from his own shame. I realise I don't need to forgive him for lying and I don't need him to give me reasons for the choices he's made. I've accepted it without judgement, but it doesn't mean my heart isn't broken.

A week later Dan phones me. His voice is dull with grief. 'I have to stay with Jolene. I can't live with the shame of what I've done. I don't know what to say, except that I will never love another woman like I love you.'

There is nothing more to say.

CHAPTER FORTY-ONE

When we are no longer able to change a situation, we are challenged to change ourselves. — Viktor Frankl

I KEEP SEEING DAN'S DESPONDENT face when I fall asleep at night, but I don't reach out to him. I can't keep anyone emotionally safe. I need to save myself. And so I decide to do something for myself that doesn't really make sense, but makes me feel excited at the prospect. I sign up for a yoga teacher-training course with Amanda's new yogi idol, in San Francisco. I want to learn how to stop the inner voice in my head that starts bitching when things go wrong. Maybe deepening my yoga practice will allow me to become more conscious of the things that I am thinking, what I am doing and saying and, most importantly, what I believe. Perhaps it will help me learn to accept the flow of my life and not keep cursing that I am in North America and I am writing, but *what now?!* Even though I told Amanda I no longer wanted to live in fear, I do. I worry. I want to learn how to stop worrying.

I'm living on credit card debt, so I book an Airbnb room in a place that looks humble but nice in the Castro.

When I arrive, the Airbnb host Tony leads me up the stairs to his apartment. His eyes are red and he's wearing a vest, something I've always, irrationally, taken as a sign of dissipation. God, I'm judgey! Tony is probably great. We step into the apartment and it's clear that the floors haven't been cleaned, possibly ever. When we walk into the lounge I see a group of people sitting, staring vacantly at nothing. Some of them seem half asleep. They are seated around a small table littered with plastic lighters and things I don't recognise. I turn away in the hope that I can forget.

'Do they all live here?'

'Nah. I met them in the park today. Never mind. Your room,' he says, pointing down a passage.

The room is narrow and looks like it was once a large cupboard. Thank God it's sunny. There's a single foam mattress on what looks like an abandoned DIY bed and the bedding is rumpled. I look around to complain, but Tony has left the room and I've already paid in full for my stay – non-refundable. The carpet feels sticky under my shoes but I'm too afraid to look at the bottom of my soles. I eye some debris on the floor. Is that eggshell?

'Come see the kitchen,' he calls.

I follow him into the kitchen.

'The listing says I'll have space in the fridge.'

'Here,' he says, opening the fridge.

I peer inside and then shy away. There is no space and it smells like a dead animal rubbed in garlic. None of the food is in containers and all of it is alive with mould.

'Where?'

'And now the bathroom,' he says, oblivious to my question, leading me on.

Heaven help me. I almost tell him not to worry: I will rather find a public bathroom to use. I have visions of a broken toilet seat, a mountain of empty bottles and tubes piling up. The reality is much better. It doesn't look too bad, aside from the rattling shower door and the grubby tiles. I fear I may get a foot disease. But that's all.

I barricade myself in my room, fall to my knees and grab the pillow positioning myself for a minor meltdown. It smells of other people's sweat. I don't care. I bury my face into it, scream and then cry.

———◆———

Although I have no intention of becoming a yoga teacher, the teacher training isn't exactly what I expected.

As the days go by, we each unravel our stories for one another to see, stories with which we need to change our relationship if we are to become teachers. The teachings remind us that everything that has happened in our lives affects us in the now. I'm surprised to hear that these happy, fit-looking young people (I've established that I'm the oldest) are carrying so much pain. The more I listen, the more I realise how critical my thoughts really are. I notice how judgemental I am of my philosophy teacher. I feel that I am constantly on the brink of snapping at him as he brags about teaching conservative Christians a real lesson. He harps on about Catholicism and how poisonous it is. Thank goodness I have a vicious bronchial infection that has made me lose my voice for a week, otherwise I'd have let him have it. Day after day, he slips moments of judgement into his lectures – stories about what some stupid conservative said to him or how he out-debated and then out-emailed a poor man he met on an aeroplane. I find myself thinking that surely, as a Buddhist, he shouldn't be so openly judgmental and small-minded. He could at least *pretend* and stop boasting about everything he's achieved.

I am physically exhausted from the training and my mind can't hold any kind of stillness with his judgments booming through the studio, which is crammed beyond capacity with students on their mats. I am seated at the back in the corner, with forty-odd students in front of me.

'A lot of people who've been living in some kind of a Catholic-inspired guilt and who identify as Catholic haven't stepped inside a church in fifteen years, and trust me I can see why they wouldn't, but now thanks to my yoga teachings –'

'Oh, for fuck's sake, not everyone had a bad experience with Catholicism!'

I've been unable to speak for a week and now these are the first words that come out of me. A judgment! Every head turns to look at me and I lower my head. It's true. Not everyone has had a bad experience with Christianity, but I did. I am pissed off with Christianity, pissed off with Jesus Christ and pissed off with my family for putting me – us – through that and for not seeing how judgemental it made us. I see myself more clearly now than I have throughout the whole summer of training and studying, as I see the reflection of my judgments in my teacher. I now see what I want.

I want somehow to *know* without doubt that God is the embodiment of love. I want evidence. I want to *know* that God – Love – is available to everyone. I don't want to hear another self-righteous and judgmental word come out of his mouth. Hell, I don't even want to listen to my own pessimistic, critical thoughts right now. I always thought that the small-minded, snarky, mean, bitchy narrative just belonged to my family, my in-laws and others like them, but my internal narrative is even more violent. All the good I've ever done in my life pales in comparison to my internal rage. I am clearly insane. Am I really calling myself insane? Isn't that a bit strong? Nope. I'm bat-shit crazy right now and I might as well admit it to myself.

There is a two-faced, vicious person that lives within me and I see her now. I need to admit her into my life and try to love her, too. I always thought I knew her, but it is only now in this public outburst that I see her true nature in a different light. I see her as part of me, a part that needs love, no matter how little she may deserve it.

After the class, a fellow student who is studying to be a Catholic Jesuit priest, comes up to me and lays a hand on my shoulder.

'I confess that you said what I was thinking,' he smiles.

All I can do is smile, shake my head and sigh.

Every day when I arrive home at the Airbnb apartment, which I now believe to be a small-time drug den, I am grateful that yoga keeps me busy from five in the morning until seven at night – and today is no different. The front door is stuck again and when I kick it open, I find myself face to face with a strange woman. Her pupils are constricted and she's grinning at me, clearly surging on heaven-knows-what.

'Hey you,' she says, coming right up to my face.

Her breath is sweet and I look past her to see Tony standing in the balcony doorway, smoking a joint.

'So, listen, I work with couples to help spice things up in the bedroom. Do you want to have a night with me? Because I can teach you things that I feel, spiritually, you really need to learn.'

I smile at her and Tony seems surprised at my warmth.

'I don't doubt that I still have to learn so many, many things in this life. I'm flattered and thank you for the offer as you are a truly beautiful human being, but this is something I have no desire to learn.'

She stumbles back towards the living room.

'Lovely meeting you, though!' I call, as she slumps down onto the couch.

Tony and I are left looking at one another.

'What a day,' I say.

'Me too. Had a rough one.'

'I'm sorry to hear that,' I say, and I mean it.

'Does my smoking weed make you uncomfortable?'

I almost say: 'No, what actually bothers me is the strangers that you openly admit you only met that day that hang out in the apartment', but I bite my tongue. I reckon Tony thinks I'm a tight-assed-never-do-anything-wrong-kinda-gal. Little does he know.

'Sometimes it bothers me. But not today. Today I'd like to join you, if that's okay.'

He smiles slowly and stuffs his pipe for me. I almost cough my lungs out and very soon I am high and exceedingly peaceful and overjoyed. We sit smiling at one another.

'Have you forgiven me for cleaning the fridge and throwing the contents down the trash chute?'

'I guess – except my balsamic vinegar I brought back from Italy.'

'But Tony, it expired over three years ago.'

'I know, but I'm still sad about it.'

It's a wonderful life, I think to myself, and when I leave, I'll miss everything in San Francisco, even this place that I have somehow come to call home for a while.

CHAPTER FORTY-TWO

Imagination is more important than knowledge. – Albert Einstein

JOURNEYS MAKE ME THINK AND the flight from San Francisco back to Toronto is no different. It's become easier to keep an eye on what thoughts and feelings are going through me since yoga teacher training. It's like it's all written down and in my daily meditation I just have to witness what's there and not judge it. The summer has been a cosmic punch to the gut. Every single day I showed up as no one else but myself, good and bad in one package. I thought that Dan was the only person who could see the bad and love me anyway, but it's not true. While he'll always be special, there are others who can love me beyond the things I've done. I wonder why I haven't felt this free to share all this with Michael. I guess I was scared he wouldn't love me anymore. Or maybe I hadn't yet accepted the pain myself.

My mind is now clear, with four things held inside it for me to focus on: writing, mountains, America and study. Being a beginner over this summer sparked a desire in me to learn something that I haven't felt since I was young. Having woken up to my life, I want to study philosophy and psychology – and learn more about what the world's greatest spiritual teachers had to say. While in San Francisco, I kept my eyes open for signs and, sure enough, one day I stumbled into a school called New Ventures West, where I could do an intensive year-long course as an integral coach, studying the union of mind, body and soul. That is what I've been flailing around trying to achieve, without a guidebook, and I am thrilled at the idea that soon I might understand more about the dark side to myself and the negative thoughts that still cause me pain. The best part is that the course would allow me to base myself in Boulder, Colorado, near Amanda, where I can safely hike year-round and travel to San Francisco for intensive lectures every few months.

And as for writing – well, nothing is going to stop me now. Getting to meet myself over the last year-and-a-half, and seeing myself mirrored in every person I meet, has taken me to a point where it's no longer a choice I have to consider making: a writer is just a part of who I am and writing makes me happy.

I look out of the plane window and down onto skyscrapers as we start our descent into Toronto. In one of those skyscrapers I met Don Johnson, a Toronto businessman who had been awarded an Order of Canada. He offered to help me find work and his secretary set up an appointment for us to meet over lunch at Canoe, a fine restaurant on the 54th floor with exceptional views over Toronto. Don offered to introduce me to some of his business contacts in the non-profit sector. Feeling deeply grateful I offered to pay for lunch to thank him for his kindness. As a regular patron, Don insisted on picking up the check. After lunch, we rode down in the elevator and he pressed me up against the elevator wall, hands on me, mouth on me, trying to kiss me. At first, I froze! The elevator descended another ten floors before I pushed him against the elevator wall. I ran out of the elevator and ranted about it in Owen's arms back at the bed and breakfast. I later came to learn that I was apparently not the only one. I remembered how over a charity lunch a few weeks after meeting Don, a few of Canada's most successful women, knowing of his transgressions, questioned why they had not had him held accountable. As I sit in my aeroplane seat, the fury I felt that day flickers inside me again. I didn't just want him to stop and be held accountable: I wanted to beat him, to smash his head against the steel walls of the elevator until it cracked. I had wanted to kill Don, to kill my dad, the perpetrators at Deloitte, to kill myself and everyone who had ever hurt me. I wanted to tear them to pieces and now I know it is this side of me that needs to be nurtured until it no longer wants to lash out at people or scream across rooms or hate myself when I am triggered. I feel that I am now ready to learn how to be more aware of my triggers and choose better responses. Although Don might have deserved a good smack nonetheless. When the elevator bumped to a stop on the ground floor, he straightened his tie and stepped out before me as though nothing had happened.

I blink and realise that the bump of the elevator in my memory coincides with the plane touching down in Toronto.

—◆—

Back in Toronto, a new friend of mine, Laura, suggests that we attend a creative workshop in New York, with a friend of hers I don't know, Inger. But at the last moment, Laura's husband has a stroke and she's unable to join us in New York. All I know about Inger is that she is Norwegian, an interior designer, and that she and her wife have a beautiful daughter. Money is tight so we've booked to share a twin room at the Holiday Inn and I'm sure it'll be a great week. I'm sitting in my seat on the aeroplane when a six-foot blonde woman whooshes past me and then backtracks.

'Oh, this is my seat.'

She's got to be from Norway, with hair so blonde it's almost translucent. This must be Inger.

'Inger, right? Hi, I'm Jacqui.'

She sits down and we start talking. We get on so well that I don't even notice the plane taking off.

'So, on the phone you said we're sharing the hotel room. You know I'm lesbian, right?'

'Ja, I do,' I say and I can't help but laugh, because that's the last thing that would bother me about sharing a room with a stranger. 'It really doesn't make a difference and I've booked twin beds. Although maybe you should be the one worried about me, because it's rumoured my family back home thinks I'm lesbian too.'

'What? That's impossible. You – gay? No,' she says, laughing. 'Some people say gaydars aren't their thing, but I've got one and you, my friend, are as straight as they come.'

'In fairness to my family, I can now see their perspective. I didn't exactly look that feminine. This whole dresses and nail polish thing is very new to me. Just take a look at my passport photo and you'll get it,' I say, and pass my passport to her.

She stares blankly for a moment and then howls with laughter, making the man across the aisle from us glare.

'Oh fuck,' she says, still laughing, 'You look like an angry dyke. And as a lesbian, I am allowed to use that word when appropriate.'

Now I can't stop laughing either. It's going to be a great week.

We arrive at the Holiday Inn Garden Court on the West Side, after laughing non-stop in the taxi from the airport. I hand over our booking confirmation and passports to the receptionist, but her face falls as she stares at the computer screen.

'I'm very sorry, but there's been a mistake: all we have left is one double-bed room. We've got no more twin beds and no king rooms.'

'That can't be right. I've booked for two single beds.'

Inger is shifting next to me. We had shared some laughs, but we barely know one another. There's no ways we can share a double bed for a whole week. We make eye contact and both seem to be thinking that this is not what we signed up for; this is too uncomfortable. But in a moment, it suddenly becomes funny.

'Ma'am, we really have nothing.'

'Don't you have a room for each of us,' Inger asks, suppressing a giggle.

'Ma'am, I'm really sorry, but as I said we only have one room left.'

'Look lady, I don't really know how to put this,' I say, struggling not to laugh. 'You see this woman standing next to me? She is lesbian and happily married.'

I'm still fighting laughter, but Inger is doubled over beside me.

'We only met at the airport two hours ago, and while it is rumoured that I am a lesbian, I am not quite ready for an intimate week in New York with a stranger. That was *not* the plan here.'

I can no longer hold back my laughter.

'I can't tell my wife that I'm sleeping with another woman,' Inger says, still laughing.

The receptionist too is now choking back laughter.

'Fine,' says Inger, still laughing. 'Just give us a lot of pillows to put between us: I am *not* spooning with her.'

Viktor Frankl was right when he said we can choose our response to any set of circumstances; beyond our individual fears in this moment, we choose joy and bond through love. Love for the sticky situation, love for ourselves, love for each other and love for what is.

CHAPTER FORTY-THREE

The wound is the place where the Light enters you. – Rumi

THE WORKSHOP IS EVERYTHING WE hoped it would be and after our first night sharing a bed, Inger and I settle into writing, drawing and meditating all day. I find that my grandmother's presence is with me all week and her tough love helps me to surrender to the process. Every day goes by too quickly, until it's finally the last day of the workshop. It's all ending too soon and what do I have to show for it? I imagine what Granny would say now.

'Oh, come on Jacqueline. Trust yourself!'

'We're going to end off our day with a meditation and then, when we open our eyes, we're going to do a speed-writing exercise,' says the instructor. 'I'm going to give you ten minutes to write a letter of love to yourselves. Ignore the manuscripts, ignore the planning, ignore your doubts. Just write something, be it a letter, a poem, a dialogue or prose that expresses love for yourself. Right, are we all ready for the meditation? Excellent. Eyes closed.'

I fall into the meditation and time stops for a while.

'Okay, you have ten minutes for your writing, starting ... Now!'

I start writing and a love letter to myself unfolds in a few minutes. I put my pen down and re-read the last line of my letter, 'I now work on a daily practice of loving you, as you are complete, whole and perfect, just the way you are with all your imperfections.' The next minute something takes control of me. The same energy that brought me back to life multiple times, that coursed through my spine at 16, that threw me off a cliff to save my friends, that walked me out of the storm back to my car, now takes my hand, lifts my pen and starts writing. I watch my hand move across the page. The words are being written of their own accord, dropping one by one from my pen. They do not come from me, but through me. My hand feels hot. Something reminds me of Olivia's letter. 'Let the light shine on your broken places.' A light is shining on me now, warm and bright. There is a poem on my page. As my pen stops writing, the instructor tells us to stop.

'All right,' says the instructor. 'We're going to go around the circle and I want you each in turn to read your love letters.'

I wonder if what has appeared on this page will look like New Age garbage to these people. The very word 'God' is difficult for me at times, because it takes me back to my family. But the God that has shown himself in this writing is universal.

'Jacqui, your turn.'

'Okay then. Here I go,' I say. I take a deep breath, ignore my letter and read the poem.

> In order to change we need to suffer forgiveness
> in forgiveness we expose and mourn our pain
> in pain we bare our soul to acceptance
> in acceptance we surrender fear to our truth
> in truth we free courage to trust our true will
> in truth will we find compassion to honour our intrinsic value
> in intrinsic value our soul nature unveils self-love
> in self-love space opens to the essential peace of life's purpose.

For this is our God-given gift
for this is choice
for this is freedom
for this is living
for this is Love.

When I finish reading, there are tears of pain and pleasure in my eyes for this journey I've been travelling. The journey back to knowing God is Love.

———◆———

After the workshop, I have a late lunch with Sylvia, a fellow student I met in San Francisco. Sylvia is aware of much of my personal journey. I tell her the story of my experience in the workshop.

'This is the journey we all travel. We have to *choose* to see this, to see love in everything and find the freedom to live with this love, to *be* Love. When we can *Be Love* for ourselves and all others then God abides in us.'

'God is Love, right,' she says.

'Yes!'

But I know it's more than this. At 16 I believed Jesus was the only way to God because I was faith healed in a Christian church. I now know that God is not limited to Christianity – or to any religion. God is quite simply not that small. God is everywhere and in all of us and manifests through us as Love. Beyond my body, mind and soul, I am nothing more than a Spirit of Love, just like everyone else.

This is what I had tried to express to Dan and what I believe he understood. Despite our shame stories, it was an unconditional love. My father and I couldn't do that for each other. As souls my father and I both suffered because our limiting beliefs withheld love from each other and based forgiveness on blame and judgement, as opposed to love and acceptance.

I can now see the underlying belief that we hold onto is what affects our ways of being in the world. I now know without doubt that God is Love; beyond religion, beyond dogma, beyond exclusion, beyond judgment.

'What was the most difficult part of your journey?' Sylvia asks.

'Finding the courage to question all of my beliefs and admit that with some of them *love* was lacking. I even realised I had a laundry list of conditions for loving myself,' I admit.

But in my heart, I know that staying on the journey with Love might prove even harder.

—◆—

Michael and I have been contacting one another intermittently and after the workshop ends, I Skype him and tell him about the poem that came to me. I'm excited that I will see him in a few months' time in South Africa.

'Mike, I love that poem of mine more than anything I've ever written. It's my favourite.'

Michael explodes with laughter, his face blurring on Skype as he rocks back in his chair.

'Jacqui, you've said that about all of them. How do you know that *this* poem is the one?'

'I know. I love everything equally – but isn't it fabulous that they're all my favourite?' I say, also laughing.

I glance at my face, blocked into a little window of pixels, and see that I am beaming. I look like a little girl who has shown someone special her homework.

'You look so happy,' Michael says.

'I am happy, Mike.'

I've reconnected with everything that I set aside at 16. I have rediscovered the Heidi in me, that child spirit to whom God's voice speaks loudest.

'I feel like I've finally fallen into my own skin,' I say.

'Jacqui, when I see you so content and so in love with life, it sounds like *you,* the you I met 18 years ago. You lost yourself somewhere along the way. I guess the unfairness of the Deloitte case broke you in two again. You broke away from yourself and now, when I look at you, I can see that you're connected again. You're whole.'

And he is right.

CHAPTER FORTY-FOUR

In Japan, broken objects are often repaired with gold. The flaw is seen as a unique piece of the object's history, which adds to its beauty. – Source unknown

MONTHS LATER, I AM BACK in New York to attend a publishing conference and everything is crystal-bright. I live in Boulder now and hike and write every day. New York still sometimes makes me feel a little lonely, as I miss the happy times I've spent here with Michael, but I pluck up my courage and remember why I wrote the book in the first place. There will be people at the conference with books that are better, more interesting, more intellectual than mine. There will be writers who will go on to win prizes and writers who have already published many books before. I know why I am doing this. Writing my story has freed me to live beyond my shame, guilt and blame stories. But even with my evidence of miracles and the knowledge that we are all connected, I feel a little lonely. I step out onto the sidewalk from Hotel Pennsylvania and a tide of people move past me on 7th Avenue. I see a light around each one of them and feel connected to them all. The differences between me and them are nothing but a permeable surface, allowing everything to float gently through. I stop on the street corner and crane my neck to see the roofs against a sky that is bright blue, despite the cold November day. The city smells like diesel and hot pretzels and feels like one great striving forwards. What do these people wish for? What is it that *I* most want? I know the answer, so why don't I just ask for it? I close my eyes and sway slightly, my toes curling over the edge of the sidewalk.

God, I'm asking for another miracle. Tonight, I want you to show me that you exist as Love. I want you to show me that you are everywhere and in everyone.

I open my eyes again and stare up at the Madison Square Gardens arena in front of me. I think of Michael and of Dan and send them both love. A part of me wishes that they were here with me, because all I want right now is to share this chilly New York evening with someone who loves me. But as I walk through the knots of people, I do feel loved. My grandmother is with me.

'It's chilly, Jacqueline. Your hands will get dreadfully dry if you don't cover them.'

I find in my coat pocket the pair of fur-lined gloves that I bought at Harrod's 27 years earlier, the trip I took with my grandmother's encouragement. I pinch them open the way she did, slip one hand in, then the next and then smooth my palms one over the other. She had this little ritual of putting on her fur-lined gloves that I used to love as a little girl. My stomach rumbles in a most unladylike fashion so I step into the first takeaway restaurant I see, *Fresh and Co.* on the corner of 7th Avenue and West 31st. I order a bowl of curried lentil soup with kale and quinoa and on my way to fetch it at the other end of the counter, I trip over a walking stick.

'I'm so sorry about that,' I say, and bend to pick it up and give it to its owner, an elegant woman who looks like she is in her mid-eighties.

'Not at all,' she says. 'I shouldn't have left it lying in your way.'

'I'm walking around in a bit of a haze today, to be honest. I've been attending a conference here in New York and I'm just exhausted.'

'There's always far too much information to be taken in at those things. Tell me, what type of conference are you attending?'

'It's a publishing conference. I've just finished writing my first book and I'm on the lookout for an agent and a publisher.'

'Well, I just can't believe it. I'll be attending a publishing conference in New York myself, but next week. Funny that we've crossed paths like this. I'm also a writer, although I'm a bit later to the game than you are. I've also just finished my first book. You're wise to have started so young.'

'Wise?' I laugh. 'Sometimes it seems mad that I've started to learn something new now, in my late forties.'

'When you get to my age, you'll realise the only thing mad about starting something new is how long you waited.'

'How did you manage to start?'

'I just realised that I didn't care anymore what people thought of me or if I never get published or any of it. I felt I had let life push me along for too many years and that I had asked for nothing. Now that I am grey, I see things in full colour.'

The woman behind the counter announces that my order is ready. I get up and fetch it – and then hesitate.

'Could I –'

'Would you like to eat with me?'

I sit opposite her, listening with my whole being to everything she tells me.

'I let life extinguish me for many years, but now I'm a flame bearer and I can see that you are too. Even if you don't find that publisher this time around, you need to keep faith.'

'How do you keep faith? How do you know that you'll get a publisher?'

'I don't: it's as simple as that. But I love writing and tinkering away on my book and that gives me courage. Faith is not about believing in what you are doing: it is when you have no doubt.'

'Do you ever feel that because you haven't published, you're not a real writer?'

She bursts out laughing and her laughter fills me with hope.

'Is a painter who never sells a single painting not an artist? Is the runner who runs for miles every day, but never wins a single race, not also a real runner? And what about the lover who is never loved in return. Is he not, too, a real lover?'

The woman sitting at the window is listening and she has started to smile, too.

'You're right. I've got to admit that I'm mesmerised by your courage.'

'And I in turn am mesmerised by you, although I am not sure what it is yet,' she says with a wink. 'My dear, if you feel that this is what you want out of your life, then there is no room for fear. I don't know you, but I know that you have somehow found the strength to wake up every day and do what makes you smile. And darling, that's what you deserve. You deserve to love your life. I have no regrets, even though I started late. If I could walk in front of you and remove every obstacle that will stand in your path, I would, but I can't. All I can do for you is send you love and encourage you to love what you do. Love is after all the answer to everything, don't doubt it.'

'I promise you that I'll try my best.'

'Well, dear, it's getting late, so I must head home and get my rest.'

I'm a little sad to see her stand up to leave, as she has filled me with hope. She pulls a pair of leather gloves out of her coat pocket, pinches them open, slips one hand in, then the next and then smooths her palms one over the other. All in one deft movement.

'It's been lovely meeting you, my dear.'

I almost ask, 'Are you an Angel?' But instead I say, 'Do you think we could keep in touch?'

'Of course. I would love that,' she says, and writes down her telephone number on a napkin.

'Thank you so much for this. But tell me, what's your name?'

'My name is Mrs Hope.'

The woman at the window and I stare at one another in amazement.

'Mrs Hope, I'm Jacqui. It's been a pleasure talking to you.'

'And you,' she says. 'My dear, I have no idea why I have to tell you this, but you must complete your book.'

'Thank you,' I say, and she smiles and then leaves the restaurant. My eyes fill with tears and as I turn to look at the woman at the window, she seems as stunned as I am.

'Jacqui,' says Mrs Hope's voice, next to me again suddenly.

I turn around in surprise and she takes my hand.

'I want you to have this. I know you understand,' she says, and she is holding out the scarf she was wearing.

Here again is a reminder of my grandmother, who had scarves for every occasion and loved gifting me them. Mrs Hope looks me in the eye, places the scarf into my hand and then strokes the top of my hand while holding it, the way my grandmother used to, but before she can leave I wrap my arms around her and hold her to me in a deep hug. She simply smiles at what she already knows: that Love is the answer to everything. And then she is gone. Tears are gliding down my cheeks now and I look again at the woman sitting at the window.

'Wow! I was amazed when she first walked out, but I can't believe the love I have just witnessed,' she says.

We can't stop staring at one another, still locked in this moment of knowing.

'You have no idea,' I say. 'I dared to ask for that.'

I step out onto the streets of New York City and know that with all that is unknown, wherever I might find myself, I am home when I am at one with Love.

———◆———

There are only 2 ways to Be in Life.
To Be Love or Not!

ACKNOWLEDGEMENTS

I OWE THE GREATEST DEBT to my mother for her unconditional love and support throughout my story-telling journey. Despite the initial discomfort I know my book caused her, I could not have completed it without her honest assessment of, and input on, my perspective. I learned so much from her during this process.

To my father, for all that we could not be for each other, I am sorry, and for all that we were able to give each other, thank you. Know that I love you.

To my ex-husband 'Michael', I will always love you. Thank you for being true to who you are.

To the writing coaches and teachers who gave their support, be it for editing, proofing, teaching or other, thank you for helping me elevate my writing and story-telling capabilities. In no specific order: Natalie Louw, Nina Geraghty, Samantha Rubenstein, Giles Griffin, Karen Schimke, Buzzy Jackson, Robyn Enright and Catherine Johnson. To Natalie Louw, this final manuscript would not exist without you. Thank you for sharing your skills, holding my tears and, when necessary, making me laugh at the same time.

To my friends and other people dear to me, thank you for reading and critiquing the multiple versions of my manuscript; my mom, Amanda Mostert, Jill Meyer, Nora Edelstein, Gerard Kisbey-

Green, Gillian Couper, Nina Geraghty, Melanie Hoare, Sihle Mbulawa, Katharine Price, Rick Badger, Mark Alexander, Rebecca Bysshe, Emily Alexander, Gavin Gobby, Jaunita Gobby, Vincent Murphy, Nathan Rous and Tracey Rous.

To Amanda, Jill, Gerard and Wayne Shonfeld, and as a professional, Jeffery Rink, who all believed in this book before the final manuscript was penned, thank you.

My thanks, too, to my dear friend, Rosmarie Baisch, for supporting me in ways too long to detail here.

To my grandmother, Dolly, and my aunts Anita, Dawn and Carol, thank you for always being there for me when mom could not be. Mom and I were both grateful for the many times you challenged me, advised me or simply made me feel safe.

To my brothers, know that I love each one of you and ask that you accept that mom loved my book, even though she felt she could not tell you this.

To 'Alison', for all that I do not know, what I do know is that I love you. May we meet again and heal our combined wound - if not in this life, then in our next.

To 'Dan' and 'Jolene', thank you for allowing your chaos to collide with mine for a moment in our lives. May your renewed commitment to each other continue to bear fruit.

To my Facebook community, thank you for encouraging me over the years to continue writing, for keeping me grounded to my committed intention that there are only two ways to be in life: *to Be Love or Not.* You keep me inspired, mostly conscious and deeply curious about the human condition, as I continue with Love in this journey called life.

To all those not mentioned by name, be it your choice, intentionally or by accident, please know that I remain grateful to each of you who have travelled with me, be it for a moment in time, for weeks, months or years. I have learned much from our experience together.

I would like to thank all the authors, inspirational leaders and spiritual teachers for the quotations I have used at the start of each chapter. A comprehensive effort has been made to ensure all of their words have been acknowledged appropriately and quoted correctly. If any acknowledgements have been omitted or I have misquoted someone, it is unintentional. If notified, the publishers will be happy to rectify any omissions or corrections in future editions.

Since coming to the understanding that Love is the answer, as a seeker I have chosen to study, read and research the works of multiple spiritual teachers, theologians, philosophers, psychologists, mystics and great leaders. Through their teachings, I have come to a deeper understanding of our purpose as human beings and the human condition. I am profoundly grateful to all those who have sacrificed so much for their message and for those who have put pen to paper over the years, ensuring that students like myself have access to the great teachings and understanding of God/Love/Universe/Source/Universal Wisdom, call it what you will.

I have chosen to share my recollection of these events, both happy and sad, as an educational tool for readers also wanting to live a life of joy, free from the shame, guilt and blame of their life stories. I can only ask that no judgments be placed on any individuals that I might refer to, despite what you might feel. While it may be tempting to judge certain characters in my book, myself included, for their actions, I believe we are all spirits of Love figuring out our journey and, in that respect, are no different from each other. By opening to this truth, I have found the ease to live in the presence of my full self, without having to suppress or deny any part of my story or my truth. In fully loving and accepting myself for all my perfect imperfections, I have opened up to unconditional love for all others, even as I navigate my own human challenges.

While I love reading about and absorbing a wide range of spiritual teachings from institutions that do not discriminate or judge the teachings of others, please note that my writings are nondenominational. I believe that access to a spiritual life with a connection to God/Love is available to all and does not require a single or specific dogma. I do not believe God/Love is that small. When I refer to or quote the work of any of the many great spiritual teachers, I do not advocate the teachings of one above any other. At the same time, I comfortably and openly have my favourites.

Lastly, thank you to my little spirit friend Sophie, for cuddling up to me at night after the long hours I spend at my desk.

I remain a student as I continue to share the message of Love.

About the Author

J ACQUI BURNETT IS AN ADVENTURER – both in journeys of the Spirit and in the world of financial strategy. Raised in South Africa, she is qualified in business studies, which has enabled her to help numerous businesses achieve their strategic and financial goals. However, Jacqui has always pursued a parallel interest in spirituality, which has guided her into her writing career.

Inspired by her discoveries on her own personal journey, Jacqui has created a successful platform called *The Dare to Be Love Journey,* which has attracted an audience of over 40 000 followers. Here, she shares her inspirational thoughts, poetry and personal life stories told through the lens of her unique *Dare to Be Love* self-development practices. Jacqui wrote her memoir in a quest to make spiritual sense of the traumatic life events she has experienced.

Jacqui lives in Cape Town, South Africa. As an impassioned student of life, Jacqui continues to practise and promote living a Spirit-led life of courage, kindness, compassion and love. Her beloved Russian Blue cat, Sophie, is a constant source of joy and inspiration.

Jacqui has a Bachelor of Commerce degree from the University of South Africa in Industrial Psychology and Economics, and a MBA from the University of Witwatersrand, including a semester abroad at Rotterdam School of Management (RSM) Erasmus. Jacqui is also a certified Integral Coach through New Ventures West, and trained as a yoga teacher with Yoga Tree, acquiring both these certifications in San Francisco, California.

This memoir, *Life's Not Yoga,* is Jacqui's first published book.

Website: https://jacquiburnett.com
Facebook: https://www.facebook.com/daretoaskjacqui
LinkedIn: https://www.linkedin.com/in/jacquiburnett/